Baseball, Barns, and Bluegrass

# Baseball, Barns, and Bluegrass

## A Geography of American Folklife

*Edited by*
George O. Carney

ROWMAN & LITTLEFIELD PUBLISHERS, INC.
*Lanham • Boulder • New York • Oxford*

ROWMAN & LITTLEFIELD PUBLISHERS, INC.

Published in the United States of America
by Rowman & Littlefield Publishers, Inc.
4720 Boston Way, Lanham, Maryland 20706

12 Hid's Copse Road
Cumnor Hill, Oxford OX2 9JJ, England

British Library Cataloguing in Publication Information Available

**Library of Congress Cataloging-in-Publication Data**
Baseball, barns, and bluegrass : a geography of American folklife /
    edited by George O. Carney.
        p.   cm.
    Includes bibliographical references and index.
    ISBN 0-8476-8600-0 (cloth : alk. paper).—ISBN 0-8476-8601-9
(paper)
        1. Folklore—United States.   2. United States—Social life and
customs.   I. Carney, George O.
    GR105.B375   1998
    398'.0973—dc21                                              97-42879
                                                                CIP

ISBN 0-8476-8600-0 (cloth: alk. paper)
ISBN 0-8476-8601-9 (pbk.: alk. paper)

Printed in the United States of America

⊗ TM The paper used in this publication meets the minimum requirements
of American National Standard for Information Sciences—Permanence of
Paper for Printed Library Materials, ANSI Z39.48–1984.

To Martha Ellen (1879–1959)
and George Washington Carney (1875–1974),
paternal grandparents,
and Madge Randel (1896–1969)
and Olney Hall Whitlow (1890–1968),
maternal grandparents,
for their influence on my folklife experiences

# Contents

# Illustrations

## Tables

# Preface

The first eighteen years of my life were spent on a 320-acre farm in Deer Creek Township, Henry County, Missouri, some six miles south of Calhoun (population 350), ten miles northwest of Tightwad (population 50), and five miles west of Thrush (population 4). My parents, Josh and Aubertine, inherited the acreage and farmstead buildings from my Grandpa and Grandma Carney, who retired and moved to Calhoun. The eighty acres to the north of the farmstead consisted of hardwood timber (walnut, hickory, and oak), Minor Creek, which flowed in an easterly direction as a tributary to Tebo Creek, and some patches of grazing land. The remaining 240 acres, south of the farmstead, were relatively rich farmland where my Dad planted and harvested a variety of crops ranging from corn and soybeans to alfalfa and oats. Classified as a diversified farmer, he also raised beef and dairy cattle, hogs, sheep, and chickens. Thus, my roots lay in a rural, agrarian way of life in the foothills of the Ozarks.

The Ozarks is a 50,000-square-mile area that encompasses southern Missouri (34,000), northwest Arkansas (13,000), and northeastern Oklahoma (3,000). Its physical geography is characterized by a hill-and-holler terrain with the highest point about two thousand feet above sea level. The most distinguishing feature of the region is its *karst* topography, including numerous caves, springs, and sinkholes created by the underlain water-soluble limestone rock. As to its cultural geography, the Ozarks is a sparsely populated, rural/small town area comprised primarily of White Anglo-Saxon Protestants. It was settled roughly 150 years ago by migrants from the Appalachian Mountains, transplanted hill people who sought a physical environment similar to what they left behind. The Ozarks and Appalachia combine to form one of the traditional folklife regions in the United States—the Upland South.

My early years fit the description that is often used to define the *folk*—a rural people who live a simple way of life, largely unaffected by changes in society, and who retain traditional customs and beliefs developed within a strong family structure. I was experiencing the *folklife* of the Ozarks. Folklife includes objects that we can see and touch (tangible items), such as food (Mom's homemade yeast rolls) and buildings (Dad's smokehouse). It also consists of other traditions that we cannot see or touch (intangible elements), such as beliefs and customs (Grandpa Whitlow's chaw of tobacco poultice used to ease the pain of a honeybee sting). Both aspects of folklife, often referred to as material and nonmaterial culture, are learned orally as they are passed down from one generation to the next—such as Grandpa Carney teaching me to use a broad axe—or they may be learned from a friend or neighbor—for example, Everett Monday, a neighbor, instructing me on the techniques of playing a harmonica.

Through this oral process, I learned many of the traditional ways from the folk who surrounded my everyday life—parents, relatives, friends, neighbors, teachers, preachers, and merchants. The most vivid memories associated with my early life among the Ozark folk are the six folklife traits selected for this anthology—architecture, food and drink, religion, music, sports, and medicine.

*Architecture* was an unfamiliar word in my youthful vocabulary. However, I knew something about the buildings, such as our two-story, cross-gabled farmhouse that was constructed by my Great Grandfather Randel. It had weatherboard siding and a rock foundation. I used the foundation to practice "grounders" by throwing a baseball against the smooth hard rock surface and it would rebound into my glove. Unfortunately, I occasionally missed the foundation and the impact of the ball would split the lower boards of the siding. This throwing mistake resulted in a whipping with switches gathered by Mom from the nearby lilac bush. The farmhouse had a full basement where Mom did the washing. It also served as storage for our harvested garden potatoes carefully spaced on a long wooden table and shelving for the canned goods, both of which provided food for the winter.

Our barn was a Midwestern three-portal type. I learned its classification after studying folk architecture in graduate school. The gabled roof was covered with sheets of tin and the wood siding was painted red. It had a central aisle (hallway) through which we drove the grain wagon. Here I scooped corn and oats into the grain cribs on the east side of the hallway. The west side of the aisle contained horse stalls and harness hangers. In the far west end were the milking stanchions, where I milked "Old Bessie" by hand after school each weekday. The hayloft, located above the hallway, provided space for bales of hay that were hoisted from the wagon to the overhead loft door and then stacked to the rafters. This task provided many unpleasant memories associated with our barn, including knots on my forehead from bumping into the low loft beams, mud dauber stings, and the sweltering heat and humidity of the summer weather. In addition to the farmhouse and barn, there were several outbuildings. The smokehouse, conveniently located near the back porch, provided storage for hams, bacon slabs, and sacked sausage after the fall butchering. The chicken house served as shelter for the hens and egg nests. Each evening I gathered eggs, and often encountered a black snake curled in one of the hen nests. Finally, there was the outhouse, or privy, a two-hole version with a quarter-moon cut in the door, and stocked with a Sears-Roebuck catalog that served dual purposes.

Additional forms of architecture that I recollect were the one-room school and church I attended. Both were simply designed, wood-framed, gable-roof buildings with weatherboard siding painted white—no bell towers or steeples—almost indistinguishable from one another. The most distinctive building in town was the Calhoun Farmers Elevator. Also constructed by my Great Grandfather Randel, it was the tallest structure in town. As I learned from studying grain elevators in Oklahoma some thirty years later, it was a wood iron-clad country style. Covered with tin siding, the elevator contained three floors of bins and was surmounted by a cupola. The workhouse, or first floor, featured the dump hopper in which I unloaded our grain for custom grinding into feed. I became well acquainted with Lillian, the office manager, as well as Zeke and Woody, elevator employees, who ground, sacked, and loaded my feed.

Perhaps the most indelible impression from my younger days was the home-cooked food prepared by the womenfolk in our family—Mom, Grandma Whitlow, and Aunt Bert—all superb cooks. Every other Sunday after church, we would journey to the Whitlows, my mother's parents, who lived near Coal. The bountiful table was laden with Southern fried chicken and cream gravy, mashed potatoes with a dollop of melted butter in the center, green beans cooked with bacon grease, wilted lettuce, and hot homemade loaf bread with freshly churned butter. Beverages included fresh lemonade or sweetened iced tea. Dessert featured cherry or apple fresh fruit pies baked in homemade pie crusts that would melt in your mouth. At the Carney holiday meals, Aunt Bert (Dad's sister) was the premier cook. Known for a variety of homemade dishes, her specialty was homemade fudge. It was a perennial blue ribbon winner at the Calhoun Colt Show and the Henry County Fair.

The neighborhood often held ice cream suppers at the one-room schoolhouse. Each family contributed a freezer of homemade ice cream. The champion ice cream maker was Tommy Kinyon, who possessed an uncanny ability of knowing the right combination of chipped block ice and rock salt, and the correct numbers of turns to produce the most flavorful and firm ice cream from his old White Mountain freezer.

Preparation and canning of vegetables from our garden was a household affair. Dad tended the vegetable garden—planting, hoeing, weeding, and harvesting. It was my job to shell the peas, stem the green beans, and shuck the sweet corn as preliminary steps in the canning process. Mom was in charge of the pressure cooker. She filled the Mason jars, adjusted the jar lids just so, and kept an eye on the cooker gauge. The newly canned vegetables were stored on basement shelves for wintertime consumption.

Rural churches abound in the Ozarks, mostly because of family feuds rather than theological disputes. Family clans would often argue with one another and eventually become dissatisfied enough to splinter from one church and form a new congregation. This was the case in the organization of the church I attended. The Eaton clan, consisting of the old "he" and the old "she" (Paw and Maw Eaton) and their seven grown children and families, had separated from a nearby church to establish the Mt. Gilead Southern Baptist congregation. The Southern Baptist denomination was attractive to rural folks because of its democratic principles. The congregation voted on all business matters from hiring and firing the preacher to spending the collection. Most rural churches could not support a full-time preacher, and because of this, Mt. Gilead shared a pastor with another rural church in the vicinity. Thus, we would have "preachin' " on either the first and third or the second and fourth Sundays in a month. The preachers were always addressed with the title, "Brother" or "Sister," followed by their last name.

On a regular basis, the preacher and the congregation would recognize a need to hold a "revival" for "backsliders" (members who did not attend regularly) or for "sinners" (those who had failed to join the church) in the community. It was at one of these special religious meetings that I "walked the aisle" and was "converted" into the faith. After a revival, it was customary to hold a "baptizin' " in Tebo Creek (no baptistries in rural churches). At an appointed time after Sunday morning services, the entire congregation would walk to the Tebo Creek bridge where they would line the banks of the creek and begin singing "Shall We Gather at the River." When it was my turn, "Brother" Wendell Mosser, our preacher, laid his white handkerchief over my nose and lowered me into the water for the "dunkin'," as several called it. After the baptism ritual was completed, a round of "Amens," "Hallelujahs," and "Praise the Lords" was shouted in celebration of the new church members.

Other activities at Mt. Gilead Church included Sunday school classes,

D. V. B. S. (Daily Vacation Bible School), and the annual "All Day Meeting and Dinner on the Grounds." My Sunday school teacher was Miss Carrie Ralston (one of the Eaton daughters). She would gather us around her in a circle and tell Bible stories, including those about Baby Moses, Cain and Abel, and Little David. Miss Carrie was an exceptional teacher because of her vast knowledge of the "Good Book" from cover to cover. I rarely missed her classes, primarily because my Dad was superintendent of Sunday school for more than fifteen years.

Bible school was the highlight of the summer for rural children because they were usually dismissed from their daily chores for two weeks. It was also a time to meet new friends and renew old acquaintances. Our leaders taught songs; prepared us for Bible drills, such as learning the books of the Bible; and conducted crafts sessions; all concluded with refreshments each day.

One of the most memorable church events was the yearly "All Day Meeting and Dinner on the Grounds." The agenda included a regular morning worship service followed by an elaborate dinner, a "singspiration" in the afternoon, and another round of preaching at night. For the dinner, each family contributed a homemade dish that was arranged by type of food (salads, meats, vegetables, bread, and dessert) on long narrow tables standing in the church yard. After the meal, the adults would visit and the children play. It was a unique opportunity for rural folk to catch up on the local gossip (births, deaths, marriages, divorces, and sicknesses).

Around midafternoon, the congregation would reenter the church for the "singspiration," a two-hour songfest where members could request their favorite hymns. It was coordinated by the church song leader, a member who could "carry a tune" as there were no professionally trained music directors. After a few piano lessons from a neighbor who was not a member of our church, I became the "official" church pianist. Requests from the congregation during the "singspiration" made me shudder because I was familiar with only a few of the traditional hymns. Therefore, we repeated the hymns I could play, such as "Heavenly Sunlight," "Rock of Ages," and "Revive Us Again."

After singing, the congregation moved again to the outdoors and ate leftovers for supper. To conclude the day, we moved indoors for another hour of old-time preaching.

Religious music was not the only form of music I experienced in the Ozarks. My first recollection of "making music" outside the church was at our neighbor's home. Everett and Pearl Monday, a jolly, gregarious couple, lived on the hillside north of our farm. Everett was a hardworking farmer who, I recall, always placed green leaves under his straw hat on hot days to keep his head cool—a folk custom he taught me. Pearl was a large woman who towered over the diminutive Everett. The centerpiece of her household was the wood cook stove on which she prepared a variety of dishes.

What I remember best about them is their musical talent. Known for her boogie-woogie style, Pearl could knock the bottom out of a piano when she tickled the ivories on such pieces as Scott Joplin's "Maple Leaf Rag." Everett, an accomplished harmonica player, would accompany her. Perhaps the most awe-inspiring fact to me was that both played "by ear." Another local musician I distinctly remember was Floyd "Peck" Shepherd, an old-time fiddler whom the Mondays always invited. Peck was short for "pecker-wood," a no-account, lazy person in Ozark lingo. But Peck could saw that fiddle on such tunes as "Sally Goodin," "Arkansas Traveler," and "Missouri Waltz." Peck's musical talents belied his "good for nothin' " character!

My folks never played musical instruments, but they were avid dancers, even though dancing was frowned upon by rural religions. Nevertheless, adults and children engaged in "play parties"—a form of activity that featured singing, clapping, and "creative movements," as one of our preachers called them. My Dad was well versed on several play party lyrics as well as the actions to them. His favorites were "Buffalo Gals," "Skip to My Lou," and "Get Along Little Cindy." At the musical gatherings, he also taught me to do the Irish jig, a variation of today's popular clog dancing. Even now, when a bouncy fiddle tune is played, I break into that jig dance that Dad passed on to me. Later, I learned to play the Appalachian dulcimer, autoharp, and mouth ("pickin'") bow. It was on these instruments that I played tunes passed down from my Ozark background—"Ballad of Jesse James," "Bile Dem Cabbage Down," and "Turkey in the Straw."

Over the years, the knowledge gained from these down-home musical experiences has become more meaningful in the "Geography of Music" course I have taught at Oklahoma State University for the past twenty years. Moreover, an appreciation for this kind of folk music, handed down by my folks and neighbors, has been instilled in my two sons, who both play guitar and sing.

Although Ozark youngsters had little time for recreation, I developed a passion for two sports—baseball and basketball—neither of which I played on an organized basis. Little League baseball and Pee Wee basketball were unheard of in the country. And because the Ozarks was a relatively poor region, we made do with as little equipment as possible. Football was virtually unknown in the Ozarks because funds were scarce to purchase the expensive equipment. Nor were the undernourished, skinny Ozark boys physically geared for the rugged demands of the sport.

My keen interest in baseball was stimulated by listening to the radio broadcasts of the St. Louis Cardinals, the only professional team west of the Mississippi. The colorful play-by-play announcing of Harry Caray ("King of the Ozarks") over KDRO radio in nearby Sedalia hooked me on the sport at the age of nine.

My Dad was not athletically inclined, however, he was willing to give me the opportunity to play baseball. We laid out a diamond in an open space on our north forty acres. Dad carefully crafted a backstop of hickory posts from our timber and chicken wire purchased from the Calhoun hardware store. The bases were gunnysacks filled with dirt. Because we had two telephones (Calhoun and Clinton exchanges), Dad was able to contact a sufficient number of boys and girls for Sunday afternoon get-togethers. On our cow-pasture diamond, we played "Work Up" and "Flies and Grounders"—it was a vision come true on my Ozarks "Field of Dreams." This story is told in full in my chapter entitled "Cow Pasture Baseball: Images of a Folk Sport Place."

Basketball was an important form of recreation for Ozark boys and girls because it required little money. All that was needed was a ball and a makeshift goal, similar to how James Naismith conceived the game. One Christmas morning I received a new Voit basketball, which instantly created an urgent need for a goal. Our timber once again supplied a hickory pole. With post-hole digger in hand, Dad set it in the ground in an open space north of the machine shed, which served as a barrier to prevent balls from rolling into the driveway. He sawed wooden slats to make a backboard, which he mounted on the pole. Then he nailed a store-bought rim to the backboard. After many games of "H-O-R-S-E" and "Round the World," the rim eventually loosened and tilted downward. After heavy rains soaked the soil around the backboard pole, it began to lean like the Tower of Pisa. Needless to say, shooting was a challenge—aiming at a tilted rim on a leaning backboard! Moreover, the ground cover of fescue grass on the playing area soon succumbed to bare earth under the constant dribbling of the ball and shuffling of feet. It was "dirt court basketball" at its finest!

Another sport that my Dad followed with great enthusiasm was foxhunting. The Ozarks version of this sport centered around the weekly meetings on Saturday night at a designated spot where hound owners would build a campfire. Here they would unleash the dogs and eventually listen to them bay in the distance, knowing they were on the trail of that elusive red "varmit." Ironically, the last time I visited the home place, our one-room country church had been razed and in its place was erected the Henry County Foxhunters Pavilion. Obviously, foxhunting had become a religion of sorts to those folks, and this monument to the sport had replaced our previous tabernacle to the "man up above." Memories of foxhunting days were recalled at my Dad's deathbed some years ago when he rolled over and spoke softly using an expression from the foxhunter's lexicon—"Son, it's time to piss on the fire and call in the dogs"—meaning his life was over.

Last, home remedies were a vital part of health care in our family. Professional physicians were few in number in our neck of the woods. "Yarb doctors" and "granny women," hillfolk who had never studied medicine, were prevalent throughout the Ozarks. My parents and grandparents had learned a variety of cures from these well-known "doctors." They relied on a number of potions and healing agents featuring various herbs, barks, roots, and other medicinal plants. Some of the more memorable remedies and cures used by my parents included a mixture of horehound leaves to relieve a cough, catnip tea for stomach cramps ("bellyache"), green walnut juice for treating ringworms, and blood of a toad to remove warts. Grandpa Whitlow had several special remedies including one for constipation. He called his concoction the "black physic," a purgative made from the root of a May apple. Because he chewed tobacco, Grandpa claimed the best poultice for a bite or sting was a chaw of tobacco. According to Grandpa, it was also applicable to boils—it would "draw the pizen" out. Grandma Whitlow passed along several treatments in our family such as soaking a cut finger in "coal oil" (kerosene), injecting a few drops of warmed castor oil into an ear for the earache, and spitting under a flat rock for a sideache. My friend, Ol Waisner, always recommended sassafras tea, made from the sassafras root, to thin or purify the blood after a long, cold winter. He always said the small fresh red roots were the best—the smaller and redder the better. It always seemed to me that the efficacy of the treatment varied directly with its unpleasantness, that is, bitter tea was always best, and the more a poultice hurt the better its cure.

Since leaving the Ozarks for the Oklahoma plains some thirty-five years ago, I have developed a greater awareness and deeper appreciation for American folklife and all its spatial manifestations. My teaching and research interests have been strongly influenced by those folk experiences of yesteryear. Students in my introductory cultural geography classes are annually given a heavy dose of lectures and slides on the folklife traits covered in this reader. My research has increasingly focused on two of these traits— music and architecture. Clearly, my roots have made a lasting impression— one that I have converted into a scholarly pursuit.

Although you may have never experienced the folklife traditions of the same magnitude that I did, I suggest you check your background for some facet of folklife that may have been passed down through your family or has been transmitted into your circle of friends. American folklife varies from place to place, however, I suspect that regardless of where you reside, some aspect of it has permeated your lifestyle. It may be the childhood rhythms of "Patty Cake" learned from your parents or the humorous blessing of "Good bread, good meat, good God, let's eat" picked up from a friend. A grandparent may have shared a personal recipe for homemade bread with you or taught you a favorite tune on the fiddle.

Despite the fact that we live in a highly urbanized, technological society, folklife remains a dynamic process in America. We refuse to allow traditions to die because they come early and stay late in the lives of all of us.

As you approach the subject of folklife, perhaps for the first time, you will be surprised to discover that interest in the field has existed for more than two hundred years, mostly among people who have examined it from vantage points related to their disciplines: language, religion, literature, anthropology, and cultural geography. Thus, the field of folklife has been formed and shaped by a variety of perspectives.

This collection of readings and my interpretation of folklife espouses no particular school or theoretical foundation. The readings represented here cover an eclectic combination of folklife traits as well as a broad spectrum of ideas produced by cultural geographers and other folklife scholars. By no means should cultural geographers claim the last word concerning folklife studies because it is truly an interdisciplinary field and to define it narrowly only inhibits others from learning about its dynamic qualities and practical applications. As an eminent folklife scholar recently stated: "Folklife is not a single topic or a single discipline; rather, its essence lies in a strong valuation of vernacular expression of all sorts, an interdisciplinary strategy for studying them, and a humanistic respect for the people who create or perform them."

Please join me now as we explore six folklife traits from a geographical slant. I hope after reading it, you will reach a fuller understanding of American folklife as well as gain a deeper respect for the folk and their traditions.

# Acknowledgments

In preparing *Baseball, Barns, and Bluegrass*, I am indebted to many people. To the folklife scholars who contributed articles to this volume, I owe a special note of appreciation. Many of them graciously provided support and encouragement, furnished photographs and maps, and responded to editorial inquiries. Among those I would especially like to thank are Steve Jett, Jon Kilpinen, Greg Jeane, Henry Glassie, Ed Price, and Dick Francaviglia.

For inspiration and guidance in the fields of cultural geography and folklife, I am forever grateful to four individuals—Archie Green, Guy Logsdon, Wilbur Zelinsky, and Terry Jordan. Archie was one of the first scholars to encourage me to pursue my folklife research interests. Guy provided me with many opportunities to participate in folklife activities, particularly the Festival of American Folklife in 1980. Wilbur's steady influence and scholarship over the years have continually stimulated my interest in cultural geography. Finally, Terry has been a constant source of ideas concerning folklife and cultural geography and permitted me to borrow many of them.

Acknowledgment is in order to Jon Sisk, editor in chief of Rowman & Littlefield, who gave me the opportunity to assemble this collection of readings on cultural geography and folklife. I want to express my sincere appreciation to Susan McEachern, executive editor, who guided me through the editorial process and lent constructive support throughout completion of the book. Scott Horst proved to be an efficient yet creative production editor.

Of the many individuals at Oklahoma State University who assisted me in the preparation of this work, none were more important than Gayle Manley, Christie Edgington, and Mike Larson. Gayle and Christie typed the manuscript and, without their diligent efforts, this publication would not have become a reality. Mike as director of cartography services waved his magic wand over the creation and revision of maps and photographs that appear in these pages. The Department of Geography is also blessed with two other exceptional professionals. Susan Shaull, department supervisor, provided organizational expertise and a positive influence throughout the duration of this project. I want to acknowledge Tom Wikle, department chair, who has consistently encouraged and facilitated my research during his tenure as departmental leader.

And last, but certainly not least, my love and affection goes to Janie, my wife of twenty-six years; Brian, my oldest son, who is in graduate school at Texas Christian University; and Mark, my youngest, who is a junior at the University of Missouri-Kansas City. If it were not for their patience, support, and caring attitude, this book would not have been completed.

Introduction

# A Geography of American Folklife

## George O. Carney

All academic disciplines are composed of their own special vocabulary. The field of folklife studies is no exception. In approaching the contents of this anthology, it is imperative to define the terminology associated with the subject matter. Attention is given to such terms as *folk culture, folkways, folk geography, folklore,* and *folklife.* Each of these is related in some way to the word *folk.*

### Folk

In the nineteenth and early twentieth century, *folk* was a word used among the lay public and popular press to describe a group of people who were old-fashioned and out of touch with modern society. Even those who studied the folk during this period defined folk as a plain group of rural, traditional people, often located in an isolated environment. Today, however, folk scholars are much less restrictive in their definition. They are now concerned with human interactions concerning traditions on all levels of society, among all ethnic, religious, and occupational groups, and encompassing all regions. Folk traditions are now considered practical, functional, and meaningful to people in their everyday lives.

Relatively few authentic folk groups still exist in the United States today because of the universalizing impacts of industrialization, urbanization, and mass communication. Moreover, the generations of intermixing of cultures, mobility of peoples, and effects of public education are additional factors that have influenced the meaning of folk. Many of the folk traditions

1

in modern society are more likely expressed by individuals than by coherent groups. In this sense, each of us may be included in the folk because we have retained some aspect of folk culture—a song, story, recipe, or superstition—that has been handed down from a former generation or passed on to us from an immediate member of our family. Several folk traditions have survived in physical form, including architecture and food, or vestiges of the folk on the cultural landscape. Furthermore, several folk traditions that were forgotten by a younger generation have been rejuvenated under the broad umbrella of "folk revivalism." Examples include folk music, dance, and dress.

In a modern context, therefore, the *folk* can refer to individuals who retain a folk tradition or to any group of people who share at least one common tradition. These traditions may relate to a variety of traits such as language, religion, occupation, or region. The common denominator is tradition.

## Folk Culture

The culture of the folk focuses on several common characteristics. The aforementioned tradition is the foremost feature. Folk culture must demonstrate stability and continuity in whatever place, whatever level of culture, or whether it is expressed by individuals or groups. Furthermore, folk culture is associated with an informal, personal, everyday lifestyle based on face-to-face communication rather than the formal, impersonal, and institutionalized way of life. In summary, folk culture is the opposite of the mass-produced, mechanized, media-conscious, popular culture of the late twentieth century.

Folk culture is categorized into separate branches. Some folk scholars use three sets including verbal, material, and customary; while others divide it into material and nonmaterial. The verbal category includes expressions people make into words, including such genres as ballads, tales, and riddles. The customary group includes expressions that exist through people's actions, such as superstitions, sports/games, and dance. Verbal and customary are often combined under one category known as *nonmaterial (mentafacts) culture.* Many of these elements are intangibles that we cannot see, touch, or smell, such as religious beliefs. In contrast, *material culture,* or *artifacts,* is a physical expression of human beings. Such expressions are tangible, physical objects that we can see, touch, or smell, such as buildings and food.

## Folkways

*Folkways* was a term coined in 1907 by American sociologist William Graham Sumner. His definition was the habitual "usages, manners, customs, mores, and morals," which were practiced more or less unconsciously in every culture. Until 1989, the term was used less frequently by folk scholars. With the publication of *Albion's Seed: Four British Folkways in America*, by David Hackett Fischer, it was revived with modifications. Fischer, a historian, used the term to examine culture as a coherent and comprehensive whole, that is, total history. He stated that folkways in the modern world may be either a material or nonmaterial culture element that retains a high degree of persistence, variability, and adaptability. He identified twenty-four categories of folkways ranging from building ways (prevailing forms of vernacular architecture and high architecture, which tend to be related to one another) to food ways (patterns of diet, nutrition, cooking, eating, feasting, and fasting). He concluded that folkways exist in both primitive and advanced cultures and have grown stronger rather than weaker as functioning systems in the modern world.

## Folk Geography

Used first by geographer Eugene Wilhelm in 1970, *folk geography* is defined as the study of land-use patterns, human/environment relationships, and reconstruction of cultural landscapes by folk groups. As a relatively undeveloped subfield of cultural geography, the term is still used in the textbook literature, but has never figured prominently in cultural geography forums.

## Folklore and Folklife

The two most commonly used terms related to the folk and folk culture are *folklore* and *folklife*. The expressive traditions from which these concepts are derived existed long before the words entered our vocabulary. A number of examples illustrate this point.

The earliest recorded histories from the Greek civilization include the often-told tales that the Greeks called myths. *Chih Cheng*, the oldest poetry anthology, dates to the time of Confucius (551–479 B.C.). These writings contain the everyday speech of the common people of China. Two Roman chroniclers, Tacitus (c. 56–120 A.D.) and Plutarch (40–120 A.D.), were among the first to compose formal essays on folklore and folklife as they wrote on the traditional customs and beliefs of the Roman people. The oldest Japanese histories, *Kojiki* (712 A.D.) and *Nihongi* (720 A.D.), serve as sources for many myths, legends, and folk songs.

During the Middle Ages and throughout the eighteenth century, noted authors, poets, and playwrights used folklore and folklife in their writings. Folk tales appear in the *Decameron* of Italian author Giovanni Boccaccio (1313–1375) and the and the *Canterbury Tales* of English poet Geoffrey Chaucer (1342–1400). Legends and myths provided subject matter for the English dramatist William Shakespeare's (1564–1616) *The Taming of the Shrew* and *King Lear*. Robert Burns, the eighteenth-century Scottish poet, collected ballads and composed poetry in the folk idiom. The Grimm Brothers (Jakob and Wilhelm) recorded tales told by their housekeeper and published them in the two-volume *Kinderund Hausmärchen*, or *Children's and Household Tales* (1812–1815). This anthology of traditional stories quickly won international acclaim and introduced the world to such well-known stories as "Cinderella," "Sleeping Beauty," "Little Red Riding Hood," and "Hansel and Gretel."

Many of the classics in nineteenth-century American literature embrace folklore and folklife. Traditional accounts of supernatural events and figures, such as "The Legend of Sleepy Hollow" (1819–1820), inspired Washington Irving. Herman Melville drew upon seafarers' tales and superstitions in writing *Moby Dick* (1851). Joel Chandler Harris derived the bulk of the animal tales in *Uncle Remus: His Songs and Sayings* (1880) from African Americans. Traditional beliefs played an important role in *The Adventures of Huckleberry Finn* (1885), authored by Mark Twain. Willa Cather included a Bohemian custom of a burial at the crossroads in *My Antonia* (1918). More recently, Alice Walker in *The Color Purple* included a conjure woman, and her other novels contain examples of African-American folk culture. Folklore and folklife thus have been a vital part of various cultures from earliest recorded history to the present.

### Folklore

The term *folklore* is of comparatively recent vintage. Englishman William John Thoms (1803–1885) wrote a letter to the periodical *Athenaeum* in 1846 in which he asked for help in documenting antiquities. Thoms proposed a "good Saxon compound, Folklore" to replace the term *popular antiquities*. He stated that folklore is the "lore of the people," and defined it as "the manners, customs, observances, superstitions, ballads, proverbs, and so forth of the olden time." Thoms and others were products of the nineteenth-century intellectual current of romanticism. Those of that age glorified the common people and took a nostalgic interest in their speech and customs for fear they were slowly vanishing.

At the close of the nineteenth century, another Englishman, Edwin Sidney Hartland, defined folklore as "the science of Tradition." He stated that its aims were to examine "the customs and beliefs, the stories and superstitions handed down from generation to generation, to ascertain how these products arose and what was the order of their development."

During the twentieth century, the number of definitions for folklore have increased and it has often been said that more definitions existed for the term than there were folklorists. A few examples from notable American folklorists illustrate this point. William Branscom defined folklore as the "myths, legends, tales, proverbs, and riddles, and a variety of other forms of artistic expressions whose medium is the spoken word" (1949). Jan Harold Brunvand described folklore as "any material that circulates traditionally among members of any group in different versions, whether in oral form or by means of customary example" (1968). Richard M. Dorson stated that it is "the hidden submerged culture lying behind the shadow of official civilization" (1968). Roger Abrahams asserted that it is the "accumulated traditions, the inherited products and practices of a specifiable group" (1983). Dan Ben-Amos affirmed it as "artistic communication in small groups" (1971). Robert A. Georges and Michael Owen Jones declared that folklore "denotes expressive forms, processes, and behaviors that we customarily learn, teach, and utilize or display during face-to-face interaction and that we judge to be traditions because they are based on known precedents and because they serve as evidence of continuities through time and space in human knowledge, thought, belief, and feeling" (1995).

## Folklife

*Folklife* is a relatively recent word in the American vocabulary. It is based on English adaptations of several European-based terms, primarily from German and Swedish sources. The German *Volkskunde* is apparently the continental European parent of American folklife. An eighteenth-century term, it literally means "knowledge of the common folk." A second German term *Volksleben* was defined by European scholars in the early twentieth century as the study of the interrelationships between the folk and folk culture as they are determined by community and tradition. These German equivalents of folklife used the prefix *Volk* as a term to denote tradition.

Use of the Swedish word *folkliv* is traced to 1847 when it first appeared in a Swedish book, *The Folklife of the Jurisdictional District of Skytt*. Subsequently introduced by scholars at the University of Lund in the early part of the twentieth century, *folkliv* was the Swedish equivalent of the German *Volksleben*, that is, the inclusion of the entire range of folk culture, both material and oral elements. Thus, when folklife studies became an academic discipline in European universities, it focused on an analysis of a folk culture in its entirety. It was intended to be a concept of broader range than folklore, which emphasized only the oral and literary aspects of folk culture, such as folk tales and folk songs, or the "lore" in folklore.

Folklife studies in Europe assembled a diverse group of disciplines, including cultural anthropology, dialectology, cultural geography, religion, sociology, and psychology. Following the German and Swedish models, British universities adopted folklife studies programs as well as initiating societies and journals, such as *Ulster Folklife* (1955) and *Folklife: Journal of the Society for Folklife Studies* (1963). Folklife research in Europe, therefore, concentrated on the study of the traditional aspects of native European cultures.

American Don Yoder, folk scholar at the University of Pennsylvania, championed the term *folklife* and launched the folklife studies movement in the United States. His paper, "The Folklife Studies Movement," published in the 1950s, became the clarion call for those interested in expanding folk culture studies. According to Yoder, folklife studies is the "20th century re-discovery of the total range of the folk-culture." His primary concern was with a preindustrial, rural community that was tied to regional and ethnic traditions. He later came to recognize "contemporary folklife" as alterations of older traditions in urban and industrial settings.

Inspired by the European models of scholarship, Yoder articulated the concept of folklife to include material and oral elements of folk culture. His paper, now almost thirty-five years old, remains the single best statement of the idea. He argued that folklife studies was a newer holistic approach that analyzed traditional cultural elements in a complex society—whether those elements are defined as folk, ethnic, regional, rural, urban, or sectarian—viewing them in the context of that larger unifying society and culture of which all subgroups and traditions are functioning parts.

In 1967, the Festival of American Folklife, jointly sponsored by the Smithsonian Institution and the National Park Service, was launched on the National Mall in Washington, D.C., to provide a "living museum" of various geographical regions and ethnic groups in the United States. By the early 1970s, a number of folk scholars led by Archie Green, Wayland Hand, and Yoder lobbied the United States Congress to establish the American Folklife Foundation. In 1973, several congressional bills were proposed to establish an American Folklife Center in the Library of Congress. Finally, in 1976, the American Folklife Center Act was enacted as Public Law 94–201 (2 January, 1976):

> American folklife is the traditional, expressive, shared culture of various groups in the United States: familial, ethnic, occupational, religious, and regional. Expressive culture includes a wide range of creative and symbolic forms such as customs, beliefs, technical skills, language, literature, art, architecture, music, play, dance, drama, ritual, pageantry, and handicrafts. These kinds of expression may be found at all levels of any culture; what makes them folklife are that they are learned orally, by imitation, or in performance, and are generally maintained or perpetuated without benefit of formal instruction or institutional direction.

As Henry Glassie, foremost folklife scholar and one of the contributors to this anthology, once described it, folklife is "the study of folk culture however expressed—in work as well as play, in craft as well as speech, in belief as well as proverb." Thus, folklife is an inclusive concept that consists of both material and nonmaterial culture. The working definition of folklife for this anthology is based on the American Folklife Act of 1976, particularly the last sentence.

## Folklife and Cultural Geography

Folklife and cultural geography share the ultimate goal of understanding cultural phenomena and cultural processes. Cultural geography seeks to understand the spatial variations among cultural groups as well as explanations for cultural diversity from a spatial perspective.

Interest in folklife by cultural geographers was spearheaded by Fred B. Kniffen and his legion of students at Louisiana State University-Baton Rouge. In 1936, he produced the first intensive study on folk architecture with his Louisiana house types article in the *Annals of the Association of American Geographers*. Almost thirty years later, Kniffen's continued fieldwork on house types resulted in the classic work entitled "Folk Housing: Key to Diffusion" in which he identified the culture hearths of American folk architecture and named many of the folk house types still in use today, such as the I-House.

In 1976, Don Yoder, eminent folklife scholar, asked Kniffen to contribute an overview essay to his *American Folklife* anthology. Entitled "American Cultural Geography and Folklife," Kniffen outlined the relationships between the two fields and cited research on the field by several cultural geographers and folklife scholars. In addition to Kniffen, Cotton Mather, John

Fraser Hart, Wilbur Zelinsky, and Matti Kaups were the pioneering cultural geographers who researched and wrote on folklife traits in the 1950s and 1960s. Most of their research focused on material culture including barns, fences, and saunas.

The most prolific cultural geographer in recent decades to explore folklife traits is Terry G. Jordan of the University of Texas-Austin. He has authored articles and books on a wide range of folklife topics including architecture, religion, and cemeteries. Jordan and other cultural geographers have delineated five basic themes in cultural geography—region, diffusion, ecology, integration, and landscape. Therefore, the study of folklife in this anthology is organized around these five themes.

## Theme 1: Folklife Regions

The folklife region is an area on the earth's surface where certain common folk cultural characteristics prevail. The folklife region is the grouping of like places to form a culturally discrete spatial unit.

Jordan has identified eleven folklife regions in the United States (fig. I.1). Although his regions are based on material culture, nonmaterial elements of folk culture are equally applicable. The eleven folklife regions and their general boundaries are:

1. Acadian French (Cajun)—southwestern Louisiana
2. Yankee—central New York, most of Vermont and New Hampshire, and the southern half of Maine
3. Pennsylvanian—Amish country of Pennsylvania and extends southwesterly into western Maryland and northern Virginia
4. Upland South—most of the Appalachian sections of eastern West Virginia, Kentucky, and Tennessee; the Appalachian sections of western Virginia and North Carolina; and the Appalachian sections of the northwestern tip of South Carolina, northeastern part of Alabama, northern Georgia, and the extreme southern portions of Illinois, Indiana, and Ohio; the Ozarks of southern Missouri, northwest Arkansas, and eastern Oklahoma; the northeastern section of Missouri, and the Texas hill country
5. Mexican—along the Rio Grande Valley from the southern portion of Texas into the southwestern part of New Mexico and southeastern part of Arizona
6. Highland Hispanic—north central part of New Mexico extending to the south central section of Colorado
7. Mormon—most of Utah and extending into southeastern Idaho

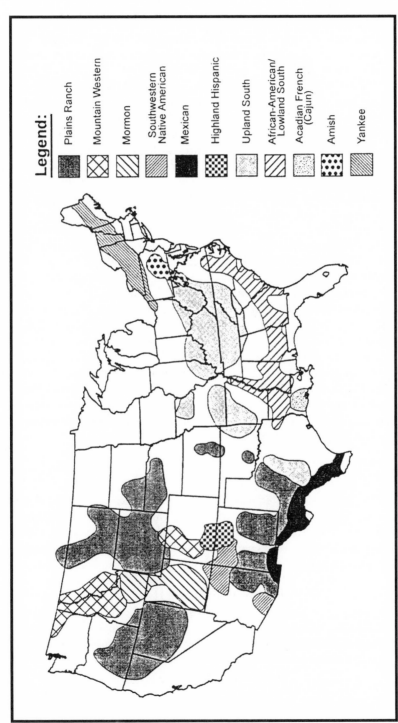

Legend:

- Plains Ranch
- Mountain Western
- Mormon
- Southwestern Native American
- Mexican
- Highland Hispanic
- Upland South
- African-American/ Lowland South
- Acadian French (Cajun)
- Amish
- Yankee

Fig. I.1. Eleven Folklife Regions in the United States. Adapted from Terry G. Jordan, et al., *The Human Mosaic*, 7th ed. New York: Longman, 1997.

8. African American/Lowland South—eastern half of North Carolina, southeastern South Carolina, southern portions of Georgia, Alabama, and Mississippi, extreme eastern Arkansas, northern Louisiana, and a small segment of east Texas
9. Mountain West—Rocky Mountain valleys of Colorado and Idaho
10. Southwestern Native American—northeastern and south central portions of Arizona and northwestern New Mexico
11. Plains Ranch—small segments in western Kansas and Oklahoma, west central Texas extending into southeastern New Mexico and eastern Arizona, a broad expanse from northern Nebraska and southwestern South Dakota to include much of Wyoming and eastern Montana, and a third large area from northern Nevada, northeastern California, and south-central Oregon

Each of the eleven folklife regions are covered by one or more readings to provide regional and ethnic breadth. Examples include: Acadian—"The Cajun Accordion" (chapter 10), Yankee—"The New England Connecting Barn" (chapter 3), Pennsylvanian—"The Amish and Their Land" (chapter 15), Upland South—"The Appalachian Log Cabin" (chapter 1), Mexican— "Plants in the Folk Medicine of the Texas-Mexico Borderlands" (chapter 18), Highland Hispanic—"Hispano Gristmills in New Mexico" (chapter 2), Mormon—"Mormon Central-Hall Houses in the American West" (chapter 4), African American/Lowland South—"Geophagy in a Mississippi County" (chapter 8), Mountain West—"The Mountain Horse Barn: A Case of Western Innovation""(chapter 5), Southwestern Native American—"Modern Navajo Cemeteries" (chapter 17), and Plains Ranch—"Sod Construction on the Great Plains" (chapter 6).

## Theme 2: Origin and Diffusion of Folklife Traits

Folklife traits, both material and nonmaterial elements, originate at certain points (hearths) and spread over space through time to other areas. Folklife traits tend to diffuse more slowly with a folk culture because of traditions and resistance to change. Examples of folklife traits covered by the readings include the origin (hearth) of bluegrass music in western North Carolina and its spread to other areas in the United States, particularly the Upland South (chapter 11). The Central-Hall House originated in Nauvoo, Illinois, one of the Mormon centers in the Midwest, and diffused to Utah via the Mormon movement westward (chapter 4). Finally, the origin of whiskey-making techniques was in the British Isles and these practices diffused to east Tennessee with migration of Scotch-Irish settlers (chapter 9).

## *Theme 3: Folklife and Ecology*

Folk culture ecology is the study of the environmental influences on folk culture and the impact of the folk as folk culture-bearers on the natural environment. Folk cultures generally possess a strong relationship with the natural environment and folk groups develop a reciprocal relationship between themselves as folklife-bearers and the natural environment, especially because of the knowledge that folk groups have of their physical surroundings. The rural folk, in particular, adapt to their natural environment by using local building materials, such as wood, stone, and sod, for their traditional architecture. Moreover, rural and sometimes urban folk often use plants from the natural environment for food and medicinal purposes. The use of plants by *curanderos* ("curers") in the Mexican-American population of the southwestern borderlands is discussed in chapter 18. Chapter 8 outlines the practice of geophagy (dirt eating) among African Americans in Mississippi. Finally, the natural environment provides a pastoral setting for the sports of foxhunting and cockfighting, two of the recreational activities covered respectively in chapters 12 and 13.

## *Theme 4: Integration in Folklife*

Integration in folklife is the analysis of all facets of folk culture and the manner in which they are systematically and spatially interconnected. Folk cultures are complex wholes rather than a series of unrelated traits—all aspects of folk culture are interdependent on one another. Integration examines how folk-culture traits interact with each other in an integrated system. Examples from the readings include the effect of the Amish religious beliefs on their agricultural practices. Thus, religion and agriculture are traits interconnected (chapter 15). The interrelationship of religion and architecture is reflected in the Mormon central-hall house (chapter 4). Many bluegrass musicians began their careers singing and playing in church. Religion and music, therefore, are intertwined (chapter 11). Finally, the integration of ethnicity and architecture and ethnicity and music are respectively demonstrated in the Hispano gristmill and Cajun accordion pieces (chapters 2 and 10).

## *Theme 5: Landscapes of the Folk*

The folk landscape consists of the forms and artifacts sequentially placed on the natural environment by the activities of folk occupants. By this progressive imprinting of the human presence, the natural environment is modified into the folk cultural landscape. Thus, the folk landscape manifests the visible imprints of folk groups on the earth's surface (human-made landscape). All six chapters on folk architecture illustrate the influence of humans on the natural environment from the Appalachian log cabin to the Mountain West barn. The folk cemeteries of the Upland Southerners (chapter 16) and the Navajo Indians (chapter 17) also produce distinctive folk landscapes.

## Folklife and Contemporary Society

The relevance of folklife to contemporary society may be seen as insignificant because of the popular perception that it is old-fashioned and out of touch with modern culture. We often see ourselves far removed, both mentally and physically, from expressions of folklife. Some examples of the six folklife traits covered in this book demonstrate their relevance to American society at present.

Folk architecture remains an important segment of our built environment. Grady Clay, former editor of *Landscape Architecture* magazine, has renovated three shotgun houses in Louisville and has attached them to make a three-room complex. The city of Louisville has completed a guidebook on procedures to bring extant shotgun houses up to housing standards for use as rental properties. Many of the remaining shotgun houses in New Orleans have been rehabilitated and sell on the real estate market for high prices, especially those with Victorian "gingerbread" detailing and in the gentrified neighborhoods of the city.

Programs of the National Trust for Historic Preservation and the National Park Service have resulted in the restoration of other forms of folk architecture. Moreover, many of these historic properties have been placed in the National Register of Historic Places. The "Barn Again" program of the National Trust has assisted in the restoration of folk barns throughout the United States, including the Amish bank barns of Pennsylvania and New England connecting barns. Although modified, many of the sod houses of the Great Plains are still in use. Finally, the log cabin concept has been rejuvenated in the form of contemporary versions.

Folk food and drink remain a vital part of the diets of many ethnic groups and an important aspect of regional cuisine in the United States. Many of the antebellum Southern foods discussed by Hilliard in chapter 7 have been revived in cookbooks and restaurants in the South, especially fried okra, boiled turnips, collard greens, and hominy grits. One of the folk foods of the South was featured in the recent motion picture, *Fried Green Tomatoes*. Corn and pork have remained staples of the Southern diet. Well-known restaurants in the South, such as Pitty Pat's Porch in Atlanta and Miss Wilke's Boarding House in Savannah, have included many of these items on their menus. Many folk foods associated with particular regions in the United States have become established items in the regional culinary traditions, such as New England clam chowder, Boston baked beans and Boston cream pie, Vermont maple syrup, and Georgia peach pie. Southern fried chicken and buttermilk biscuits have become standard fare in the fast-food franchise system. Finally, "chitlins" are now commercially packaged and sold in supermarkets.

Perhaps the most recent interest in any of the six folklife traits focuses on folk medicine, currently referred to as "alternative" medicine. The retail store shelves are filled with herbal teas, and herbal aromatic therapy is in vogue. Medical reports indicate an increased use of midwifery in delivery of babies. The use of *curanderos* as paramedics in the Rio Grande Valley has increased, a phenomenon discussed in chapter 18. The importance of ginseng as an export to East Asian countries is outlined in chapter 19. Finally, there is the controversial issue of the medical use of marijuana. Advocates extoll its usage for nausea from cancer chemotherapy, improving appetites of AIDS patients, and lowering pressure inside the eye due to glaucoma. This presents yet another example of folk-derived medicine.

Although the Amish are associated with the central valley of Pennsylvania, this religious folk group has spread into the American Midwest with new colonies in Illinois, Iowa, Missouri, and Oklahoma. With this colonization has come the increased popularity and sale of Amish-made goods to the "English" (non-Amish) in the form of quilts and furniture. Retail stores, especially groceries and restaurants, owned by the Amish are featuring traditional Amish foods. Folk cemeteries also have become significant with a renewed interest in seeking one's "roots." The growing hobby of tracing family genealogy has led to such practices as "rubbing gravestones."

Folk music has progressed through several revival periods, mainly in the 1960s with the so-called folk music renaissance. Several forms of folk music from traditional country to bluegrass to blues were included in these revivals, including Flatt and Scruggs in Carnegie Hall to the Cajun Balfa Brothers at the Newport Folk Festival. Publication of such magazines as *Old-Time Country*, *Living Blues*, and *Bluegrass Unlimited* indicate a growing audience for folk music. A reawakening interest in blues music is witnessed by annual blues festivals across the country, such as the Chicago Blues Festival, which draws a half-million visitors each year, and the emphasis on their blues heritage by such artists as Eric Clapton. Finally, bluegrass, a folk music tradition once considered unacceptable by the country music industry, now graces the stage of the Grand Ole Opry each weekend in Nashville. The impact of bluegrass on the new generation of country music superstars was recently acknowledged at Bill Monroe's funeral at the Ryman Auditorium when Vince Gill, Ricky Skaggs, Alison Krauss, and Patty Loveless paid tribute to Monroe, the "father of bluegrass."

Although illegal, cockfighting remains an important gaming pastime in isolated sections of the rural South. Moreover, the legal raising of gamecocks is evident throughout the South from Oklahoma to Georgia. Fox and coon hunting as well as the breeding and raising of hound dogs has become a serious hobby and business for many suburbanites as well as rural residents of the South. Playground basketball games, such as "H-O-R-S-E" and "Round the World," have endured in the rural towns of Indiana, to the inner-city pavements of New York. And children still play sandlot baseball games, such as "Work Up" and "Grounders and Flies." Finally, even though baseball has evolved into a major business with professional players making millions, the folk aspects of the game have been retained by many players who believe in superstitions, such as not touching the foul lines when they enter or leave the field.

## A Preview

This anthology is a collection of nineteen previously published articles selected from the most prestigious journals in geography and folklife, including the *Annals of the Association of American Geographers*, *Geographical Review*, *Pioneer America*, *Landscape*, *Journal of Cultural Geography*, *Sport Place*, and *Material Culture*. The chapters are authored by some of the most notable cultural geographers and folklife scholars in America.

The nineteen chapters are organized into six parts, each covering a different folklife trait: architecture, food and drink, music, sports and games, religion and cemeteries, and medicine. These six by no means represent all the folklife traits studied by cultural geographers and folklife scholars. Others that could have been considered include folk speech, folk dress and apparel, folk tales, folk dance, and folk art; however, little research by cultural geographers has been completed on these topics. The six selected traits represent a cross-section of material (e.g., architecture and food) and nonmaterial (e.g., music and religion) elements. Thus, the anthology strikes a balance between these two divisions of folklife. Headnotes for each part contain a brief synopsis of each reading and its relationship to one or more of the five themes of cultural geography. At the end of this volume is a selected annotated list of references for further reading on each folklife trait. Finally, reprinted articles appear as they were originally published, though some minor changes were made to enhance readability and update ethnic-and-gender-specific language.

# Part I: Folk Architecture

Cultural geographers interested in folklife have researched and written more on folk architecture than any other folklife trait. Cultural geographer Fred B. Kniffen, the dean of American folk architecture, pioneered the study of traditional building techniques, identified traditional buildings based on their shape and form, and eventually provided names for many of the folk building styles.

Folk architecture is built by someone who carries a cognitive, or learned, model of the way houses, barns, bridges, or fences should look when finished. Construction techniques and form are handed down from generation to generation, or learned from a neighbor. Often referred to as "architecture without architects," folk architecture is not from the drafting tables and blueprints of professional architects. It is not spectacular, decorative, or revolutionary; rather, it is conservative, functional, and traditional. Finally, it is a reflection of a folk culture's identity and values, priorities and aspirations, and technology and economy.

As to its relationship to the five themes of folklife, folk architecture is an extension of a traditional people and their *folklife region*. Folklife regions have spawned various folk architecture styles, for example, Upland South and the log cabin and Yankee and the connecting barn (chapters 1 and 3).

As to the *origin and diffusion of folklife traits* theme, Kniffen stated that folk architectural styles originated on the American East Coast and diffused westward to the interior. Human migration was the catalyst for the spread of these styles as an item in the "cultural baggage" of folk groups as they moved from place to place. This is exemplified by the Mormon Central-hall House as it spread from Nauvoo, Illinois, where it was known as the "Nauvoo-style house," to the Mormon country of Utah after the 1840s (chapter 4).

The theme of *folklife and ecology* is reflected in folk architecture's harmony with the natural environment. Folk groups used locally available building materials (e.g., wood, stone, and sod) and adjusted to the local climate, such as the addition of front porches and elevated floors off the ground, both of which provided ventilation in warm, moist areas. Chapter six demonstrates the reliance of settlers on sod cut from the Great Plains earth and used as a building material where little timber or stone was available. The heavy sod materials provided warmth in the winter, and con-

17

structed on a southern hillside location, protected the house from the cold winter winds from the north.

*Folklife integration*, the relationship between one or more folklife traits, is portrayed in chapters 1 and 2. The ethnicity of folk groups played an important role in folk architecture. Log construction techniques were introduced to America by the Swedes, Germans, and Scotch-Irish during the seventeenth and eighteenth centuries, according to Glassie (chapter 1). The Hispanic folk of the northern New Mexico highlands developed a unique type of gristmill with horizontal waterwheels and lack of any gear mechanism. These log-housed gristmills represent an interrelationship of folk architecture with the ethnic-based Hispano folk culture of the nineteenth century (chapter 2).

Finally, architecture is a major force in the forging of *folk landscapes* and an important indicator of a folk culture's way of life. Folk architecture is the most dominant component of the folk landscape. The Mountain Horse Barn, an innovative building type developed in the Rocky Mountain valleys, is an identifiable feature of the Mountain West folk landscape (chapter 5).

Of all the traits that make up folklife, architecture is one of the most visible parts of our material culture. It provides important statements and examples regarding the five themes of folklife.

# 1

# The Appalachian Log Cabin

## *Henry H. Glassie*

In the nineteenth century, the log cabin was a symbol of America and, although it has been replaced in most of the nation by the suburban development and steel mill, it remains a symbol of southern Appalachia. Recorded music made for the mountain person who moved to the northern city nostalgically remind him of "the little old log cabin in the mountains," and a log cabin is on the seal of the Southern Highland Handicraft Guild. As some aspects of southern Appalachian culture have been studied in great detail since the days of Cecil Sharp, noted ballad collector, it is surprising that very little has been written about the architecture of the mountains, and surprising that the little bit that has been written is for the most part erroneous. To clear up a great many misconceptions about the log cabin, to perhaps generate a bit of interest in the fading old structure, and to show that it is most certainly a fit symbol for the Appalachian Mountains, its development is here outlined.[1]

Upon arriving in America, the English built rude huts in imitation of Indian dwellings, which were in no way related to the log cabin. As soon as possible, they constructed half-timber houses of the type they had known in England. The half-timber house is one heavily framed with the spaces between the timbers filled with mud and sticks. It was found that American soil lacked the lime of the English soil and the filling between the timbers was unsatisfactory. The practice of covering the framed building with clap-

Reprinted by permission from the author. Originally published in *Mountain Life and Work* 39 (1963): 5–14.

boarding, as was done in certain sections of England, thus became the rule throughout the English colonies.

In the mid-seventeenth century, a group of Swedes settled on the Delaware River and built houses of horizontal log. When the English settled nearby in Pennsylvania, they had little intercourse with the Swedes and, although the Swedish log house was easier to build and sounder than a frame one, the English continued to split boards from logs and laboriously construct houses as they had done in England. Thus the Swedish form of log construction never spread beyond New Sweden.

Throughout the eighteenth century great numbers of Germans and Scotch-Irish arrived in Pennsylvania.[2] They immediately moved west of the area settled by the English and began constructing the type of house each had known in Europe. The Scotch-Irish probably built the mud or stone cabins they had known in Scotland and Ulster. The Germans, like the English, brought the half-timber tradition, but they also possessed the medieval tradition of horizontal log construction. Thus, unlike the English, they were able to abandon the half-timber form in favor of the more economical log form.

The German log house (fig. 1.1) was rectangular with a three-room division of the first floor. It always had a central chimney and was often built on a hillside, producing a partially below-ground lower level like that of the great Pennsylvania barn. A few examples of this type of house remain in eastern Pennsylvania and the Valley of Virginia.

Upon arriving in America, the Germans and Scotch-Irish had similar histories of religious persecution, economic unrest, and disastrous warfare; and, having similar religions, ideals, and hardships in the New World, they soon became politically and socially aligned against the English. Although great numbers of Germans remained in the rich farmlands of eastern Pennsylvania, many moved westward with the Scotch-Irish, and by 1732 a mixed German and Scotch-Irish settlement had been established in the Valley of Virginia. Within thirty years the Valley, the Blue Ridge from Maryland to about Roanoke County, Virginia, and the lands just east of it were settled. Settlers from the Valley, directly from Pennsylvania, and Germans and Scots from eastern North Carolina soon had settled the North Carolina Piedmont. The Battle of Alamance (1771) began the great movement from the Piedmont into the mountainous Watauga area of northwestern North Carolina and northeastern Tennessee. Before the Revolution the Watauga area had been settled and people had begun moving south down the mountains, and east into the valleys.

The hardships of American Indian wars and agricultural settlement mutually endured by Germans and Scotch-Irish broke down any prejudice that

Fig. 1.1. Pennsylvania German Log House

existed between the two and there occurred a natural borrowing and meshing of cultural elements. The Germans almost fully adopted the British
music and gave in return their musical instrument, which was to become
the Appalachian dulcimer. The similar German and British folktale traditions were combined, producing a stronger folktale tradition than that
which had been known in Germany or Britain. In this way the German and
Scotch-Irish cultures meshed, producing the basis of the southern Appalachian culture, which has been changed from the original by the early addition of English and Indian elements and the later addition of African-American and urban twentieth-century elements.

The log cabin stands as a symbol of this meshing of German and Scotch-
Irish cultures. The Scotch-Irish, having inferior construction modes and
few skilled artisans, quickly adopted German horizontal log construction,
which utilized skills similar to those of British military and half-timber construction. The Scotch-Irish did not fully adopt the German house form, but
rather made certain changes in accordance with their architectual traditions
which were reinforced by the arrival in the mountains of the English in
about 1800. The house was constructed on a more square plan and had one

large rather than three small rooms. The chimney was moved from the inside, as in German tradition, to the outside, as in British tradition, where it could be more quickly and easily built. The result was, therefore, a house built upon a British plan using German construction techniques, which became the typical house of all settlers from Maryland to Alabama (fig. 1.2).

Not all cabins are log, nor are all log houses cabins. "Cabin" is an Irish term applied to a small one-room house, and large log houses, called "log castles" on the frontier, were often built in a fashionable form with numerous rooms. These grand log houses are rare in the mountains but many remain in the Valley of Virginia and the Tennessee Valley.

Wherever the Germans and Scotch-Irish moved after they had left eastern Pennsylvania, the first house they constructed was a temporary one that

Fig. 1.2.  Appalachian Log Cabin

most people consider to be the authentic log cabin. It was low with a shallow pitched roof and was built of round logs, roughly notched, with overhanging ends (fig. 1.3). It had a dirt floor and a mud and stick or crude stone chimney. This dwelling could be raised in a day and served as a shelter until a better house could be built. Cabins of this type are still rarely built as hunting cabins and are called "pole shacks" to distinguish them from the much more neatly made log cabin. A few of these cabins remain in the Great Smoky areas settled in this century, but they are quite rare in the older sections as they were not built to last, and a pole shack twenty years old is likely to be in worse repair than a log cabin two hundred years old.

The log cabin is a rectangular house averaging about sixteen by twenty feet, although there is great variation in size. In areas where the English influence is great, the log cabin is often about sixteen feet square, which is the traditional medieval English single-bay house size. It is almost always one and one-half stories high (fig. 1.2), although it rarely attains a full two-story height. It was most usually built about a foot off the ground on a stone foundation and thus had a wooden floor. At the southern end of the Appalachian Mountains, the cabin was often built up on stone or log piers rather than a solid foundation. The German practice of building on a hillside, although useful, was time consuming and was abandoned in house construction although retained in some smaller outbuildings. The cabin usually had one large chimney of fitted field stone, although in some areas of eastern Tennessee where the clay was proper, brick chimneys were built. Often next to the large fireplace, which frequently had a fine mantelpiece, was a steep stair, very rarely a ladder, which led to the loft above. The stair may have been placed anywhere about the one large room but almost always has a small closet under it. The roof was generally lightly framed and covered with "shakes," which are long shingles split out of a short log.

The feature that most distinguished the log cabin from the pole shack was the log construction itself. In the pole shack the logs were round and the corners formed by simple saddle notching (fig. 1.3). In the log cabin the logs were much larger and were hewn square or split and hewn flat on two sides. The spaces between the logs, which were often quite narrow, were filled, "chinked," with clay or mud and often pieces of wood split off like shingles. The logs were joined neatly at the corners in variations on a dovetail pattern (fig. 1.3). The ends of the logs were cut off flush producing a square corner in which no rainwater could collect and thus the corner could not rot out as so frequently happened with saddle notching.

In studying any cultural element, some variable feature must be decided on by which one may learn about its development and geographical distribution. In architecture the form of the building is usually that feature but,

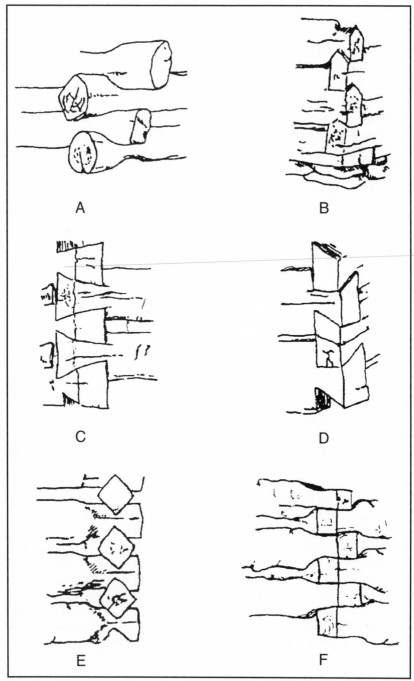

Fig. 1.3. Log Corner Notching Types: A. Saddle  B. V-Notch  C. Full Dovetail
D. Half Dovetail  E. Diamond  F. Square

as there is little difference in form from cabin to cabin, form is of little use in the study of the log cabin. The most distinguishing variable feature is the method of corner timbering, the way the logs are joined at the corners. In eastern Pennsylvania, three forms of corner timbering may be found, all of which are traditional in Germany. One is the saddle notching of temporary buildings and barns. The two others, V and full dovetail, are the types found on all log houses in eastern Pennsylvania. The V-corner timbering (fig. 1.3) was associated in early times with the Schwenkenfelders, although other German groups probably used it. V-corner timbering was carried into the Valley of Virginia and virtually every log cabin in the mountains of Maryland and Virginia was constructed with this corner timbering. Full dovetail (fig. 1.3) is not common outside of eastern Pennsylvania as it was early developed into half dovetail (fig. 1.3), which could be more easily made and, as it had no inward-sloping surfaces to hold water, was longer lasting. Half dovetail is virtually the only type found in the western North Carolina Piedmont from whence it was carried into the Watauga area and thence south and west. Many of the settlers of the Watauga area came directly from the Valley so that both V and half dovetail, with extremely rare instances of full dovetail, are found there, whereas north of Watauga, only V may be found, and south, generally half dovetail. There are, of course, exceptions owing to unconventional migrations. The reason for this division is unclear, as the bulk of all the settlers came from eastern Pennsylvania. Perhaps the settlers of the Valley left before full dovetailing was introduced into Pennsylvania. Perhaps the influence of the Germans and Swiss from eastern North Carolina caused the division. It remains, however, a mystery.

In eastern American log construction, there are two remaining corner timbering types. Diamond-corner timbering (fig. 1.3) is perhaps of Scandinavian origin. It is found from the Tidewater to the eastern North Carolina Piedmont, but no example has been found in the mountains. When the English encountered the horizontal squared log tradition, they developed square-corner timbering (fig. 1.3), which was similar to the types of joining used in British half-timber and fort construction. This type is found in eastern Virginia and areas of the South settled by eastern Virginians. It is rarely found in the mountains, and when encountered it is more usually found on newer buildings that have sawn rather than hewn logs, as square-corner timbering was easily made with a saw.

The log cabin, although sturdy, was not large and from the beginning of its development additions were made onto it. The most common form of addition, well within the British tradition, was a rear shed addition. Another British form, favored by the Pennsylvania Germans, was the ell addition.

These additions, which were often kitchens, are rarely found of log, but are common in frame, indicating that they were for the most part added after the introduction of milled lumber.

In medieval British house-building tradition, the one-room, single-bay house was most usually enlarged by means of a one-room addition onto the end of the original house producing a two-room house with a chimney on each end. This form of house was popular in the early English colonies, but was rarely built of log. The existence of a few log houses in south-central Virginia reflects the attempts made by the English to build familiar houses with unfamiliar but economical log construction techniques.

Frame additions were occasionally made onto the ends of log cabins. Unlike framed construction, when an addition of log is made to a log house, the old and new logs cannot be fitted into each other. Thus, an end addition could not become an integral part of the old house but could only be built as close as possible, the area between the old and new sections usually being filled with vertical logs and chinking. One solution was to make the addition onto the chimney end as was often done in British tradition. The chimney thus joined the two rooms and supplied both with heat. This house is called a "saddlebag" and is found westward from the Watauga area and sporadically throughout the mountains where the addition is of frame as often as of log (fig. 1.4).

Another solution to the log end addition was the "dog trot" house (fig.

Fig. 1.4. Saddlebag House

Fig. 1.5. Dog Trot House

1.5). The second room, or "pen," was not built up to the end of the first but rather was built some feet away and the two were covered with a common roof. The result was two log cabins, each with its own chimney, with an open covered passage between them. It bore a remarkable resemblance to the German double crib barn found throughout the mountains, which may have been in some way an inspiration. Houses thus divided into three sections were common in northern Europe and Britian and so the form quickly became popular. This house seems to have sprung up west of the Blue Ridge and is very common from southeastern Tennessee through much of Mississippi and Alabama. The few examples found in the North Carolina Piedmont and the exceedingly few found along the Blue Ridge were probably brought from the West.

Thus, the log cabin is a fitting symbol of southern Appalachia because it brought together the best of German and British architectural traditions. In this day of functional design, it may be established as an architectural ideal in that it was molded by tradition and necessity into the perfect dwelling for our pioneers, whose craft and hardiness it reflects.

## Notes

1. I have read the few works on the subject but, to avoid mistakes of their authors, I have spent more time studying the old houses firsthand than I have in libraries.

2. The Germans referred to throughout this article are the Pennsylvania

Germans, also called the Pennsylvania Dutch. The Pennsylvania Germans came primarily from the Rhenish Palatine and Switzerland, but also from Alsace, Wurtemburg, Hesse, Saxony, and Silesia. The Scotch-Irish were Lowland Scots who settled in Ulster before coming to America. The Scotch-Irish include small numbers of English, Irish, and Highland Scots.

2

# Hispano Gristmills
# in New Mexico

## Charles F. Gritzner

Few parts of the United States are more rewarding for the student of folklife than the area of Spanish settlement in the Rio Grande Valley and adjacent highlands of northern New Mexico. Hispanic colonists began moving northward into the region from Mexico as early as the seventeenth century. Many pioneer traits remain within the contemporary culture, and often stand in marked contrast to those practices that were of aboriginal or Anglo-American provenance.

Northern New Mexico has retained its distinctive folk culture for a variety of reasons. Paramount is the tenacity with which Hispanos have clung to traditional practices. Its relative geographical and cultural isolation, a paucity of those resources that stimulated Anglo settlement elsewhere in the West during the nineteenth century, and the widely perceived "backward" nature of the region have also kept outside cultural intrusion to a minimum until recently.[1] The region remains one of the most distinct folk cultural enclaves in the United States.

A rapidly decreasing number of small, log-housed gristmills are among those folk relics that link contemporary Hispanic culture with an earlier era. These mills are unique because of their horizontal waterwheels and the absence of any gear mechanism. The mills have been ignored by most lay or scientific writers. Perhaps they seem like insignificant rustic oddities amid a

Reprinted by permission from the *Annals of the Association of American Geographers* 64 (1974): 514–24.

plethora of such romanticized features as well-preserved aboriginal ruins, inhabited pueblos, adobe construction, centuries-old religious and public buildings, and a wealth of folk arts and handicrafts.

Such mention as they received in the narratives of nineteenth-century travelers was superficial and generally disparaging, and no detailed analysis of the presence, origin, nature, and economic function of the gristmills has yet appeared in the literature of the region.

This lack appears to have resulted from historical circumstances and perhaps human nature. Spanish Americans themselves have written very little about their culture, which as the accepted norm has been unworthy of special notation. The great majority of nineteenth-century English-speaking visitors to the region confined their travels, and hence their observations and written accounts, to such well-established routes as the Rio Grande Valley and the Santa Fe Trail. With few exceptions, they failed to penetrate the more remote villages where folk practices abounded.[2] The "Mountain Men" who trapped the region between 1820 and 1840 almost certainly acquired locally milled wheat flour and firsthand knowledge of the outpost settlements, but no reference to milling methods has been found in the scant literature contributed by these hardy individuals.

The dearth of written information on gristmills is in keeping with the general lack of detailed reference to many other more mundane aspects of the Spanish-American culture. In New Mexico, perhaps to a greater degree than elsewhere in the United States, writers have tended to overlook the fundamental components of peasant society and focused their attention on the exotic.[3]

## Description

The earliest description of a New Mexican gristmill appears in the 1847 report of J. W. Abert. The mills that he observed in Manzano (Torrance County) were

like everything else in New Mexico . . . of very primitive style. There is a vertical axis, on the lower end of which is the waterwheel; the other end passes through the lower burr, and is firmly connected with the upper stone, which, as the axis turns, revolves upon the lower stone. Above all this, hangs a large hopper of ox-hide, kept open at the top by a square frame, and narrowed off towards the bottom, so as to present the form of an inverted cone. In the extremity of the bag is a small opening, and this is fastened to a little trough. One end of this trough being supported by its connexion with the hopper, the other end, or mouth, is sustained by a horizontal strip of wood, of which an extremity rests on an upright, and the other is upheld by an inclined stick that rests on the upper burr, so that the motion of the burr gives a jostling motion to the trough and hopper; thus the grain falls into the opening of the centre of the upper burr, and passes out between the two burrs. [4]

William W. H. Davis described a similar mill near Peña Blanca (Sandoval County) in 1855:

> In my rambles around the village, I came across an old-fashioned Spanish grist-mill, the first one of the kind I had seen in the country, which was something of a curiosity in a small way. The building was not more than ten or twelve feet square, with one run of stone, turned by a small tub-wheel [sic] by water from a neighboring acequia. The upper stone was made in the form of a basin, with a rim around it some four inches wide, and fits down over the lower stone, made fast to the floor, and is about eighteen inches high. The grain is mashed by the revolution of the upper stone, and the meal falls down into a box built of bull-hide, and fastened to the beams overhead. [5]

Some notion of the mills' efficiency, as well as the negative manner in which the majority of Anglo travelers perceived the New Mexican's techno-logical level, can be gained from Bourke's observation of mills in the vicinity of Santa Cruz (Santa Fe County) in 1881:

> Two of the main acequias crossed the road and near the bridges we saw Mexi-can flour mills; these were cottonwood log edifices, about 12 feet square and 7 feet high, built over the ditch to allow the water to turn a small turbine wheel. I should conjecture that in an emergency, under the stimulus of a Gov-ernment contract (that is to say a man smoking a cigarrito, a small boy scratch-ing his nose, and a big dog scratching his ribs), and running full time, one of these mills could grind a bushel of wheat in a week; the ordinary output can't be over half that quantity. [6]

The few mills that remain intact differ little from those examples described during the nineteenth century. A wooden hopper seems to have been re-placed with one of oxhide. In time, the millstones became encased within a wooden box, and metal tended to replace a wooden shaft in the axle. In operation, however, there was little change.

## Mill Housing

The millworks were housed in simple crib structures of horizontal notched logs. There is no indication that any other building material, such as stone, adobe, or lumber, was ever employed for this purpose. Construction was generally crude, a clear indication that the housing was little more than a shell to protect the mill, grain, and flour from wind and rain, and perhaps pilfering (fig. 2.1). The comfort of the miller was of little consequence, since ice prevented milling during subfreezing weather. Corner timbering was often haphazard; several modes of notching were frequently employed in a single wall, and logs were often reused, as is attested by the number of nonfunctional notches that appear on log members extending beyond the corner joints.

Floor plans were normally square, or nearly so, with measured outer-wall dimensions varying from nine to fifteen feet (2.7 to 4.6 m). Ceilings were quite low, measuring some seven to eight feet (2.1 to 2.4 m) above the floor, and were only the exposed underside of a flat roof (*azotea*), which is common to much Hispanic architecture of the Southwest. Floors were constructed of planks, and many were covered with adobe to prevent the loss of grain that might otherwise have spilled through cracks. Doorways were low, a trait common to the Hispanic tradition, and many required one to stoop upon entering. Windows were small openings, and many were only

Fig. 2.1. The 100-Year-Old Cordova Mill Near Vadito (Taos County) Is the Only Remaining Mill Still Fully Functional at Its Original Site.

wide interstices between logs, or narrow incisions on the facing sides of adjacent logs.

## Mill Site and Power Source

Mills were built astride a small ditch (*acequia*) or trough into which water could be diverted from a nearby stream. No elaborate dam, millpond, or extensive system of canals was needed to provide adequate power. *Acequias* scarcely a foot wide (0.3 m) and less than a foot deep were able to provide enough water to turn the wheels. The gradient of the ditch was of little significance. A sufficient velocity to power a mill was achieved by water rushing down a millrace directed beneath the structure at a sharp angle and with a descent of four to six feet (1.2 to 1.8 m). Rocks, horizontal logs, and vertical posts, commonly in combination, provided the necessary support for the downstream portion of the mill housing. Water that had passed beneath the mill was diverted for irrigation, or channeled back into the stream. It is not uncommon to find two or more mill sites on a single *acequia*, although the number of mills along a channel was determined by population and economic necessity rather than by water volume.

The flow of water to the mill wheel was always controlled. Waterwheel, axle, and runner (upper millstone) were a fused unit. The millstone could not remain stationary while the waterwheel continued to rotate, as in mills with gear mechanisms and a clutch. Continued rotation when not in use would have caused the rapid deterioration of both stones. The flow was controlled by diversion at the ditch head or at some point along its course above the mill or, if the mill were on a ditch that was also used for irrigation, the water was diverted from the waterwheel itself. This diversion was accomplished by using a moveable sluice, or by securing a horizontal diversion board atop the mill wheel if the sluice itself was stationary.

## Functional Components

Grain was fed from a suspended hopper into the "eye" of the upper stone, or "runner," which rotated upon a stationary lower stone, or "bed stone" (fig. 2.2). The runner was fixed to a straight spindle or shaft whose lower extremity was connected to the waterwheel. There was no intermediate gear mechanism; the runner and waterwheel rotated at the same speed, which was determined by the volume and velocity of water permitted to play upon the wheel and the amount of friction created at the stones' inter-

Fig. 2.2.  Upper Components of a Hispano Gristmill (Grain Hopper, Upper and Lower Stones, Paddle or Agitator, and Flour Bin)

face. The weight of the entire shaft was supported by a single-point bearing at its base.

Waterwheels varied in dimension, although they were remarkably similar in design. The nine wheels found intact ranged in diameter from thirty-two to forty inches (0.8 to 1.0 m) and in width from five to eight inches (13 to 20 cm). Hubs were made from modified wagon wheels, with wooden paddles, or flat flanges, placed at a slight angle in order to present a nearly perpendicular face to the flow of water from the sluice. An outer rim of wood secured the extreme end of the paddles. In all instances the sluice was directed to rotate the waterwheel and millstone in a counterclockwise direction.

Millstones were hewn from abrasive rocks of volcanic origin, which were available in most communities. They were cut by individual mill owners; their cutting appears to be a lost skill. Interviews with former *molineros* failed to identify a single individual who had actually fashioned a stone. The average diameter of millstones was approximately thirty inches (0.76 m), with extremes of twenty-three and forty inches (0.58 to 1.0 m). Top stones, or runners, varied from three to five inches (8 to 13 cm) at the center and tapered to a thickness of two to three inches (5 to 8 cm) at the rim. Bedstones were of the same diameter, flat in cross-section, and considerably thicker than runners, with extremes of six and twelve inches (15 and 30 cm). The life of a millstone varied from several years under heavy use and unskilled operation, to a lifetime. Runners wore out faster than bedstones. Their useful life was determined by the quality of the rock, the amount of use, and the skill of the miller. All stones required frequent sharpening, or regrooving, because abrasion burned, or shallowed, the vital grooves. These grooves permitted the free flow of meal across the bottom stone to its periphery, where it fell into a collecting bin.

## Origin

The few folk historians who have commented upon New Mexico's Hispanic gristmills appear unified in the belief that they were of relatively recent Anglo-American introduction. A noted authority on the region's folk architecture, Bainbridge Bunting, has observed that "from [the] Territorial Period [approximately 1865 in terms of architectural considerations] came . . . a series of interesting water-driven grist mills. Housed in simple log structures . . . these buildings are of no great architectural significance."[7] Though not stated per se, the implication is that the mills were among the numerous architectural introductions of that period that resulted from increased Anglo settlement and cultural influence. Bunting was evidently influenced by his belief that any form of log housing in the state had to be of Anglo-American origin. I have argued, however, that horizontal notched-log housing was practiced in New Mexico well before the earliest north European settler arrived in the area, and that the trait was diffused northward from Mexico by Hispanic settlers.[8]

Wheat was introduced into New Mexico by Oñate at the very outset of early seventeenth-century Spanish settlement.[9] Flour was probably ground by hand using the *metate* and *mano*, or querns, during the first century of settlement. The earliest known reference to a water-powered gristmill dates from 1756: "One of these mills [in Santa Fe] was built by Vicar Roybal just above the villa and was donated by him in 1756 to Felipe Sandoval."[10] Santa Fe had three operational mills in 1776: "The water [of the Santa Fe River] runs three mills which are located at the foot of the Sierra just below our convent. Although they do not grind large quantities, at least they lighten the labor of grinding by hand."[11]

Two small mills were in the village of Chimayó (Santa Fe and Rio Arriba counties), which supported a population of seventy-one families in 1776, for a mill-to-families ratio of approximately one per thirty-five, though any such figure is highly speculative. The will of Antonio José Ortiz, dated 2 August, 1806, bequeathed the *molino* on the family estate in Pojoaque (Santa Fe County) to his son.[12] Zebulon Pike, in 1807, was the first Anglo-American traveler to comment on the mills. In the vicinity of Ojo Caliente (Taos County), he noted that "this village had a mill near it, situated on the little creek, which made very good flour."[13] On the basis of these accounts, it appears that water-powered gristmills were functioning in New Mexico prior to the earliest Anglo-American penetration. I believe the mills were introduced by Hispano settlers who moved into the region from Mexico sometime during the early- to mid-eighteenth century.

The direction of waterwheel rotation is significant. Mills with horizontal waterwheels rotate clockwise in northern Europe, whereas in the Mediterranean region they operate exclusively counterclockwise.[14] The clockwise tradition was universally maintained throughout the eastern United States, whereas the counterclockwise rotation was continued throughout the Spanish areas in the New World.[15] If the early settlers of New Mexico had lacked knowledge of such mills, and if the technology had been attained directly from Anglo-Americans, the clockwise rotation probably would have been adopted. Some support for the hypothesis may also be inferred from the nineteenth-century references by Davis to a "Spanish gristmill," and Bourke to "Mexican flour mills."[16]

A final factor arguing against an Anglo provenance for the mills is the lack of evidence that the "tub-mill," which was widespread in the eastern United States, was ever introduced to New Mexico. All Anglo-American mills in the region were larger, more efficient, driven by vertical waterwheels, and commercial. It is difficult to envisage Anglo Americans introducing a more primitive technology to Hispanic residents that not only produced lower yields for equivalent labor, but also would have competed directly with the commercial Anglo milling operations.

Gristmills with horizontal waterwheels were common in the Spanish realm, thereby providing an adequate technological reservoir for their diffusion into New Mexico. Townsend's *Travels*, published in London in 1791, indicated that such mills were functioning in eighteenth-century Spain: "In the ravines through which we passed I observed that all the mills have horizontal water wheels . . . they place many near together, and the same little stream, having communicated motion to one wheel, passes in succession to the rest."[17] These mills were associated with peasant cultivation of small grains in the New World. They existed in the Central Andes as early as 1539, were accepted in Peru, Bolivia, and Ecuador during the sixteenth century, and in much of Spanish America by the early seventeenth century.[18]

The question of gristmilling practices in Mexico requires more intensive analysis. Numerous references have been made to "gristmills," "flour mills," and "*molinos*," but only a few have more detailed information. In view of the lack of evidence from Mexico, I postulate that the *mano* and *metate* were the major means of peasant milling in areas where maize was the dietary staple. The Spaniard preferred wheat flour, however, and large *haciendas* probably had higher yielding vertical-wheel gristmills for the provision of this staple, whereas peasant farmers relied upon the smaller mills for this purpose, as did their counterparts throughout much of Spanish America.

## Function

Folk milling practices should be judged within a particular social, economic, and technological context. The low-yielding gristmills were no doubt considered to be an improvement over the quern, or *mano* and *metate*. The New Mexican peasant farmer of the eighteenth and nineteenth centuries possibly considered a high-yield, commercial, vertical-wheel mill just as impractical for his or her particular needs as most "progress-oriented" Americans would have viewed the crude mill with horizontal wheel.

Dominguez quoted a price of one *peso* per *fanega* of flour ground by a watermill in 1776.[19] When mills were unable to function because of subfreezing temperatures, a *fanega* of wheat was exchanged for hand grinding an equivalent amount of flour. One *fanega* of wheat was worth four *pesos*.[20] It may be deduced, therefore, that during the eighteenth century watermilling represented a fourfold reduction of cost when contrasted with handmilling.

Elderly Hispano informants indicate that a variety of customs prevailed regarding the cost of milling. Most of the mills have been inoperative for several decades and the elapsed time has jaded the memories of both buyer and miller. Most often, the miller was paid in kind. Estimates go as high as "one for three," but one part in ten seems closer to the norm.

The yield of the mills was determined by the quality and type of grain, the volume of water, the condition of the millstones, and the skill of the miller. Elderly *molineros* say they could have ground fifty pounds (23 kg) per hour, with a daily maximum of approximately three hundred pounds (136 kg) of flour. Milling was seasonal, determined by the flow of water and the availability of grain. Streams were normally frozen in the higher villages from November to April. Late summer and early autumn were the periods of maximum milling activity.

Most mills closed during the 1930s and 1940s. Cash incomes became more common, easier travel between villages and cities made commercially milled flour available at a reasonable price, and the region experienced a high rate of out-migration and farm abandonment.

## Distribution and Number

There is no way of determining the precise number, or historical distribution, of New Mexico's folk gristmills. I cannot agree with Roland F. Dickey that "mechanical grist-mills were not widespread . . . only a few communities were equipped with these water power mills."[21] I have located approximately fifty mills or probable mill sites by a survey of the historical literature, interviews, and field observation. This figure probably represents fewer than half the number that were operational during the nineteenth century (fig. 2.3). Locational prerequisites include (1) a Spanish-American agricultural settlement, (2) a population of sufficient number to justify the operation, and (3) a stream with sufficient volume and reliability during summer and autumn to provide adequate power.[22] Mills were therefore restricted to the Pecos River and the Rio Grande and their main tributaries.

The housings of at least twelve mills remained at their original sites as recently as 1968, although most had been stripped of their milling apparatus. By 1973 this number had been reduced by at least five. The wood of abandoned log buildings, including mills, has been used for fuel, fencing, or the construction of other buildings. The log housing and components of two mills have been removed from their original sites in Talpa (Taos County) and Truchas (Rio Arriba County), and reconstructed at El Rancho de las Golondrinas Spanish Colonial Outdoor Museum near La Cienega, some ten miles (16 km) south of Santa Fe. These mills and one other that was original to the location are now fully operational.

Only one mill remains functional at its original site (fig. 2.1). A brief history and description of this mill, which has been designated as a New Mexico Cultural Properties Site, appeared in *New Mexico Architecture*:

About 100 years ago, Mr. Acorcino Cordova and his wife, Genoveva Romero y Cordova, lived on their land at the foot of U. S. Hill near Vadito [Taos

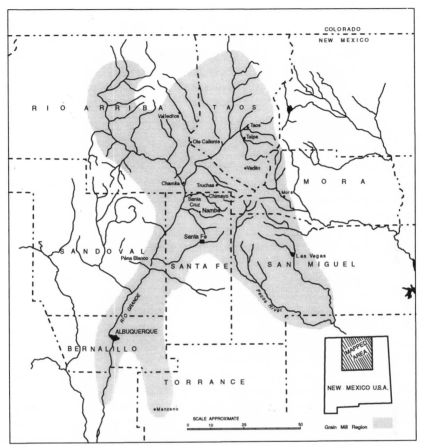

Fig. 2.3. Probable Distribution of Hispano Gristmills in New Mexico During the Nineteenth Century

County]. Here on the bank of the Rio Pueblo, Mr. Cordova built his mill. The logs for the millhouse were cut in the nearby mountains, and about 20 miles away, near Dixon, he found the proper kind of rock for his millstones. There he chipped and fashioned two stones. Each stone was about 30 inches in diameter and six inches thick. The undersurface of the top stone was smooth for grinding while the top of the bottom stone had shallow grooves chiseled into it to carry off the ground meal or flour. After the stones were finished, he could only haul one stone at a time on his small cart back to the millsite. After the death of Mr. Acorcino Cordova, the mill became the property of his son, Laureano Cordova, present owner and miller. Mr. Laureano still dresses the stones, replaces rotted logs, and keeps the mill in excellent condition and in operation.[23]

# Conclusion

The significance of New Mexico's log-built gristmills with horizontal waterwheels lies not so much in their architectural form as in their historical importance. Eighteenth-century documentation of these mills in Santa Fe and nearby communities, the exclusive use of horizontal notched logs in the mill housing, and the counterclockwise rotation of waterwheels and millstones indicate that this form of technology was introduced northward into the region by Hispano settlers, rather than from the eastern United States as has been generally believed.

Horizontal gristmills served a basic economic necessity. Their construction required only the time, skill, and labor of the individual builder. Costly metal components, which were imported for the Anglo-American commercial mills, were unnecessary. The operation of the mill was a relatively simple and easily learned task. Any breakdown, other than cracked millstones, could be repaired immediately by a local craftsman using materials that were readily available. The residents of a single small village could not support a large commercial mill, and transportation between villages was so poor that a number of small, though less-productive, local mills better served their needs.

There appears to have been no decrease in the number or importance of these folk mills from the earliest period of commercial milling in the mid-eighteenth century until their ultimate decline, which was prompted by economic and settlement changes beginning in the 1930s. Though small, awkward in appearance, and low in yield, these mills with horizontal waterwheels adequately performed an important function within the Hispanic hearth of northern New Mexico.

# Notes

1. The more isolated communities in northern New Mexico have experienced little Anglo-American influence. The village of Truchas, founded during the mid-eighteenth century, reportedly accepted its initial Anglo-American resident in 1931, even though it is one of the largest mountain communities. The village of Lower Colonias (San Miguel County) did not receive transmitted electrical power until 1969, although it was founded around 1750 and had a population of some two hundred persons for several centuries. A continuing national ignorance of the political affiliation of New Mexico prompted the State Motor Vehicle Division to add "U.S.A." after the state name on license plates in 1972.

2. A survey of more than fifty nineteenth-century travel narratives failed to disclose a single in-depth account of conditions in any of the isolated mountain communities. Even the noted observer and recorder, Josiah Gregg, rendered several inaccurate judgments of the region because his travels were limited to the Santa Fe Trail and the Rio Grande Valley (*Commerce of the Prairies* [New York: J. B. Lippincott Company, 1844]).

3. Notable exceptions include Alice Bullock, *Mountain Villages* (Santa Fe, N. M.: The Sunstone Press, 1973); Roland F. Dickey, *New Mexico Village Arts* (Albuquerque: University of New Mexico Press, 1949); and numerous works by Elizabeth Boyd, Bainbridge Bunting, and J. B. Jackson, who have made substantial contributions to our knowledge of cultural practices in Hispanic New Mexico over several decades.

4. J. W. Abert, *Report of J. W. Abert, of His Examination of New Mexico, in the Years 1846–1857* (Albuquerque, N. M.: Horn & Wallace, 1962), 107–8.

5. William W. H. Davis, *El Gringo: Or New Mexico and Her People* (Chicago: The Rio Grande Press, 1938; reprint of 1857 ed.), 187.

6. L. B. Bloom, "Bourke on the Southwest, VIII: Chapter XIII, A Visit to the Shoshonees," *New Mexico Historical Review* 10 (1935): 299.

7. Bainbridge Bunting, "The Architecture of the Embudo Watershed," *New Mexico Architecture* 4 (1962): 25.

8. Charles F. Gritzner, "Log Housing in New Mexico," *Pioneer America* 3 (1971): 54–62. The Roybal mill in Santa Fe, which was constructed in 1756 and stood until the 1920s, was of horizontal notched log housing, (Elizabeth Boyd, personal correspondence, 1974).

9. George P. Hammond and Agapito Rey, *Oñate, Colonizer of New Mexico, 1595–1628* (Albuquerque: University of New Mexico Press, 1953), 116.

10. Fray F. A. Dominquez, *The Missions of New Mexico, 1776*, ed. and trans. by E. B. Adams and Fray A. Chavez (Albuquerque: University of New Mexico Press, 1956), 40.

11. Dominquez, *Missions*, 40.

12. Data obtained from the Ortiz Family Papers, New Mexico Department of Records and Archives, Santa Fe, New Mexico. I am indebted to Dr. M. E. Jenkins, director of Archives, for her translation of the handwritten unnumbered passage and her estimate that the mill was constructed during the 1760s.

13. Elliott Cories, ed., *The Expedition of Zebulon Montgomery Pike* (New York: Francis P. Harper, 1895; reprinted, Minneapolis: Ross and Haines, Inc., 1965), 600.

14. E. C. Curwen, "The Problem of Early Watermills," *Antiquity* 18 (1944): 130–46 and John Storck and Walter Dorwin Teague, *Flour for Man's*

*Bread: A History of Milling* (Minneapolis: University of Minnesota Press, 1952), 97.

15. Daniel W. Gade, "Grist Milling with the Horizontal Waterwheel in the Central Andes," *Technology and Culture* 12 (1971): 43–51, and personal correspondence from Professor Gade.

16. Davis, 187, and Bloom, 299.

17. Quoted in J. P. O'Reilly, "Some Further Notes on Ancient Horizontal Water-mills, Native and Foreign," *Proceedings, Royal Irish Academy* 24 (1902–4): 76.

18. Gade, 44–45.

19. A *fanega* was a dry measure of 1.5 to 2.5 bushels, the amount varying with locality, (Dominquez, 31).

20. Dominquez, 245.

21. Roland F. Dickey, *New Mexico Village Arts* (Albuquerque: University of New Mexico Press, 1949, reprinted 1970), 87.

22. A number of streams, or portions thereof, which flowed during the nineteenth century are now dry or intermittent as a result of clearing or overgrazing, the building of small earthen dams to entrap water for livestock, or the construction of larger dams on major streams.

23. "A Continuing Heritage—The Cultural Properties of New Mexico," *New Mexico Architecture* 13 (1971): 19–21 and 26.

3

# The New England
# Connecting Barn

## Wilbur Zelinsky

Observers of the New England rural landscape have been aware for some time that one of its striking features is the physical linking of the farmhouse with one or more barns; yet no attempt has been made to ascertain the cultural or geographical significance of such "continuous architecture." Throughout the remainder of Anglo-America, houses and barns are set apart from each other, probably in conformity with such British example as early settlers may have had, and there is no ready explanation for the New England departure in farmstead pattern. In their approaches to the agricultural scene, American geographers, historians, and architects alike have neglected the barn, in spite of its ubiquity, bulk, and manifold promise for the student of regional cultures. Aside from the relatively abundant literature on the Pennsylvania German country and its large, picturesque barns and a few brief geographical articles on other areas, the record remains blank.[1]

We have, then, only the dimmest conception of the origin of any of the non-Teutonic barn types that have become established on this continent; and there is even much work still to be done on the process by which the Pennsylvania barn was transplanted from the Rhineland to the New World. In preparing for the field reconnaissance reported in this paper, the writer searched all available travel and general descriptive accounts, both old and new, dealing with New England for references to barns and related topics,

Reprinted by permission from *The Geographical Review* 48 (1958): 540–53.

but with the meagerest of results.[2] Apparently, the barns of the region failed to make an impression on either visitors or native observers before the present century, even those who were expressly concerned with agricultural questions.[3] Unfortunately, the sheer bulk of primary sources on New England history prohibited a systematic exploration of this material, but one of the few scholarly contributions on early New England agriculture based on such sources offers this significant observation:

> The New England barn was neither very commodious nor very conveniently arranged considering the great variety of uses to which it was put. It was often attached to the house, a rather dangerous practice—so much so that one town ordered [1649] that, 'there being manni sad ascidantes in the Contree by fire, to the great damming of manny, by joining of barnes and haystackes to dwelling houses, therfor no barne nor haystacke shall be set within six polles of anni dwelling house opon panillte of twentie shillings.'[4]

The field evidence presented below by no means excludes so early a date for the connecting barn.

In the modern literature on New England, the connecting barn appears fairly frequently in both text and illustration, but with scant discussion of origin or meaning. In particular, certain of the Federal Writers' Project state guides refer to or illustrate it and Eric Sloane has pictured connecting barns in both words and sketch; but the most informative single source is probably Congdon's *Old Vermont Houses*.[5]

The traverse route followed during the summer of 1957 in collecting data on the connecting barn (fig. 3.1) was designed so as to chart the outer limits of the area of frequent occurrence and to provide a cross section through the center. Because of the scarcity of background information, the itinerary was improvised as the field work progressed. In the main, secondary roads were utilized and the larger urban communities avoided. The type of barn, separate or connecting, was noted for each farmstead visible from the road; and in the case of connecting barns, the physical details of both house and barn were recorded. A total distance of about 2,600 miles was covered in the six New England states and in New Brunswick and Quebec, and notes were taken on 4,376 farmsteads, of which 897, or 20.5 percent, had connecting barns. Because of the necessarily haphazard pattern of the traverse route, the results afford only a first approximation to a portrayal of the true areal and statistical characteristics of the New England connecting barns and the basis for further, more methodical exploration.

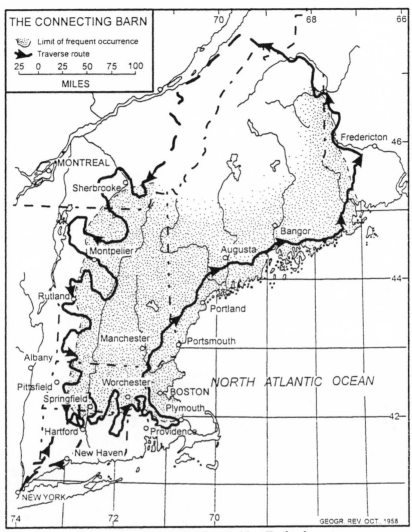

THE CONNECTING BARN

Limit of frequent occurrence
Traverse route

25  0  25  50  75  100
MILES

Fig. 3.1. Distribution of the Connecting Barn in New England

## Characteristics of the Connecting Barn

The connecting barn is, by definition, any barn that is physically joined to the farmhouse; there is great variety in its size, shape, and construction, and in the manner of its connection with the house.[6] Basically, almost all the barns of New England are simple rectangular structures with gabled roofs. Their style occasionally reflects some Pennsylvania German or Middle Western influences, but by and large the barns are elementary and functional in design and strongly resemble many of the older, humbler barns found elsewhere in Anglo-America. An overwhelming majority are of frame construction with board siding, but in eastern New England there is an interesting minority of barns—and houses—with shingle siding. The only nonframe connecting barns encountered were one built of brick and one of concrete block; none were made of stone, and in contrast to the South, West, and parts of the Middle West, none were of log. The frequency of painted barns would seem to be rather higher than in most other parts of the country (fig. 3.2): 610, or about 68 percent of all connecting barns observed, were painted, 400 of them white, 175 red, and the remainder green, tan, or yellow. Another 42 were covered with asbestos or asphalt siding.[7]

In size, the connecting barn ranges from a unit scarcely larger than a

Fig. 3.2. Combination of White Frame House and Connecting Red Frame Barn Is Quite Common (near Pelham, New Hampshire)

garage to some rivaling the largest barns of Wisconsin, but the average is smaller than most Middle Western barns. It must be stressed that, from general observation and the meager statistics gathered during this study, there are no significant physical differences between connecting barns and the general-purpose detached barns of New England. Certain specialized barns are almost never joined to the house, among them the widely distributed poultry barn (fig. 3.3), the tobacco barns of the Connecticut Valley, and the potato barns of the Aroostook Valley. The principal functions of the connecting barn, as of most other American barns, are the storage of farm implements, crops, and feed, the housing of livestock, and, more recently, the garaging of automobiles and the storage of household goods.

The connection between house and barn takes many forms. The most elaborate, and one of the less common, is a corridor or gallery that is roofed but may be open along one side.[8] More frequently, the house and barn are contiguous and share the full extent of one wall, forming a long, straight unit. Even more commonly, the two meet along only part of a wall, *en echelon*. In both cases there is usually a door opening from the house directly into the barn. Many houses and barns simply touch each other at a corner or are connected by a short board fence. Whatever method is used

Fig. 3.3. Poultry Barn Attached to this Farmhouse Is a Unique Example of the Conjunction of a Dwelling with a Specialized Barn (near Belfast, Maine)

to join house and barn, each preserves its individuality, as is evidenced by the separate roofs; they are *not*, like some dwellings of Central Europe, integrated into a single structure under a common roof.

In New England, accretion need not stop at a single barn. Two, or even three or four, barns may extend out from the farmhouse, but they invariably lie at the rear or at one side; no houses were encountered set *between* two barns. The ground plan of the house-barn combination may run parallel to the road or at right angles, or it may assume an L or T shape; but none of these layouts seem to have any functional or geographical significance. Frequently, the farmstead that has a connecting barn may also have barns standing apart, again without any prescribed spatial pattern.

Inasmuch as New Englanders seldom inscribe dates on houses or barns, it is difficult to guess either the absolute or the relative age of contiguous buildings except by studying architectural styles or techniques and the general condition of the structures.[9] It would seem that as a rule the house is older or is contemporary with the first of the connecting barns; if there is more than one barn, the terminal units have often been added at a later date.[10] The relative scarcity of the connecting barn on recent farmsteads, except, possibly, in eastern Maine, leads one to suspect that its popularity may have fallen off sometime in or after the last quarter of the nineteenth century.

One of the interesting things about the connecting barn in New England is the abundance of both full-fledged examples and transitional types, not only in the attenuated *Strassendörfer* but even in fairly large settlements. Farmsteads embedded within expanded villages are a common sight in New England, where town and country have always been peculiarly intermingled. The transitional house-barn complex in a quasi-urban setting generally consists of a substantial house to which is appended a structure that may originally have been either a small barn or just a stable and carriage house but is now almost invariably a garage, storage shed, or workshop. Another intermediate form, most often found around the fringes of the boundary depicted on figure 3.1, is the wholly rural farmhouse that has a garage, small workshop, or some sort of lean-to attached to it. It might be noted parenthetically that the attached garage, which is a prominent feature of many recently built houses throughout the country, is unrelated in origin to the connecting barn.

## Distribution of the Connecting Barn

The field traverse indicates that connecting barns are found with some frequency in northern and eastern New England and the adjacent strips of

Quebec and New Brunswick and that only occasionally can one be found beyond the line shown on the map. Toward the south, the boundary runs west from Plymouth to a point northwest of Hartford without ever straying far from the south edge of Massachusetts. It is clear from field reconnaissance and the statements of informants that the connecting barn is unknown southward from this line in Connecticut and Rhode Island, but the situation in southeastern Massachusetts is less clear-cut. The sparseness of agricultural settlement makes it difficult to establish the absence of any farmstead trait, but if connecting barns do occur in the Cape Cod region, they must be rare. After leaving Connecticut, the boundary trends almost due north through western Massachusetts and central Vermont to the Canadian border as it follows rather closely the rugged spine of the Green Mountain range and its southward extension into Massachusetts. In Quebec the line bends gradually eastward as it approaches the unpopulated highlands along the Quebec-Maine border. The segment of the Eastern Townships included within the connecting-barn territory was evidently settled in good part by American pioneers early in the nineteenth century, and the area to its north by emigrants from both the United States and the United Kingdom.[11] In any case, the connecting barn is superseded in the north by other Anglo-American barn types, rather than by the distinctly different barns found among the French Canadians farther north.[12] A fair number of isolated examples of the connecting barn are to be found elsewhere in the Eastern Townships and in northwestern Vermont.[13] Indeed, the connecting barn appears to have spread over much of New York north of the Mohawk Valley as a minor element in the rural landscape; but even though New England settlement was strong throughout much of the upper Middle West, this barn type seems to have fallen by the wayside west of the Adirondack region. In southern New York, northern New Jersey, and northeastern Pennsylvania, areas that presumably drew Yankee migrants from southwestern New England only, the connecting barn is wholly unknown.[14]

Because of the virtual absence of agricultural settlement in most of northern and central Maine, no boundary line was drawn through the state, but it is assumed from limited observation that the connecting barn is universal in the settled southern and southeastern parts.[15] It is missing in the upper St. John Valley and the northern part of the Aroostook Valley, regions now strongly French-Canadian in character, but reappears south of Caribou, Maine, and in much of the area between the St. John River and the Maine-New Brunswick border. The New Brunswick segment of the line is sharply defined in the field and separates the connecting-barn territory from an area of detached Anglo-American barn types to the east. However, farther northeast in Maritime Canada it is reported that connecting barns appear in localities occupied by New England emigrants during the eighteenth century, specifically along the south and west coasts of Nova Scotia from Lunenburg to Digby and, particularly, north and east from Digby.

> From Digby east through the Annapolis Valley and around the shores of the Minas Basin and Chignecto where the New Englanders took over completely from the Acadians in the late 50's and early 60's of the 18th Century, the connecting barn is even more common, although by no means universal. One finds it occasionally also inland in Hants County. Colchester County and Cumberland County, and occasionally along the southern shore of Halifax and Guysborough, where I suspect it has New England origins.[16]

Clark also reports that the connecting barn appears in some parts of Prince Edward Island, presumably by cultural diffusion from the mainland, rather than by migration of New Englanders.

Within its primary distribution area in northern and eastern New England, there are pronounced variations in the incidence of the connecting barn. In the marginal parts, roughly the outer ten to twenty miles, between 5 and 25 percent of all farmsteads have connecting barns. In the areas of Vermont and western Massachusetts traversed from this study, the percentage ranges from 24 to 50. The frequency is greatest in the eastern part of the territory: from 50 to 70 percent in eastern Massachusetts and in New Hampshire and from 50 percent to as high as 85 percent in Maine. With an average of about 65 percent of its observed farmsteads having connecting barns, Maine would seem to contain the strongest concentration at present.

## Some Problems of Origin

In attempting to explain the origin and historical geography of the connecting barn, we must rely almost solely on the current distributional pattern and on what is known of migrational trends during the early years of settlement. As was previously noted, our knowledge of the barns erected in the colonial period by English-speaking settlers is of the haziest sort, and even less is known about their relationships with possible Old World antecedents. Sloane may be correct in asserting that these early barns were "entirely American" and "unlike anything built anywhere else."[17] Although substantial barns were used by large landowners in the British Isles and on the Continent and by the peasantry at large in certain areas of Central Europe, it is likely that few seventeenth-century pioneers in New England with an agricultural background had much of a barn-building tradition. Valuable insight into the barn situation in Pennsylvania comes from the pen of Peter Kalm, a Swedish naturalist endowed with an encyclopedic curiosity, who toured the Atlantic seaboard during the years 1748 to 1751 and who had the opportunity to interview survivors of the first generation of Pennsylvania settlement.

> Yet, notwithstanding it was cold . . . all the cattle were obliged to stay day and night in the fields, during the whole winter. For neither the English nor the Swedes had any stables; but the Germans and Dutch had preserved the custom of their country, and generally kept their cattle in barns during the winter. Almost all the old Swedes say, that on their first arrival in this country they made barns for their cattle, as is usual in Sweden; but as the English came and settled among them, and left their cattle in the fields all winter, as is customary in England, they left their former custom, and adopted the English one.[18]

American winters being what they are, even the English settlers eventually saw the wisdom of adopting barns. The most logical hypothesis regarding the connecting barn is that it came into being in or near the original Massachusetts Bay Colony by the middle of the seventeenth century. Its absence in Rhode Island, southeastern Massachusetts, and most of Connecticut could be explained by the fact that these areas were settled before the connecting barn was firmly established in its source region or that they received most of their settlers directly from the British Isles. An examination of the best available maps of the advancing New England frontier and of the migrational routes followed indicates the strong possibility that the connecting-barn territory correlates fairly well with the area settled largely by migrants fanning out from eastern Massachusetts.[19] Beyond the highland crest in Vermont and western Massachusetts that marks the western limit of the connecting barn, the population was apparently drawn chiefly from Connecticut and even, to some extent, from New York. In southeastern Quebec and Maritime Canada, the limit of this barn type seems to have coincided with the high-water mark of strong New England settlement. From the beginning of the English Civil Wars until the middle of the nineteenth century, migration from the Old World to New England was negligible, and such interregional movement as occurred was outward from New England to the newer frontiers of North America. Hence, no alien influences were at work to lessen the popularity of the connecting barn. In more recent years it seems to have lost ground to types prevalent in neighboring regions. Its strong persistence in Maine may be attributed to relative isolation of the state.

Obviously, the connecting barn is a highly practical device in any locality such as New England with severe, snowy winters.[20] The reduced exposure to snow, mud, wind, and cold is certainly a convenience to the farmer and a powerful argument for the connecting barn, only partly canceled by objections to it on hygienic grounds or as a fire hazard. What is puzzling is the fact that similar barns were not in vogue elsewhere; for connecting barns would have meant a gain in both comfort and efficiency for almost any area farther north than, say, Philadelphia.[21] It is paradoxical indeed that the Pennsylvania Germans, who had been accustomed to building house and barn under a single roof in their homeland, should have dropped the practice in America.[22] In particular, there are the most persuasive climatic reasons for connecting barns in the St. Lawrence Valley, where almost none appear; and winter conditions in northern New York and northern Ohio—both of which derived much of their pioneer population from New England—would amply justify their use. If this were a matter of pure climatic determinism, then the optimum region for the connecting barn would logically be northern New York, where winter temperatures tend to range below those in New England and a total seasonal snowfall averaging between 60 and 150 inches well exceeds the 30 to 90 inches recorded for the latter area.

We are forced to accept the suggestion that in the Middle Atlantic states, Connecticut, Rhode Island, and the parts of Canada with no strong influx of New Englanders, the early settlers, for reasons that may never be entirely clear, preferred to build their houses and barns at some distance apart. As settlement advanced westward, the emigrants from New England naturally tended to preserve their traditional barn-building ways; but as they became increasingly diluted among settlers from other sources, they began to adopt the material culture of the dominant majority. If this majority had been wholly rational in adapting its farming techniques to the climate of northern North America, the New England connecting barn would have been copied far and wide. As it is, we can add another triumph for conformity to many instances in culture history where conformity and practicality have conflicted.

## Notes

1. The subject has been covered with great care in Alfred E. Shoemaker, ed., *The Pennsylvania Barn* (Lancaster, Penn.: Pennsylvania Dutch Folklore Center, 1955), a volume containing valuable bibliographic material. See also Loyal Durand, Jr., "Dairy Barns of Southeastern Wisconsin," *Economic Geography* 19 (1943): 37–44, and J. B. Jackson, "A Catalog of New Mexico

Farm-Building Terms," *Landscape* 1 (1952): 31–32. Farmstead layout, but not barn morphology, is considered in Glen T. Trewartha, "Some Regional Characteristics of American Farmsteads," *Annals of the Association of American Geographers* 38 (1948): 169–225.

2. John K. Wright, ed., *New England's Prospect* (New York: American Geographical Society, 1933) remains one of the best general treatments of the region. However, two more volumes are indispensable to the student of New England geography: Hans Kurath, *Handbook of the Linguistic Geography of New England* (New York: AMS Press, 1973) and John H. Thompson and Edward C. Higbee, *New England Excursion Guidebook* (Washington, D.C.: Seventeenth International Geographical Congress, 1952). Kurath's work is notable for its bibliography. The following are valuable for special aspects of New England geography or history: L. K. Mathews, *The Expansion of New England: The Spread of New England Settlement and Institutions to the Mississippi River, 1620–1865* (Boston: Houghton Mifflin, 1909); Ralph H. Brown, *Historical Geography of the United States* (New York: Harcourt, Brace & World, 1948); G. F. Dow, *Every Day Life in the Massachusetts Bay Colony* (Boston: Society for the Preservation of New England Antiquities, 1935); and Edna Schofield, "The Origins of Settlement Patterns in Rural New England," *Geographical Review* 28 (1938): 652–63.

3. Eric Sloane in his *American Barns and Covered Bridges* (New York: Funk & Wagnalls, 1954) transcribes without any documentation a "Letter to England, 1786," which states that "these people live near their animals . . . it is difficult to tell where their house ends and their barn begins," and he also quotes an anonymous "English traveler" of 1800 to the same effect.

4. R. R. Walcott, "Husbandry in Colonial New England," *New England Quarterly* 9 (1936): 233.

5. *Vermont: A Guide to the Green Mountain State* (Boston: Houghton Mifflin, 1937); *Massachusetts: A Guide to Its Places and People* (Boston: Houghton Mifflin, 1937); and *New Hampshire: A Guide to the Granite State* (Boston: Houghton Mifflin, 1938). See also Sloane, *American Barns and Covered Bridges*, 51 and 56–57, and Eric Sloane, *Our Vanishing Landscape* (New York: Ballantine, 1955), 16. Also Herbert W. Congdon, *Old Vermont Houses* (New York: Knopf, 1946). Reprinted in 1968 by Noone House, Peterborough, N.H.

6. To the best of my knowledge, there is no vernacular name for this barn type, and the probable absence of any is indicated by the omission of barns in Hans Kurath, *Linguistic Atlas of New England* (New York: AMS Press, 1972), which offers data on most everyday objects with distinctly regional names or pronunciation of them.

7. We have an early report that many of the barns and stables seen on

the road between Boston and Albany were painted red. See Duc de La Rochefoucault-Liancourt, *Travels through the United States of North America . . . in the Years 1795, 1796, and 1797* (London: R. Phillips, 1799, 2 vols.), vol. 1, 396.

8. Congdon, 72–73, fig. 60, gives an unusually good example.

9. Only two of the connecting barns inspected bore any visible data— 1855 and 1883, to be specific—and both were in eastern Maine.

10. Congdon, 79, briefly documents an example of such a gradually elongated series.

11. T. L. Hills, "The St. Francis to the Chaudiere, 1830—A Study in the Historical Geography of Southeastern Quebec," *Canadian Geographer* 6 (1955): 26.

12. Much of this area, both north and south of the international border, is being steadily occupied at present by French-Canadian migrants, but with little visible effect on barn types.

13. Correspondence with Theo L. Hills, McGill University, 1957.

14. Correspondence with John E. Brush, Rutgers University, 1957.

15. The unoccupied parts of Maine and other New England states are shown in detail on the two maps accompanying L. E. Klimm, "The Empty Areas of the Northeastern United States," *Geographical Review* 44 (1954): 325–45.

16. Correspondence with Andrew H. Clark, University of Wisconsin, 1957.

17. Sloane, *American Barns and Covered Bridges*, 51, and correspondence with Eric Sloane, 1957.

18. Peter Kalm, *America of 1750: Peter Kalm's Travels in North America; The English Version of 1770* (New York: Wilson-Erickson, 1937), 236. It is a matter of the keenest regret that Kalm did not see fit to include New England on his 1750 itinerary (he traveled from Pennsylvania to Quebec via the Hudson-Lake Champlain route), since he was one observer who would almost certainly have furnished us with a detailed account of New England farmsteads. However, Kalm's avoidance of New England was not an isolated instance. The region may have been commercially important throughout the eighteenth century, but it did not begin to attain cultural or scientific eminence until the dawn of the nineteenth century. Most scholarly visitors were attracted instead to such relatively advanced communities as Philadelphia, New York, or Baltimore. Cf. D. J. Struik, *The Origins of American Science* (New York: Cameron Associates, 1948).

19. See Mathews, *Expansion of New England*; Kurath, *Handbook of the Linguistic Geography of New England*, plates 1 and 2; and Stanley D. Dodge, "The Frontier of New England in the Seventeenth and Eighteenth

Centuries and Its Significance in American History," *Papers of the Michigan Academy of Science, Arts and Letters* 28 (1942): map facing 436.

20. Congdon, 95; *Vermont: A Guide to the Green Mountain State*, 65; and Sloane, *American Barns and Covered Bridges*, 57.

21. A possible explanation for the localization of the connecting barn in New England that may merit some investigation is military security. According to this hypothesis, such a structure would afford the beleaguered farmer safe access to his livestock and the various goods stored in barns in a region that experienced more than its share of alarums and excursions during the colonial period.

22. This point is discussed in Shoemaker, 9. Shoemaker was able to locate only three isolated references to house-barn combinations in his detailed study of early records for Pennsylvania.

4

# Mormon Central-Hall Houses
# in the American West

## Richard V. Francaviglia

Perhaps the most distinctive house type in the Anglo-American West is
what Kniffen has called the "I" house. The western "I" house has a symmetrical plan and facade, is one and a half to two stories high, only one
room deep, and usually has a chimney at each end (fig. 4.1). Very similar in
appearance to the true "I" house, and very much related, is the "Four over
Four" plan, which is two rooms rather than one deep. Both the "I" house
and the "Four Over Four" are subtypes of the general "Central-hall" house
type (fig. 4.2). According to Glassie, they are related to Georgian architectural influences, which profoundly affected American folk architecture.[1]

The Central-hall house type was well established in the eastern United
States by the end of the eighteenth century.[2] Kniffen implies that this type
became so modified as to be disappearing when it reached the frontier portions of the Midwest.[3] Perhaps its disappearance as an important feature in
the cultural landscape of the American West would have been complete
had it not been for the Mormon pioneers who took it to Utah with them.

Present-day folk terminology implies its association with the Latter-Day
Saints. Mormons in the Intermontane West locally refer to this type of
house in three ways. First, it is sometimes called a "Nauvoo-style house,"
referring to Nauvoo, Illinois, the town from which the Mormons fled to the
West in the 1840s. There are many homes of this type in Nauvoo. Second,

Reprinted by permission from the *Annals of the Association of American Geographers* 61 (1971): 65–71.

Fig. 4.1. A True "I" House at Fountain Green, Utah (Two Rooms Wide and One Room Deep with a Symmetrical Façade) has the Characteristic End Chimneys and Fine Brickwork Often Seen in the Mormon West (Built c. 1890)

it is sometimes called a "polygamy house," referring to the legend that there was "a chimney for each wife." The early Mormons may have found this house useful for polygamy, since it was symmetrical and sometimes divided into two equal halves, each having a front door, with no interior communication between the two halves of the house. Nevertheless, Spencer refuted this theory in his study of southern Utah house types.[4] Third, this house type is simply called an "old Mormon house," again reflecting a vernacular awareness of the correlation between it and the Mormons.

The Central-hall house type is indeed very closely correlated with pre-1900 Mormon settlement, as Meinig has defined it.[5] It appears in Idaho in the north, through the Mormon heartland of Utah, and south in Arizona (fig. 4.3). It is in fact a dominant house type in Utah. The highest concentration of Central-hall houses in the entire West is found near the center of the Mormon region. In the Mormon towns of Spring City, Scipio, and

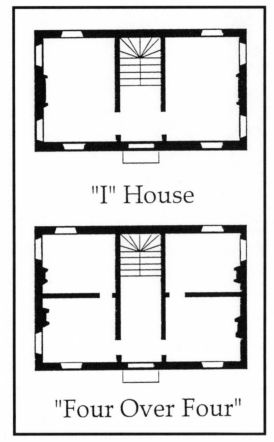

"I" House

"Four Over Four"

Fig. 4.2.    First-Floor Plan of Two Central-Hall
Houses: "I" House and "Four Over Four"

Fountain Green, Utah, almost half of the houses are of this type. Such high
percentages are rare, however, and only about 15 to 20 percent of the
houses of most early Mormon towns are Central-hall houses. The percentage generally decreases toward the periphery of the Mormon region, which
was settled later. It is at best a minor landscape element outside the Mormon West.

Some Central-hall houses outside the main Mormon area can also be
traced to Mormons. They appear in the Manassa and Sanford area of Colorado, towns that were settled by Mormons in the 1880s. Likewise, the presence of this type at Mackay, Idaho, is traceable to a Mormon settler who

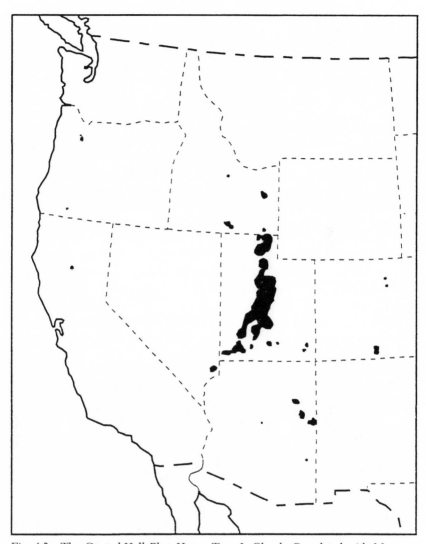

Fig. 4.3. The Central-Hall Plan House Type Is Closely Correlated with Mormon Settlement

moved there from Utah around 1904 and built a house type that had long been outmoded elsewhere in the United States.

Although Central-hall houses were built in the early days of Anglo-American California, these were never very common, and were affected by Spanish influence. Large porches and changes in floor plan were obvious modifications. Central-hall houses were built in Oregon and Washington in the 1840s, but were soon superseded by other types. A similar story is revealed for all of the Gentile West, which was more generally affected by Victorian styles and the Gothic revival. By comparison, these styles had only a slight impact on many a Mormon town until just before the turn of the century.

Slight variations characterized Central-hall houses in the West, even among the "homogeneous" Mormons. Wood, stone, and brick were common building materials in the East. In the West, adobe must be added to the list.[6] A fine adobe building tradition arose, especially in the southern portion of the Mormon culture region. These solid old homes were often well constructed; some are still standing after more than a century. The Central-hall adobes in the Virgin River country of southwestern Utah, especially those at Santa Clara and St. George, are examples of a now almost lost art.

The early Central-hall homes in many Mormon communities are true folk architecture (fig. 4.4). Differences in craftsmanship can be detected

Fig. 4.4. Central-Hall House in Logan, Utah, Built c. 1875 (Asymmetrical Façade and Solid Course of Darker Stone Separates First and Second Stories)

throughout the area, but there is a general uniformity of building type and external appearance. Availability of different types of building material helped to create some diversity and individuality, bringing out the best or the worst that an artisan might have to offer. The fine stone homes in and near Willard, Utah, in the Cache Valley, and in Spring City, Utah, are examples of some of the finest masonry in the entire West. The solid fired-brick homes in the Mormon communities of Oakley, Idaho, and Snowflake, Arizona, also reflect the fine local workmanship of days gone by.

The Central-hall house underwent a definite evolution in the Mormon West. Although elaborations of plan were common in the East during the first part of the nineteenth century, the early Mormon settlers in the West found the basic Central-hall type cheap and easy to build. The simplest change involved the addition of the wing, creating a "T" plan. This drastically altered the simple rectangular geometry of the home, but the original central block could still be detected. Lean-to additions were common in earlier days, but by the turn of the century the incorporation of several additions helped disguise the basic plan. The resulting "L"- and "H"-shaped plans, accompanied by the relocation of chimneys, marked the end of the simple Central-hall type, which was not, to my knowledge, built after about 1910 even in the Mormon West.

The presence of the Central-hall house in Mormon country can only partly be explained by the fact that general Mormon agricultural settlement was earlier than Gentile. As was noted, the Mormons built this type even into the 1870s and 1880s. The survival of architectural forms in the Mormon village, however, is noteworthy. In many Mormon towns one often finds the original buildings dating from earlier periods of settlement. Gentile towns, by contrast, are more often progressive and older structures are removed. "Save everything," a concept now firmly part of the Mormon religion, has had its impact on the architectural character of the Mormon West. However, why did Mormons persist in building Central-hall houses long after they were unfashionable in the East and Gentile West? There are several reasons, and these fit into a religious-cultural framework.

The religious factor involved the association of this type with Nauvoo. Although Nauvoo was not architecturally unique, to the Mormons it was a Holy City based in part on their prophet Joseph Smith's plan for the City of Zion.[7] They were forced to leave Nauvoo after the martyrdom of their beloved leader, but were not about to forget the fine homes they had there.

In building Zion in the West, the Mormons used techniques similar to those they had used in Nauvoo. Early church leaders in the western theocracy called "Deseret" requested that the Saints build substantial permanent homes. Joseph Smith had specified brick and stone as the building materials for all homes in the City of Zion, and Utah leaders attempted to continue this tradition.[8] The Central-hall house became a favorite in the Mormon West, not by specific recommendation from the Church, but because it was an easy style to translate into masonry, and lingered in the mind, associated with Zion.

Architecture was related to religion, also, because of the Church's unique proselyting campaign. The early Utah Mormons were hardly "typical" Americans, because a large number of converts came directly to the West from England, the Scandinavian countries, and Holland.[9] For example, the records for Nephi, Utah, reveal that over half of the early settlers had come from England.[10] Spring City, Utah, less than forty miles (64 km) distant, was called "Little Denmark," because over half of its population was from Scandinavia. Mormon converts brought building traditions with them directly from the Old World. Indeed, the president of the Church, Brigham Young, requested missionaries to seek converts with building skills.[11] The fine brick and stone work in the Mormon West reflects the quality of these builders who were converted to the ways of the Church, bringing traditional building styles with them. The Mormon West has a treasure trove of Old World traits, transported there over a century ago, and the Central-hall house type was reinforced, as was Mormon settlement in general, by Old World tradition.[12]

Another factor in the persistence of the Central-hall type was the dynamic character of Mormon colonization. Many settlers who had proven their worth in one area were, after but a few years, requested to settle other areas in the same fashion. The Mormon people were highly mobile even after their "trek" to the West. There are records of settlers moving three, four, or even more times. Leaving one's home and setting out to build another, perhaps hundreds of miles away, was part of the "building of Zion." These moves partly account for a definite visual repetition in Mormon settlement. A house in one area may have been built by a Mormon who had built two or more houses like it somewhere else in the West.

The final factor was the isolation of many Mormon settlements. Partly because they were so busy building Zion, and partly because they wanted to be self-sufficient and communications were poor, Mormon towns missed or generally rejected much contemporary American culture. Some of the rejection was deliberate; Mormon leader Erastus Snow, for example, urged the Saints at Manassa, Colorado, to "become self sustaining, and endevor to build houses for themself and dose become independent of maney of the enfluences that now surround them."[13] This suggestion must have been followed; the architectural difference between Mormon and non-Mormon towns, both settled at about the same time, is striking. Because the Central-hall type had proved sufficient, was firmly rooted in the past, and exemplified the solid and substantial in domestic architecture, it persisted as an important element in the cultural landscape of the conservative Mormon towns.

Thus, the Central-hall house, along with the "Mormon hay derrick," the "Mormon fence," village patterns, and religious architecture, is an important cultural trait, and a very effective indicator of cultural and religious traditions. Its presence in the Intermontane West generally reflects Mormon settlement, for both religious and cultural reasons. Indeed, the entire Mormon landscape contains a series of unique elements either not present, or only poorly developed, in Gentile settlements in the West.[14]

## Notes

1. Henry Glassie, "The Impact of the Georgian Form on American Folk Housing (Abstract)," in *Forms upon the Frontier: Folklife and Folk Arts in the United States*, eds. Austin Fife and Henry Glassie (Logan: Utah State University Press, 1969): 23–25.

2. Peirce F. Lewis, "The Geography of Old Houses," *Earth and Mineral Sciences* 39 (1970): 33–34.

3. Fred Kniffen, "Folk Housing: Key to Diffusion," *Annals of the Association of American Geographers* 55 (1965): 549–77.

4. Joseph E. Spencer, "House Types of Southern Utah," *Geographical Review* 35 (1945): 448. The Utah folklorist Austin Fife also believes that there is no correlation between number of doors and number of wives (personal communication).

5. Donald W. Meinig, "The Mormon Culture Region: Strategies and Patterns in the Geography of the American West, 1847–1964," *Annals of the Association of American Geographers* 55 (1965): 191–220.

6. A brief but interesting analysis of this topic is David Winburn, "The Early Homes of Utah: A Study of Techniques and Materials," unpublished B.A. thesis, University of Utah, 1952.

7. According to Robert M. Lillibridge, Nauvoo was architecturally typical of many towns at that time. See his article, "Architectural Currents on the Mississippi River Frontier: Nauvoo, Illinois," *Journal of the Society of Architectural Historians* 19 (1960): 109–14.

8. Smith's architectural specifics for the City of Zion are found in C. L. Sellers, "Early Mormon Community Planning," *Journal of the American Institute of Planners* 28 (1962): 24–30 and John W. Reps, *The Making of*

*Urban America: A History of City Planning in the United States* (Princeton, N.J.: Princeton University Press, 1965): 466–72.

9. J. A. Olson, "Proselytism, Immigration and Settlement of Foreign Converts to the Mormon Culture in Zion," *Journal of the West* 6 (1967): 189–204.

10. Official Church "Record of Members" for Nephi, Utah, 1852–1854. Church Historian's Office, Salt Lake City, Utah.

11. M. B. DeGraw, "A Study of Representative Examples of Art Works Fostered by the Mormon Church with an Analysis of the Aesthetic Values of these Works," unpublished M.A. thesis, Brigham Young University, 1959, 2.

12. The Central-hall type has been assumed to have originated in Western Europe. Both Kniffen and Glassie, for example, have used the term "English I House." The origin of the Central-hall plan in European and American domestic architecture, however, has never been properly documented and remains obscure, as does its supposed transport to America.

13. Historical Records, Manassa Ward, Book A, 1877–79, 29. Church Historian's Office, Salt Lake City, Utah.

14. Richard V. Francaviglia, "The Mormon Landscape: Definition of an Image in the American West," *Proceedings of the Association of American Geographers* 2 (1970): 59–61.

# 5

# The Mountain Horse Barn:
# A Case of Western Innovation

## Jon T. Kilpinen

In settling the high valleys of the Mountain West in the late-nineteenth century, Anglo-American pioneers encountered environmental conditions unlike those found in much of eastern North America. Western settlers often responded to these conditions in creative and innovative ways. Rocky Mountain cattle ranchers, in particular, adapted their livestock-managing techniques and material culture to the high valley setting. Of their material innovations, which included various hay stackers and certain fence types, one of the most unique was the mountain horse barn.[1] An altogether new type, this log barn was designed to house the many horses used on mountain valley ranches, as well as to store a modicum of hay to feed them during the harshest periods of winter. From its source areas in the Rockies, the mountain horse barn spread to other ranching districts, most notably those of central British Columbia.

Key to Rocky Mountain high valley settlement was the development by ranchers of a distinctive adaptive strategy. Through this system, ranchers responded to the often unfavorable conditions of this cold, semi-arid environment. Based on my analysis of this ranching system and its greater material artifacts, I contend that early mountain western culture had roots in both the diffusion of eastern cultural elements and the invention of altogether new ones.[2] Diffused items of material culture, clearly revealing an

Reprinted by permission from the author and the *Pioneer America Society Transactions* 17 (1994): 25–32.

eastern heritage, included worm fences and log construction techniques like V-notching and square notching. On the other side of the ledger, in the category of innovation, were such western inventions as the Mormon hay derrick, the Beaverslide haystacker, and the buck fence. As I have discovered, another prime area of western innovation involved the development of new kinds of barns.

Folk geographers have devoted considerable attention to the barns of much of North America, especially the eastern portion of the continent, linking many types to specific cultural groups or regions. Four studies in particular, however, demonstrate the usefulness of barn types in the present discussion. Wilbur Zelinsky identified what he called the New England connecting barn, demonstrating the correlation between this barn type and the New England settlement area (see chapter 3).[3] Joseph Glass went a step further in his study of the forebay bank or Pennsylvania barn, essentially using the distribution of this type to define limits of the Pennsylvania culture region.[4] Robert Ensminger recently added additional insights to the origin and broader distribution of the Pennsylvania barn and the possible geographic extent of Pennsylvania German culture.[5] Finally, Peter Wacker utilized the architectural forms of Dutch barns in New Jersey to identify culture and to trace cultural diffusion.[6] Folk barns, then, can be valuable indicators of cultural heritage and diffusion, as well as of regional variation.

Nevertheless, while scholars have treated many eastern barn forms in their work, very few have paid attention to western barns. In fact, remarkably few studies of western barns exist. Richard Francaviglia, in an exceptional study, examined the architectural form and climatic adaptations of a half-dozen different western barn plans and subtypes.[7] He noted that these types apparently originated in the eastern United States but were modified in the West to meet local environmental conditions. Francaviglia's barns, however, consisted mainly of frame construction, and thus appear to be more recent forms than the log structures so common throughout much of the Mountain West. In another study, Harold Knudson examined the barns of western Montana, utilizing them as indexes of ethnic origins.[8] Carried out on a very limited scale and targeted at European immigrant groups, Knudson's study lacked a broader scope and failed to address the greater, nonethnic western landscape.

A great many western barns, however, constructed roughly between 1880 and 1910, survive throughout the Rockies and other mountain ranges. I surveyed nearly three hundred of these between 1989 and 1991. A great variety of floor plans typify these structures, but by and large they bear very little resemblance to historic eastern barn types. The western landscape is home, for example, to many eave-entry log barns, types that were not typical of much of eastern North America. Western barns are generally larger than most traditional eastern barns. Finally, western barns appear to have served new and different functions compared to their eastern predecessors, including the storage of large amounts of hay and the stabling of numerous horses. If they are different from traditional eastern types, are western barns innovative components of the built landscape? I believe they are, mainly due to the dissimilarities they exhibit when compared to eastern barns.

A type I have chosen to call the "mountain horse barn" was one of the most common and distinctive barns in this innovative category (fig. 5.1). Consisting of but a single log crib, the mountain horse barn averaged twenty-five to thirty feet in width and an impressive forty feet in length, though some examples were even longer. Such immense size required builders to obtain huge logs, some of which were well over a foot in diameter. The barn's rectangular plan was split down the center by a long, narrow runway situated directly beneath the ridgeline. At either end of this runway, centered in each gable wall, was a door, while individual animal stalls and a tack room flanked the runway. From two to five small windows often lined the barn's eave walls for illumination. Some mountain horse barns lacked windows altogether, and a few had only one gable entrance, revealing variations in the treatment of the structure's ground level. Above the main floor

Fig. 5.1. Mountain West Horse Barn in Montana's Big Hole Valley, Built c. 1900 (Note the Round Logs, Chinking, Small Eave Window, Massive Hay Door and Loft, and Hay Hood above the Door)

was usually a sizable hayloft, with a hay window or door in the main gable end.[9] Early prototypes consisted mainly of round logs, though hewn log examples also existed. Still more recent mountain horse barns appear in frame construction.

Clearly linked to mountain valley ranching, the purpose of this barn type seems clear. Western ranching required a great deal of horsepower, for both livestock herding and haying operations. Stockraisers used the ground level of the mountain horse barn to house these animals, especially during the cold alpine winters. The upper loft, on the other hand, permitted ranchers to store a modicum of hay, likely enough to sustain their horses through the winter.[10] In fact, some of the mountain horse barns I examined had mangers lining the outer walls of the horse stalls. Some of these could even be filled from the upper story through slots in the floor of the hay loft.

Though impressive in size, the mountain horse barn was not very common. In fact, only about 10 percent of a sample of nearly three hundred barns consisted of the mountain horse subtype. While not a significant number of barns overall, about a third of the sample consisted of various random, innovative multicrib barn plans—most of which were unlike other established types and each other—making the mountain horse barn the most common innovative type. In addition, the mountain horse barn was highly concentrated within the West, occurring mainly in the Rocky Mountains and in the Cariboo/Chilcotin country of south-central British Columbia, as my preliminary survey revealed (fig. 5.2). For this reason, I consider it another example of western innovation, as does Jordan.[11] It exhibits the same sort of limited, intraregional distribution as the Beaverslide haystacker, the Mormon hay derrick, and other innovations. Typologically, the mountain horse barn bears some resemblance to the transverse-crib barn of the eastern United States, possibly suggesting some influence. But if this were the case, the influence was only minimal. These two types of barns, though similar in layout, served vastly different functions.

A second large single-crib barn plan, similar to the mountain horse barn in some ways, also occurred in the Mountain West. In contrast to the mountain horse barn, this second type was characterized by a single-eave entrance. It was generally smaller and more nearly square than the mountain horse barn, and it lacked the linear stall arrangement and eave-side windows of its gable-entry counterpart. Accordingly, it represents an altogether different barn plan. To be sure, many of these large eave-entry barns served as horse barns with large hay lofts; some even bore a striking resemblance to the gable-entry version.[12] Large eave-entry barns, however, were rare. I observed only a dozen examples of this plan—a mere 4 percent of my sample. Most were located in ranching areas in the Rockies.

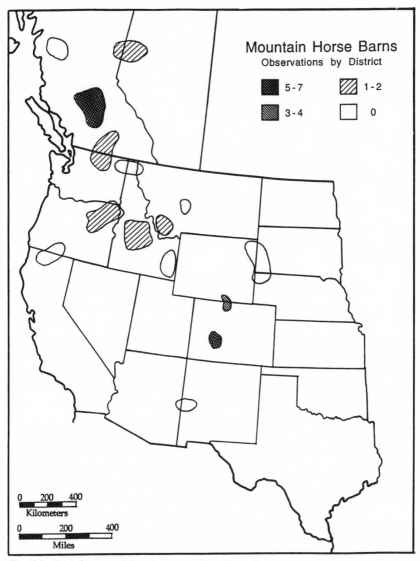

Fig. 5.2. Distribution of the Mountain West Horse Barn

In an earlier study, I suggested that this eave-entry plan may have been a forerunner of the mountain horse barn.[13] But based on the larger sampling of the present study, I now feel the two types were contemporary western innovations, emerging in the Rocky Mountains as ranchers settled the high valleys. With its gable entrances and stall layout, the mountain horse barn apparently proved better adapted than the eave-entry barn. Accordingly, the mountain horse barn gained a somewhat wider acceptance, even spreading north into the ranching country of the Cariboo and Chilcotin districts of British Columbia and to the Peace River Country of Alberta. While a relatively unsuccessful adaptation, the large eave-entry barn of the Rocky Mountain chain embodies the innovative character of the West.

In sum, western barn plans, especially that of the mountain horse barn, reveal little in the way of diffusion from the East. Hardly any of the standard eastern log-barn types, like the single-crib barn or the double-crib barn, occur in the Mountain West consistently. This is not to say, however, that the diffusion was altogether absent, for it was not. The log carpentry of these barns was decidedly eastern, with clear roots in the Pennsylvania-derived Midland log-building tradition.[14] Many of the best examples of the mountain horse barn exhibit diagnostically Midland corner notching, especially crowned V-notching, and chink construction. Still, western barn floor plans indicate a fairly high degree of experimentation or innovation. The emergence of such new types as the mountain horse barn attest to this.

The innovation evident in western barns is surely linked to newfound needs in regional agricultural pursuits. In particular, the need ranchers felt for stabling their horses and storing feed and haying equipment during alpine winters encouraged experimentation since these needs had not really existed in the eastern United States. Most traditional eastern log barns were simply too small for these applications, and ranchers responded adaptively to replace them. Barns, then, suggest that innovation contributed significantly to the distinctiveness of the western cultural landscape.

## Notes

1. Jon T. Kilpinen, "Traditional Fence Types of Western North America," *Pioneer America Society Transactions* 15 (1992): 15–22.

2. Jon T. Kilpinen, "Material Folk Culture in the Adaptive Strategy of the Rocky Mountain Valley Ranching Frontier," unpublished M.A. thesis, University of Texas at Austin, 1990, and Jon T. Kilpinen, "Material Folk Culture of the Rocky Mountain High Valleys," *Material Culture* 23 (1991): 25–41.

3. Wilbur Zelinsky, "The New England Connecting Barn," *Geographical Review* 48 (1958): 540–53.

4. Joseph Glass, *The Pennsylvania Culture Region: A View from the Barn* (Ann Arbor, Mich.: U. M. I. Research Press, 1986).

5. Robert F. Ensminger, *The Pennsylvania Barn: Its Origin, Evolution, and Distribution in North America* (Baltimore, Md.: Johns Hopkins University Press, 1992).

6. Peter Wacker, "Folk Architecture as an Indicator of Culture Areas and Culture Diffusion: Dutch Barns and Barracks in New Jersey," *Pioneer America* 5 (1973): 37–47.

7. Richard Francaviglia, "Western American Barns: Architectural Form and Climatic Considerations," *Yearbook of the Association of Pacific Coast Geographers* 34 (1972): 153–60.

8. Harold Knudson, "Barns as an Index to Ethnic Origins in Western Montana," unpublished M.A. thesis, University of Montana, 1969.

9. Kilpinen, "Material Folk Culture in the Adaptive Strategy of the Rocky Mountain Valley Ranching Frontier," 132.

10. Kilpinen, "Material Folk Culture of the Rocky Mountain High Valleys," 38.

11. Kilpinen, "Material Folk Culture in the Adaptive Strategy of the Rocky Mountain Valley Ranching Frontier," 142. See also Terry G. Jordan, "The North American West: Continuity or Innovation?" in *The Dauphin Papers: Research by Prairie Geographers*, Brandon Geographical Series No. 1, Department of Geography, Brandon University, 1991, Brandon, Manitoba, eds. John Welsted and John Everitt, 1–17.

12. Kilpinen, "Material Folk Culture in the Adaptive Strategy of the Rocky Mountain Valley Ranching Frontier," 142–144.

13. Kilpinen, "Material Folk Culture in the Adaptive Strategy of the Rocky Mountain Valley Ranching Frontier," 139.

14. Terry G. Jordan and Matti Kaups, *The American Backwoods Frontier: An Ethnic and Ecological Interpretation* (Baltimore, Md.: Johns Hopkins University Press, 1989).

6

# Sod Construction on the Great Plains

*Roger L. Welsch*

A visit to the Great Plains of the north-central United States can be a shock even to twentieth-century travelers because much of it remains treeless and sparsely settled, so imagine what it must have been like seventy-five years ago. Crossing the Missouri River was as substantial a psychological agony as physical, because it marked the eastern boundary of the Great American Desert. Today it is in fashion to laugh off that label, for the land has proved to be fertile, but two factors have changed since the early days of settlement: (1) techniques have been developed to ease harsh prairie conditions: house insulation, gas and electric heat and cooling, rapid and large-scale transportation of people and freight, irrigation, and river stabilization, among many others; (2) we who live on the Great Plains now have come to accept its severity as ordinary. Thus, the Great American Desert is no longer what it was and we are not the people the nineteenth-century settlers were. With its nomadic Indians, treeless wastes, blowing sands, meager rainfall, poisonous snakes and mighty bison, severe winter cold and summer heat, tornadoes, grasshopper plagues, cacti, and ferocious storms, the northern plains fulfilled in every way the pioneers' concept of "desert." Their hopes then were not to exploit a garden but rather to create a garden from a wilderness.

The settlers came from northern Europe, eastern America, and the east-central states; they were used to building materials in abundance—if not excess. At their previous homes they perhaps had to pick up stones from

Reprinted by permission from the author and *Pioneer America* 1 (1969): 13–17.

the plow's furrow at virtually every step or they had to fight trees as weeds, burning, hoeing, grubbing, cutting. Wood and stone were always at hand for houses, barns, and fences.

But in the north-central-states area there were no trees. Trees on the Oregon Trail, which cuts lengthwise, east to west, through Nebraska, along the south side of the Platte River, were so rare that they had names and served as unmistakable landmarks. Even along the rivers, where one would certainly expect to find stands of wood, there were only low scrub bushes and willow wands. Only in some canyons could one find groves of ancient, gnarled cedars.

Although good clays were available for brick, there was no fuel to fire them. Stone suitable for construction is found only in the extreme eastern regions and the great distances of the Great Plains, and the lack of commercial transport forbade large-scale moving of cut stone.

Since the acquisition of homestead lands required construction of a permanent dwelling within a limited time, would-be settlers had to develop some technique for home building: they used sod.

The Mormons, when they first crossed into Nebraska in 1846, found the Omaha and Pawnee Indians living in great earth lodges—heavy timber frames with a sod covering, and since the Mormons also built sod houses during their first winter here, it may well be that they picked up the idea from the Indians, while they were also bartering for food and animals. On the other hand, the Mormons and later settlers may have borrowed the concept from English or European antecedents, low turf and stone huts used especially for temporary field-housing.

Whatever the origin, the technique developed rapidly and spread throughout the region, where it dominated for fifty years. A special plow, the "grasshopper" or cutting plow, was developed to cut the sod cleanly and lift it gently from the earth; the turning plow had been designed after all to destroy sod, tumbling and breaking it. From crude dugouts the soddies developed into fine, permanent houses, many of which are still in use today. Indeed, centuries of grass roots grasping the sticky loess soil proved to be a superior construction material, supplanted by lumber only when it became prestigious to have a frame house—a sure sign of affluence because it cost so much to haul in the lumber and it took a fortune to heat the vastly inferior frame house. This is still reflected in today's buildings on the Great Plains: stone quarries of fine limestone lie unworked all about Lincoln, Nebraska, and a brickyard that provides a handsome, inexpensive product has a difficult market in the face of lumber imported from a thousand miles away.

Priorities developed for certain kinds of sod for house building: late-fall

sod was preferred, because the roots were woodier than they might be earlier in the year; slough grass, buffalo grass, and blue stems were considered
the toughest; and valley sod was better than hill sod because the earth was
usually more moist and the sod was therefore more solid during handling.

The site for the house was leveled with hand spades and tamped with
fence posts and wagon tongues after the gopher and snake holes had been
filled with loose dirt. As the sod came off the plow like a long, fourteen-
inch wide, two- or three-inch-deep ribbon, it was cut into manageable
blocks (called "sods" or "bricks") with a spade. The sod was loaded and
moved as it was cut. More than a day's supply was never cut at one time,
for the sods would dry quickly in the sun and wind and they would then
crumble when lifted to the wagon or sledge. Oxen were preferred to horses
for the sod cutting, for they pulled more slowly and evenly; I am told that
the sound of the cutting plow slicing through the sturdy grass mat was like
the opening of a huge zipper.

The sods were piled like bricks for the wall, grass down, usually two deep,
always staggering joints to discourage animal, insect, and climatic invasions
(fig. 6.1). All walls rose evenly, the surfaces shaved smooth with the ubiquitous spade. Window and door frames were propped into place and the walls
rose around them. Later, rods were driven through the frames into the walls
to hold the frames firmly in place. A buffer space, filled with grass, rags, or
paper, was left between the tops of the frames and the overlying sod to
prevent the settling walls from jamming the window.

Roofs, usually hipped but sometimes gabled, were held to the walls with
rods driven down into the walls (fig. 6.2). Some commercial tarpaper, shin-

Fig. 6.1. A Great Plains Flat-Roofed Sod House

Fig. 6.2.  A Great Plains Gable-Roofed Sod House

gles, and cut lumber was used in roofs, but more often three, five, or seven beams of cedar posts were overlaid with willow or plum brush, grasses, and sod (this time grass up). A layer of fine alkali clay discouraged leaks, but the most common complaint about sod houses is the fact that during rains the window wells were the only dry places and that, even after a storm let up, it continued to "rain" inside the house from the heavy sod roof for days after the rain stopped outside.

Refinements were a cloth ceiling, plastered and papered walls, white-washed or beveled window casements (to permit more light to enter the dark interior of the house through the three-foot-thick walls), a puncheon or lumber floor, potted plants in the windows, and a rack of elk horns in the front yard or on the roof. Pioneer housewives, seeking color in the prairied world of endless blues, greens, and browns, threw flower seeds on the roof, where they bloomed in the spring; in one case, a roof of dandelions (grown from seed sent to the pioneer from Maine) converted a drab soddy into a Great Plains beacon.

Most Nebraskans can boast of a visit to a sod house or have heard tales of their parents' life in one, and, as mentioned above, many still live in them. Now, as in pioneer years, the soddies are cool in the summer and warm in the winter, totally impervious to brutal Great Plains storms and winds.

Although I have been able to give only a simple outline of the construction here, as I learned about it from interviews, letters, and early photographs, I have been again and again impressed by the ingenuity and practicality of the techniques of building with sod. The soddy deserves mention when discussions arise about factors that permitted the settling of the Great American Desert.

# Part II: Folk Food and Drink

Wilbur Zelinsky, a preeminent American cultural geographer, reported more than twenty years ago that the geographic cupboard was relatively bare when one looks for literature on food and drink. Despite the lack of attention by cultural geographers, other folklife scholars, especially Don Yoder and his legion of students at Pennsylvania State University, have focused on traditional food and drink as a significant indicator of folk cultures.

The study of folk food and drink includes a wide range of factors, including foodstuff production, preparation, preservation, consumption, and social/psychological functions. Folklife scholars have combined all these components into a useful term known as "foodways."

Foodways then is the everyday, domestic food traditions that are obviously the opposite of the commercial and institutional versions of food preparation and consumption. While food and drink are themselves elements of material folk culture, the customs and holidays associated with them are considered nonmaterial aspects.

Although Americans today have developed an eclectic and homogenized "American" diet, folklife scholars have identified regional variations of foodways based on differing ethnic backgrounds and climatic/soil conditions. Food and drink associated with *folklife regions* that illustrate place-to-place variations include a comparison of the combined Upland and Lowland South with the Pennsylvanian. The Upland and Lowland South folk cultures (chapter 7) relied heavily on the frying pan and stew pot in the preparation of a restricted range of foodstuffs, namely hog meat and corn. Where vegetables were grown, okra, turnips, and potatoes added variety to the American Southerner's diet. In contrast, the folk culture of Pennsylvania (chapter 15) represented a different method of preparing foods ranging from sauerkraut (fermented cabbage) to schnitz (dried apples).

Okra, one of the folk foods discussed in chapter 7, presents an interesting pattern of the *origin and diffusion* theme. With its definite hearth in West Africa (known there as *nkru* in the Ashanti language), okra diffused either directly to the American South or indirectly through the West Indies. Because of its versatility, okra is today used by folk groups in a variety of ways from the cornmeal-coated fried version in the Lowland South folklife region to a thickening base agent for gumbo in the Acadian French (Cajun) folklife region.

The *folklife and ecology* theme accounts for the diversity of foodways because the natural environment (climate and soils) establishes a basic framework concerning the availability and feasibility of producing food-stuffs. Chapter 8 explores geophagy (dirt eating), the conscious consumption by humans of soils. Local folk cultures, especially in the Lowland South, identify certain clays that are extracted and prepared (usually baked) for eating as a food. Thus, the natural environment serves as a source for a folk food custom, primarily among poor Black and White Southerners, who consume it for nutritional purposes. A second example reflecting the *folk ecology* theme is found in chapter 9. Corn (maize) as a basic staple was adopted from the American Indian because of its adaptability to the poor soils and growing season of the Upland South. Mountain moonshine, or "corn likker," is a corn-based distillation. Moreover, cold running water was an absolute necessity, therefore, stills were located near hillside springs. Thus, corn served not only as a primary foodstuff, but also as a folk drink for Upland Southerners.

The *interrelationships of foodways with other folklife traits* is represented in several of the readings. Mountain moonshine is often consumed at Southern sporting events, such as two of those covered in chapter 12 (fox-hunting) and chapter 13 (cockfighting). Additionally, the distribution of mountain moonshine was instrumental in the development of a third Southern sport—stock car racing. During Prohibition, haulers of corn whis-key required modified vehicles in order to outrun the "revenuer." Conse-quently, they removed all seats to transport more cases and souped up their engines for higher speeds. It is theorized, therefore, that the hauler's whis-key-running autos were the forerunners of the basic American stock car—an intriguing interplay between the folklife traits of drink and sport.

Foodways and the *folk landscape* are illustrated again by the production of "white lightning." The mountain valleys of Tennessee, Kentucky, and North Carolina were once dominated by the whiskey-making stills. In a very intricate production process, the still contained several components that were present in the mountain moonshine landscape, including a furnace, heater box, flake stand, copper boiler, thump barrel, dry barrel, and a trough to transport water from a nearby spring.

In conclusion, foodways offers one of the oldest and most evocative sys-tems of folk culture identification, defining ethnic, regional, and religious differences throughout America.

7

# Hog Meat and Cornpone:
# Food Habits in the Antebellum South

## Sam Hilliard

*There is a pleasant land, not far from the sea-shore of a celebrated
Southern State, watered by the Waccamaw, Great Pedee, and
Winyah, noble rivers. . . . A land it is of jonny-cakes and waffles,
hoe-cakes and hominy, very agreeable to look back upon.*[1]

An essential element in any discussion of Southern culture is the distinctive
character of its food habits. Nowhere in the nation has a culture trait become so outstanding nor certain foods become so identified with a single
area as in the South. While it is true that recent trends indicate a mass
homogenization of American food habits, the notable food preferences of
eighteenth- and nineteenth-century Southerners and the persistence of
these choices into the twentieth century have consistently distinguished
the region from other parts of the country. Perhaps owing to low production
costs or ready availability of certain foods, the area developed and maintained strong food preferences. Most Southern foods were not unique;
many were frontier staples in other parts of the country. Yet the South came
to depend so strongly upon items such as pork, corn, turnips, sweet potatoes, okra, and peas that they often are regarded as "Southern" foods. This
paper deals with the development of Southern food habits and describes
foodways as they existed during the antebellum period.

Reprinted by permission from the *Proceedings of the American Philosophical Society*
113 (1969): 1–13.

The scientific study of diet is essentially a post–Civil War phenomenon. Detailed information is not available for the antebellum period, leaving us the problem of extracting bits of material from scattered sources that do not deal specifically with food habits. Some information can be gleaned from the writings of travelers in the South, who commented frequently on food they encountered while touring the area. More comes from the extant diaries and daybooks of planters and farmers who kept records of foodstuffs produced or purchased. Finally, a number of studies published toward the end of the nineteenth century and in the twentieth century indicate fairly precisely the food habits in a few specific areas.[2] From these rather scattered sources it is possible to glean bits of information about Southern food habits, and with what we know about contemporary food habits we can sketch a generalized picture of conditions as they existed during the pre–Civil War period.

Southern food habits stemmed in part from those existing in the eastern seaboard during the late eighteenth and early nineteenth centuries and were tempered by frontier conditions and the availability of food items suited to conditions in the South.

During the early years, food choices were dictated by frontier conditions and the state of agricultural settlement. Since settlement was not instantaneous, frontier conditions varied from place to place and from time to time. In Virginia, along the South Carolina coast, and in lower Louisiana, settlement was accomplished quite early and the inhabitants enjoyed a variety of foods. In the interior lower South, no such conditions existed. Even as late as 1840, parts of Georgia, Alabama, and Mississippi were scarcely inhabited and few amenities were available. Our best, though most critical, descriptions of the interior come from travelers. Much of the area was considered wilderness and was avoided by all but the most adventurous travelers. Those who did venture into the interior found conditions changing markedly as they moved from the more settled areas into the back country. Before 1835 or 1840, many travelers reported an almost total lack of luxury items in the interior and often complained about the coarse food. On an overland trip from New Orleans to Charleston in the 1830s, Thomas Hamilton described the food in the interior of Alabama: "We were now beyond the region of bread, and our fare consisted of eggs, broiled venison, and cakes of Indian corn fried in some kind of oleaginous matter."

He reported this menu again and again, though at times there were no eggs.[3] In the back country there was a strong dependence upon game, and travelers found it wherever they went.[4] This was also true of the more-settled areas. Fanny Kemble, while a resident on the Butler plantation in Georgia in 1838 and 1839, stated that their "living consists very mainly of wild geese, wild turkeys and venison."[5] This fare was not exclusively a rural one, as there was a sizable market for venison in the port cities. Tyrone Power described the Mobile market as "abundantly supplied with provisions, fish, and game of every variety."[6] New Orleans markets were similarly stocked with "game of all kinds, venison, woodcock, pheasant, snipe, plover, etc."[7] Even in the more settled areas, game was not entirely absent from the urban market. In 1840 the *Southern Cabinet* described the Charleston market as being "abundantly supplied with game . . . as in former years."[8] Nearly two decades later Frederick Olmsted found deer still plentiful in South Carolina. In the up-country he referred to a farmer who had "lately shot three deer," while near Charleston the sons of his host returned from a night hunt "with a boatload of venison, wild fowl and fish." He added that "the woods and waters around us abound . . . with game."[9]

The transition from wild to domestic food was gradual, with most people depending less on forest and stream as their farms began to produce and as the supply of game diminished. During the first year on a farm or plantation, practically everything was in short supply; even corn had to be brought in from the settled areas or purchased from neighbors who were already producing.[10] Most settlers, whether large or small landholders, planted corn as soon as possible to provide food for the coming year. They usually owned a few cattle and hogs, which were expected to increase and provide dairy products and meat.

Pork was the most common domestic meat during the early years, and a stock of hogs was considered essential on all new holdings. These increased rapidly and, even in remote areas, salt pork competed very strongly with venison. In the 1830s, Harriet Martineau complained that travelers found "little else than pork, under all manner of disguises."[11] One complained about the toughness of Virginia chickens, but remarked that they would have been relished "in Alabama, where bacon and sweet potatoes constitute the only delicacies."[12] He described a meal offered him near Columbus, Georgia, which, with possible exception of the milk, probably represented the usual fare.

> In the middle of the table was placed a bottle of whiskey, of which both host and hostess partook in no measured quantity, before they tasted any of the dishes. Pigs' feet pickled in vinegar formed the first course; then followed bacon with molasses; and the repast concluded with a super-abundance of milk and bread, which the landlord, to use his own expression, washed down with a half a tumbler of whiskey. The landlady, a real Amazon, was not a little surprized to see a person refusing such a delicacy as bacon swimming in molasses.[13]

In 1837 a traveler near Berrien, Georgia, reported the addition of rice to the usual "fryed middlen, cornbread, and coffee."[14] Early settlers in Mississippi could seldom offer much variety, as James Creecy complained: "I had never fallen in with any cooking so villainous. Rusty salt pork, boiled or fried . . . and Musty cornmeal dodgers, rarely a vegetable of any description, no milk, butter, eggs, or the semblance of a condiment—was my fare often for weeks at a time." Again, "But few, indeed, of the early settlers gave a thought to gardens or vegetables, and their food was coarse corn-meal bread, rusty pork, with wild game . . . and sometimes what was, most slanderously, called coffee."[15]

Corn and pork were dietary mainstays and were the domestic food items most avidly sought. Other foods were added as settlers devoted more time and space to gardens, orchards, and poultry, but the primary foods were still corn and hog meat. A good crop for new settlers was turnips. Providing greens in only a few weeks, the plants were ideal for new clearings and were quite common on newly opened landholdings. The overseer of a new plantation in Mississippi proudly reported to the owner that he had "sode four acre of turnips," which would serve as food.[16] Even if the prospective farmer or planter arrived at the site in late summer or fall, there was always time for sowing turnips.

As more land was cleared for farming, a greater variety of foods became available. A garden was planted; orchards were set out; the cattle and hogs increased; and poultry became more common. Moreover, the sale of cash crops such as cotton made possible the purchase of a few luxury items. Thus, the typical fare of new settlers underwent gradual improvement in variety. During the first year or so there was almost complete reliance on nondomestic foods and pork, corn, sweet potatoes, turnips, and a few chickens, but most farmers had to wait a few years until sufficient stock of animals was accumulated, thus providing an abundance of meat. Perhaps by the third or fourth year the garden began to yield adequately, and by the fifth or sixth the orchard trees were bearing. But a decade might pass before the farm or plantation could offer a good variety, although only the most foresighted could maintain an assorted fare throughout the year.

While the more settled parts of the South underwent some change in food habits as the variety of foods increased, most farmers and planters retained a number of their frontier eating habits, keeping game, fish, and gathered food from the large areas of unimproved land on the table up until the War Between the States. Moreover, corn and pork, the frontier staples, were retained throughout the antebellum period and, indeed, into the twentieth century.

The primary meat in the South was pork. In fact, this could be said for the remainder of the country as well. Not only was it the most important meat on American tables, but the total consumption of meat was very high in comparison with other countries. This heavy consumption of meat together with the preponderance of pork tended to give European travelers the impression that Americans consumed little else. Mrs. Trollope, in commenting on the diet in America, remarked that "They consume an extraordinary quantity of bacon. Ham and beefsteaks appear morning, noon, and night."[17] Some estimates place per capita pork consumption during the period at three times that of Europe.[18] In the South and West, the tendency was to rely even more strongly on pork, most White people having it every day. One story has it that an immigrant Irishman wrote home that he commonly took meat twice a day. When asked why he did not state the truth, he replied that if he said "three times a day" he would have been called a liar.[19]

In the Deep South, pork was the undisputed "king of the table." Olmsted stated that bacon "invariably appeared at every meal."[20] Emily Burke believed "the people of the South would not think they could subsist without their [swine] flesh; bacon, instead of bread, seems to be THEIR staff of life. Consequently, you see bacon upon a Southern table three times a day either boiled or fried."[21]

Many people thought pork to be high in "energy" and considered it the best for working people. And, though some physicians were beginning to plead for less pork and more vegetables in the diet, most thought it best for heavy laborers and slaves.[22] Dr. John S. Wilson of Columbus, Georgia, one of the most outspoken doctors in the South, frequently attacked the overuse of pork. In one of his numerous articles on diet and health, he delivered a scathing attack on pork eating and cooking with lard.

The United States of America might properly be called the great Hog-eating Confederacy, or the Republic of Porkdom. At any rate, should the South and West . . . be named dietetically, the above appellation would be peculiarly appropriate; for in many parts of this region, so far as meat is concerned, it is fat bacon and pork, fat bacon and pork only, and that continually morning, noon, and night, for all classes, sexes, ages, and conditions; and except the boiled bacon and collards at dinner, the meat is generally fried, and thus supersaturated with grease in the form of hogs' lard. But the frying is not confined to the meat alone: for we have fried vegetables of all kinds, fried fritters and pancakes . . . fried bread not infrequently, and indeed fried everything that is fryable, or what will stick together long enough to undergo the delightful process . . . hogs' lard is the very oil that moves the machinery of life, and they would as soon think of dispensing with tea, coffee, [or] tobacco . . . as with the essence of hog.[23]

The dominance of pork led to a great deal of experimentation with production, slaughter, and preservation methods. The system of pork-packing that had developed in the Ohio River Valley was well organized by 1840 and, because of the dominance of large packing houses, exhibited considerable uniformity. But with no organized packing industry in the Deep South, pork production was largely confined to farms and plantations; consequently, variety was the order of the day, each person having his own "pet" methods of slaughtering and curing. The carcass was cut up into six or more pieces, placed in a meat box, and covered with salt. After a few weeks (sometimes as long as six), the meat was removed, washed, and hung in the smokehouse over a light fire. Though not a universal practice, some producers preferred to sprinkle lightly with salt and let the meat lie overnight to "draw out the blood" before placing in the meat box.

An alternative was pickling in casks filled with brine solution. Pickling permitted slaughtering in warmer weather without fear of spoilage and eliminated the laborious process of salting, hanging, and smoking. Moreover, awkward pieces, such as the head, could be preserved more easily than by smoking. While pickled meat was less likely to become spoiled than smoked meat, it required soaking in water to remove enough salt to make it palatable.[24] Moreover, most Southerners much preferred the salt-smoke process since it produced, to their taste at least, better flavored meat. Consequently, it must have been the most commonly used method. Emily Burke reported from Georgia: "Pork in the South is never to my knowledge, salted and barreled as it is with us, but flitches as well as hams are hung up without being divided, in a house built for that purpose, and preserved in a smoke that is kept up night and day."[25]

These general descriptions of pork processing hardly do justice to the myriad individual variations that existed. The methods described above were employed commonly in making large quantities of pork, such as the slave meat on plantations, but meat destined for planter or farmer use received special treatment. The carcass was carefully dissected, the joints trimmed to shape, and the spine, ribs, and tenderloin were separated from the abdominal sides, which were cured into bacon. Excess fat was rendered into lard while lean pieces went into sausage, "souse," and "head cheese." The backbone and ribs, liver, tongue, and brains often were eaten fresh. The kidneys, heart, and lungs were occasionally eaten, but most southerners did not care for them. Chitterlings (the large intestine), reputedly treasured only by Blacks, were relished by Whites too, and the traditional "chitlin supper" came to be an annual event. Curing techniques were matters of personal pride, each farmer or planter adding his or her own flourishes to the basic method. Pepper, alum, ashes, charcoal, corn meal, honey, sugar, molasses, saltpeter, mustard, and a host of other seasonings were added, and each producer fancied his or her own meat to be "not inferior to the best Wesphalian hams."[26] The preferred cuts were the hams, shoulders, sausage, and perhaps the tenderloin, but each part of the animal had its devotees and all were consumed in one manner or another through the winter and well into the summer.

On occasion the entire animal was roasted. Apparently, the famous Southern barbecue was in practice before the war; a young bride in North Carolina wrote her parents in New York: "Not until you come here can you imagine how entirely different is their mode of living here from the North. They live more heartily. . . . Red pepper is much used to flavor. . . . the famous barbarque [*sic*] of the South . . . which I believe they esteem above all."[27]

The use of meat other than pork by the White people of the Deep South is easy to underestimate. Beef was not relied upon very heavily because it was hard to preserve in a manner to suit Southern tastes. Most beef was eaten fresh, but it was occasionally pickled and there is some evidence that it was also dried.[28] In order to prevent spoilage, fresh beef has to be consumed rather quickly. On a farm or plantation with a large labor force, beeves were slaughtered one at a time and the meat divided among the families, to be consumed in a few days. Occasionally, planters and farmers formed cooperatives in which each family killed periodically and divided the meat among the participants.[29] Apparently, this became a common practice among the French in Louisiana.[30] In other cases, neighbors simply borrowed fresh meat and repaid later as their own animals were slaughtered.[31]

Owing to the tendency to run short of pork in summer, there was probably a rise in beef consumption in the season. Cattle were fatter in summer and, after months of salt pork, beef was a welcome relief.[32] One Southern writer, pleading for agricultural reform, cited planters who were forced to kill beeves so often that "the cows are afraid to come home at night."[33]

Such frequency was not the rule and, except the piney woods grazers who kept large cattle herds, it is unlikely that beef was eaten regularly by the poorer Whites. Among the diversified farmers and better planters, beef was more common. Most operators slaughtered one or two animals each year while the large planters may have killed more.[34] Susan Dabney Smedes refers to beef as if it were common, and it is likely that beef-eating was the rule among the herders in the southern portion of the Deep South.[35] Beef consumption by most Southerners, however, must have been sporadic and the total amount small relative to pork. However, this was not true where cooperative slaughtering was practiced, but one questions just how widespread the cooperative system might have been.

Apparently, there were no regionally characteristic ways in which Southerners prepared their beef. Travelers referred to "beefsteaks" but seldom with any hint as to the preparation.[36] In restaurants or hotels it was prepared in a variety of ways. Olmsted noted entrees on the menu of the Commercial Hotel in Memphis that included a number of beef dishes: corned beef, Kentucky Beef (roasted), beef heart, and kidney.[37] Frying was a common cooking method and was well suited to places where few utensils were available.[38]

Traditionally, Southerners have not been considered consumers of mutton. In fact, Lewis C. Gray states that "there was a strong prejudice in the South against mutton, a prejudice that must have been widespread, judging from frequent references to it."[39]

While there is little doubt about mutton being a minor food on Southern tables, its use was not uncommon and, in many areas, it was actively sought.[40] One visitor along the Rice Coast remarked, "So far from mutton being dispised, as we have been told, it was much desired."[41] In Louisiana mutton was well liked, and even in the interior of the Deep South there appears to have been a sizable demand.[42] In fact, there is evidence that sheep were kept primarily for their flesh rather than for wool. Solon Robinson met a planter in Louisiana who kept two hundred to five hundred sheep to feed his slaves and he hinted that the practice was common along the Mississippi.[43] In writing to the Patent Office, a Mississippi agriculturist revealed a surprising concern for mutton sheep: "Few planters keep more sheep than enough to supply their own tables with that most excellent dish, a saddle of Mississippi mutton."[44] Another wrote, "I do not think it an object with our planters to increase their flocks to a greater extent to supply their family wants. The sheep is valued with us more for his flesh than for his fleece. The mutton, we think, is quite equal to any in the world."[45]

Mutton probably was more common among the affluent than among poorer Whites and slaves. The larger farmers and planters were more likely to keep sheep. They planned to slaughter several each year, so that mutton became a periodic supplement to the regular meat supply.[46] Some planters, however, kept sheep enough to have lamb or mutton quite often. Fanny Kemble, while visiting along the Rice Coast, remarked that, "we have now not infrequently had mutton at table, the flavor of which is quite excellent."[47] A Mississippi planter butchered as often as twice a week during spring and summer.[48] On *Rosedew*, a Georgia coastal plantation, lambs were slaughtered weekly and sent to market, indicating some demand in urban areas.[49]

While mutton and beef offered periodic respites from pork, poultry served as a regular meat dish throughout the year. Chickens, turkeys, ducks, geese, and guinea fowl were common on most Southern landholdings and were important to the White diet, possibly more than either beef or mutton. Even if the total quantity of poultry did not equal the amount of beef and mutton consumed, it was available more regularly and was more important in breaking the monotony of the usual meat routine.

Poultry was regarded as a semiluxury item and the implication of the term "chicken on Sunday" was probably accurate. The larger farmers and planters were able to have poultry frequently, and the visitor was plied with both chicken and turkey.[50] Most planters had their own flocks and some supplemented their diet with purchases from their slaves who kept poultry. The smaller landholder had fewer fowls, but still depended upon poultry for special occasions. Southern pots were often filled in expectation of the preacher or other guests. For example, Olmsted's request for breakfast in northern Mississippi was promptly fulfilled after a group of Black children chased and caught a hen in the backyard.[51] The occasional visitor, the family get-togethers on Sundays, or the periodic visits by the preacher were times for slaughtering a fryer or nonlaying old hen. A favorite story in the rural South portrays barnyard fowls becoming so "educated" to the Sunday slaughter that when a "genteel-looking" person approached the house they fled to the woods.

The preparation of poultry meat was simple, with few Southern flourishes added. The most notable dish was fried chicken, but frying required a young bird, which was not always available. Those too old and tough for frying were roasted or boiled until tender, and leftover chicken or turkey carcasses were converted into pies with large dumplings made of wheat flour. While poultry flesh helped relieve the monotony of a pork-dominated diet, eggs added more variety. Commonly used as ingredients in breads, cakes, and pies, they also were used as food items themselves and were surprisingly common as food for travelers.[52] Though the quantity of eggs consumed is unknown, they must have been eaten regularly during summer by most White families. Unfortunately, the seasonal character of egg-laying meant a dearth in the winter.

While Southerners took game of all kinds throughout the year, fall and winter were the preferred hunting seasons. This provided game during the period when poultry and eggs were least abundant. Thus, wild turkey, rabbit, and squirrel tended to replace domestic poultry and eggs in the diet. The cooking of game was similar to that for domestic meats. Frying was a favorite method of preparing young rabbit, but older animals were boiled.[53] Squirrel meat is tougher than rabbit and requires more cooking, but the results were considered superior to rabbit dishes. Squirrel broth and pie with dumplings were considered delicacies.[54] Opossum was certainly not confined to the Black diet. Most Whites ate the animals and many sought them eagerly. One can imagine the satisfaction of the Southern hunter who proudly entered in his diary the results of the night's hunt: "Caught three fine Possums last night."[55] Young ones could be fried, but the preferred method was roasting and serving with sweet potatoes. An ex-slave commented on their gastronomical worth: "But verily there is nothing in all butcherdom so delicious as a roasted 'possom.' "[56]

Perhaps the game most sought was the various kinds of fowl. Along the Atlantic coast and Mississippi flyways, waterfowl were most numerous and offered excellent food. However, wild turkey was the favorite since it abounded throughout the area. A South Carolina hunter revealed his enthusiasm for the hunt: "Today I saw a lot of wild turkeys . . . among the others was one fine goblar [sic]; I have marked him as mine—and if he does not leave the neighborhood I will be sure to eat him."[57]

Like game, fish and other seafoods were important minor foods in much of the area. However, near the coasts and in the larger rivers, they were relied on quite heavily. While the oyster was the easiest of the marine foods to harvest, other kinds were taken by nets and seines in large quantities. Shrimp and mullet were taken with "cast nets" and, with luck, a large catch could be had in a few hours' casting.[58] One source describes a bachelor Carolina planter who owned five or six slaves and lived off fish, shrimp, potatoes, and game. Apparently, he spent "half of his time hunting and fishing and the rest in making shrimp nets and fishing tackle."[59]

Farther inland the catfish became the prize catch. They were found in all rivers including those of the Tennessee, Mississippi, and Alabama-Tombigbee systems as well as the streams that flow into the Atlantic. River "cats" were easy to catch and many were large enough to feed an entire family. And, while some Whites expressed disgust upon seeing their first live catfish, their reservations disappeared when confronted with steaming platters of fillets or steaks. Both Whites and Blacks came to relish catfish, and, indeed, it has come to be the fish commonly identified with the area. The fish were taken in large quantities, and considerable evidence indicates that many people depended strongly upon them for food.[60] Catches could be quite large; on the Davis plantation in Alabama, several dozen were caught daily. Occasionally, large cats were caught weighing thirty to forty pounds.[61] In the Mississippi River's channels and tributaries, extremely large fish sometimes were taken. On one plantation two were caught that weighed 104 and 108 pounds.[62]

During season, shad were taken from the Atlantic-flowing streams of the South. From the James to the Altamaha, these fish moved upstream annually to be taken by seine and net. Charles Stevenson states that they moved as far as four hundred miles upstream and were taken in large quantities to be consumed fresh and salted for later use.[63] This estimate on distance would have placed shad above the Fall Zone cities and well within the reach of many inland inhabitants, and there is evidence that they were caught far inland. Shad are extremely easy to catch and, given any constriction in the channel, dip nets can yield dozens of fish in a night.[64] In coastal North Carolina, shad fishing was quite well developed, with many planters gaining considerable income from fishing; some even issued regular fish rations to their slaves.[65]

Frying was the most common method of preparing fresh fish and, no matter what the species, the fish was rolled in cornmeal and then fried. Saltwater fish were treated in the same manner. Near the coast, shellfish, too, were so prepared, though often they were roasted unshucked over an open fire or made into a stew.

As mentioned previously, Indian corn (maize) was the companion food to pork and together they were dietary mainstays of the South. Corn was utilized in myriad ways. While still green during early summer, it often was boiled on the cob or cut off the cob and creamed (called "fried corn"). Frequently it was simply roasted in the shuck.[66] After the ears had ripened and dried, there were other ways to prepare it. The most common was to grind it into meal from which an almost endless variety of breads was concocted. The most common was cornbread, which, in its simplest form, was a baked cake of "pone" made from meal, salt, and water. Variations upon this included the addition of milk, buttermilk, shortening, or eggs. After hog-killing, bits of crisp "cracklings" left over from the lard-rendering process were added to make crackling bread. The variations were legion and, even today, one encounters dozens of recipes for Southern cornbread.

The dominance of cornbread as *the* bread for the Deep South is unquestionable. Whether in the mountains or near the coast, Olmsted constantly commented about being fed cornbread, and apparently it was the bread he most often encountered.[67] U. B. Phillips refers to corn as the food of the "plain people," but there is little to indicate that cornbread was exclusively a poor man's food. It is true that the more affluent could afford wheaten bread, but most did not abandon cornbread as they "moved up" to the use of other cereals. Charles Lyell found that even in "some rich houses maize, or Indian corn, and rice were entirely substituted for wheaten bread."[68] Harriet Martineau, in describing a fantastically sumptuous plantation menu, lists "hot wheat bread . . . corn bread, biscuits" as if both corn and wheat bread were commonly served together.[69] Gosse, while visiting in Alabama, concluded that it was "even preferred to the finest wheaten bread."[70]

The popularity of cornbread is not easy to explain. Its use for slave food presumably was due to the cheapness of cornmeal compared with wheat flour, but one wonders why it was so well liked by all. It was very easy to make, but, unlike most European breads, did not remain fresh very long. Perhaps this is one of the reasons why Southern housewives cooked hot bread at every meal. In the absence of other reasons for its popularity, one can only presume that Southerners learned to like the taste of cornbread when it was all they had and have continued to demand it though they might well have afforded wheaten bread. However, such persistence was not notable in other areas such as the Old Northwest where corn was the principle "frontier" cereal.

Besides cornbread, cornmeal was used to make a number of other items. Some, such as corn dodgers, hoe-cake, corn muffins, and egg bread, were simply variations of cornbread, while other dishes were quite different.[71] Often cornmeal was made into mush (porridge), griddle cakes, or waffles.[72] It was sometimes mixed with wheat flour and occasionally with rice to make bread. In some cases, meal was mixed with milk or water, put in a warm place to sour, and made into "sourings," which served as bread.[73]

In addition to the use of corn as meal, Southerners converted it into hominy and grits. This involved a lye process that removed the husk from the grain. Hominy consisted of whole grain corn boiled and eaten as a vegetable. When hominy grains were dried, ground into a coarse meal, and boiled, the dish was called grits. The preparation of grits varied depending upon personal preference but usually were cooked into a thick porridge. Contrary to popular opinion, neither grits nor hominy ever came close to being universally used in the area prior to the War. Both were common, but, compared to the use of corn ground into meal, they were certainly subordinate. Since the Civil War, grits have come to be a common complementary dish to ham, sausage, or bacon and eggs for breakfast, but there is little evidence that grits were used nearly as much as cornbread during the antebellum period.

Other cereals had much less notable places in the Southern diet. Wheat and rice were the most common minor cereals. Wheat bread was commonly used by Virginia and Carolina colonialists, and this tendency was retained throughout the antebellum period, but the relatively low production of the grain within much of the area and the high cost of imported flour tended to cut down wheat consumption. Visitors often complained about the lack of wheat bread and when available it was considered "doughy" because of the addition of too much shortening.[74] Wheaten bread undoubtedly was more commonly used in the older states of the South than in the later settled areas. More wheat flour was consumed in Virginia and North Carolina than in Georgia, and more in Georgia than in Mississippi or Alabama. Wheat bread and other wheaten items were by no means rare, but among the less-affluent people they were "something special," available perhaps on Sundays or two or three times each week. The day-to-day bread was cornbread. Moreover, much of the wheat flour was used for pastries, cakes, waffles, and pancakes.

Rice consumption was quite high along the Carolina and Georgia coasts, yet outside the "rice area" it was a minor item. Extremely high production along the coastal counties and correspondingly low costs—especially for the less-marketable kinds—made it a staple in the diet of both Blacks and Whites. Charles Lyell noted that it, together with cornbread, replaced wheaten bread in the rice area of South Carolina.[75] Olmsted commented quite favorably upon a breakfast roll made with rice flour.[76] Another visitor noted that it was one of the principal dishes: "I always eat from this dish of rice at breakfast, because I know it to be very wholesome. People generally eat it with fresh butter, and many mix with it also a soft-boiled egg."[77]

This high consumption of rice in limited areas of the South is an excellent example of a food preference being determined by the ready availability of an item. Though rice is no longer grown in these Georgia and Carolina counties, this local preference has persisted to the present day. Buckwheat, rye, oats, and other cereal grains have never been particularly liked and were seldom used.

The favorite Deep South vegetables were sweet potatoes, turnips, and peas. More than any others, these were the items to which Southerners turned for vegetable food. The sweet potato (commonly and confusingly referred to simply as "potato") was useful in that it was highly nutritious, kept well during winter, and could be cooked in a number of ways. Baking or roasting in ashes was a common method of cooking. This left the skin on the tuber, making it easy to carry and quite suitable for hunting trips or for snacks. Olmsted noted both Black and White boys roasting potatoes in the ashes of a campfire at a religious service; later the children crawled around on the church floor carrying "handfuls of cornbread and roasted potatoes about with them."[78]

Turnips were grown for the roots and greens and both were eaten in large quantities. Both were invariably boiled, and Southerners preferred the greens boiled with a large "chunk" of bacon in the pot. Cabbage, collards, other greens, beans, and peas (field peas or cowpeas) were all cooked in this manner. A by-product of this process of boiling with a piece of bacon was the "potlikker." This was a concentrated broth combining juices from both the vegetables and meat and was eaten with cornbread. Although this practice might not appeal to today's discerning tastes, it was extremely important that the more nutritious juices were consumed rather than discarded. In addition to boiling, many vegetables were fried, including white potatoes, eggplant, okra, squash (Southerners preferred the yellow summer squash) and even sweet potatoes, sliced and rolled in meal.

Fruits and melons were popular in season and were easily preserved for winter use.[79] For desserts, fruits were made into pies or served fresh. Surplus fruits were either dried or preserved by some sugar process. Dried peaches, apples, and other fruits were served in winter, while apples, peaches, scuppernongs, muscadines and other grapes, blackberries, strawberries, and even watermelons were converted to sweets for off-season use. Additional sweetening came in the form of molasses, syrup, and honey (both wild and domestic).[80] The molasses and syrup used in the Deep South were of two basic kinds. In areas near the South Atlantic and Gulf Coasts and especially in Louisiana, the most common syrup was molasses made from sugar cane. It was an important trade item and was the sweetening most frequently issued to slaves. The major sources were Louisiana or the West Indies. On landholdings not producing sugar, syrup was made from sorghum cane and was referred to as sorghum, ribbon cane, cane syrup, but occasionally as "molasses," too.

The Southern attitude toward beverages has changed markedly since antebellum times. While there was a small temperance movement before the War, the great, almost universal condemnation of alcoholic drinks came in the late nineteenth and early twentieth centuries. During the antebellum period, whiskey and wine were consumed in huge quantities by all Whites who could afford them, whiskey being preferred by the less well-to-do.[81] Wine was very common among the affluent. A number of visitors noted its use, and apparently claret was the favorite.[82] This preference for claret is further confirmed by the statistics for wines imported into the country that show the major part of the claret moving into New Orleans.[83]

Nonalcoholic drinks included coffee, tea, and milk. Coffee was a favorite but tea was fairly common. Milk was consumed fresh, sour (curds), or made into buttermilk. Both sour milk and buttermilk were quite popular and, even today, a favorite dish is cornbread crumbled into buttermilk to make a soupy mixture.[84] It was common to serve plain water at meals and, between meals, a gourd of cool spring water was a summer treat invariably offered to visitors.

A number of towns and cities offered a variety of luxury foods not available in the more remote rural stores. The most outstanding cities were New Orleans, Mobile, Savannah, and Charleston. Smaller inland towns functioned much as did the coastal cities but on a smaller scale. These places included Raleigh, Columbia, Augusta, Macon, Milledgeville, Columbus,

Montgomery, Selma, Florence, Decatur, Jackson, Vicksburg, and Natchez. Such places were centers where a number of luxury foodstuffs were available. Stores, restaurants, and hotels were sources for imported wines, liquors, spices, cheese, and other items for the more affluent. Atherton's study of stores in the South revealed a surprising variety of goods. While all stores carried sugar, coffee, tea, salt, and whiskey, a number went far beyond this simple list. Some towns had specialty stores where luxury items were sold. A house in Huntsville advertised "loaf and lump sugar, pineapple cheese, allspice, ginger, pepper, raisins, almonds, nutmegs, mustard . . . tea, and wine."[85] In Talladega, a store advertised "liquors, brandies, wines, whiskies, ale, porter, . . . schnapps."[86] A wholesaler in Athens listed an almost unbelievable array of gourmet items. Furthermore, many towns had confectioners where "candies, cordials, fruit cakes" were offered.[87] Buckingham noted (even in the 1840s) that Columbus, Georgia, had "more than the usual number of . . . 'Confectionaries,' [*sic*] where sweetmeats and fruits are sold." He apparently found a similar situation in Alabama but noted that the cordials were alcoholic and that some confectioner's shops were only gentlemen's bars.[88]

Perhaps the most notable innovation affecting good tastes was the availability of ice. It became available in port cities early in the century and by the 1850s had penetrated the interior as well. It was for sale in Selma in 1840 and by 1855 had reached most urban places located near rivers or on railroads.[89] The availability of ice increased the variety offered by the confectionery, and the true soda fountain came into being. Just prior to the War, an Alabama store advertised: "The subscribers have put up a soda fountain in their establishment, and have arrangements to be be supplied with ice. . . . The syrups will be of the richest and most choice variety, consisting of rose, lemon, pineapple, and strawberry, vanilla, sarasparilla, sassafras, ginger, almond, and peach."[90]

As ice became available the year round, ice cream making became possible. It was made in the area before the 1840s but few machines were in use. A freezer, roughly the same as the freezer now used, was being sold during the 1840s and presumably some moved into the South.[91]

With such items available, the urban inhabitant as well as planters and farmers living nearby had opportunities to vary their food intake with unusual or exotic goods. It is unlikely that people indulged in such luxuries very often, but there must have been occasions when even small farmers purchased a few special items. The occasional trip to town, the birthday, or the trip to take a son away to the academy, were occasions calling for treats that offered a welcome variety in the day-to-day fare.

The availability of these items together with a disparity of wealth among

Southerners led to variations in habits among economic classes. Unfortunately, most detailed menu descriptions come from the pens of affluent planters or writers who visited the large and better-managed plantations, most of which were in the old or more-developed settlements such as the Carolina Coast or lower Louisiana. Such descriptions reveal an almost incredible opulence. At one meal on the Alston plantation on the rice coast a sumptuous table was laden with:

> Turtle soup at each end, [and] two parallel dishes, one containing a leg of boiled mutton and the other turtle steaks and fins. Next was a pie of Maccaroni [sic] in the center of the table and on each side of it was a small dish of oysters. Next . . . were two parallel dishes, corresponding with the two above mentioned, one of them turtle steak and fins, and the other a boiled ham. When the soups were removed, their place was supplied at one end by a haunch of venison and at the other by a roast turkey. . . . [A second course included] bread pudding . . . jelly . . . a high glass dish of ice cream . . . [and] a pie. . . . [After the second course came] two high baskets . . . one of bananas and the other of oranges. One larger . . . of apples.

During the meal madeira, sherry, and champagne were served and, after dessert, hermitage, madeira, and cordials.[92] Grimball describes another meal for eight with four courses that included two soups, ham, turkey with oyster sauce, a leg of mutton, a haunch of venison, three wild ducks, turtle steaks and fins, four vegetables, apple pudding, custards, cheese, and bread. All this was followed by dessert.[93] Apparently overindulgence was not unknown for he complained of another meal: "Dined yesterday with Mr. Vanderhorst . . . the table absolutely groaned under the load of meats . . . the wines were good. . . . I mixed the wines and drank more that my stomach would bear, and when I came home was made quite ill."[94]

The tables of the less wealthy were not so abundantly supplied, yet it was common to have more than one meat. A traveler in Mississippi in the 1850s reported: "Here we have excellent ham, boiled whole, a surloin [sic] of Venison, and a dainty steak from 'Old Bruin.' "[95] Small planters and farmers served abundant and wholesome but not sumptuous meals. In Virginia, a traveler was fed soup, cabbage, and bacon (boiled together), fowl, both wheaten and cornbread, potatoes, green corn, and apple dumplings for dinner. Breakfast was made up of "coffee, small hot wheaten rolls [probably biscuits], batter bread, and hoe-cake . . . milk, eggs, and rashers of bacon."[96] But these modest meals were not available to all Whites. Many Southern tables saw only pork, cornbread, and a vegetable or two day after day. This was particularly true in winter when vegetables were fewer and there was a strong dependence upon cured meat and semiperishable cereals and vegetables.

Perhaps the most significant aspect of Southern foodways is the persistence of food preferences once they were established. The most obvious characteristic was the strong dependence upon corn and pork, which persisted throughout the nineteenth century and, indeed, well into the twentieth. During the colonial period, both were staples all along the Atlantic Coast including New England. Both were staples in the South and West during the first few decades of the nineteenth century. But by the 1830s or 1840s food habits in the East and West were undergoing significant changes. There was a general rise in standard of living after about 1840, with a consequent change in food habits. Better methods of food preservation and transportation increased the varieties available to the consumer. At the same time, waves of immigrants from all parts of Europe introduced new food habits to the increasingly complex cultures of the East and West. The South, on the other hand, shared little in these changes. Instead of being strongly affected by these factors, it became increasingly isolated during the years prior to the Civil War. Perhaps even more important was the continuation of these processes after the War. Emancipation did little to alter the economic position of Blacks, nor did it greatly alter the agricultural commodity emphases. If anything, there was an intensification of the cotton economy. Moreover, the effects of sharecropping reduced many former White landowners to tenancy and a lower level of living. Without the "cultural shock" of immigrants moving into the South and handicapped by a lower level of living than other regions, many elements of the Southern diet persisted through the nineteenth and well into the twentieth century. Thus, the traditional Southern foods have survived the settlement years, a civil war, and more than a century of time to become a frontier "relic."

## Notes

1. An anonymous English traveler quoted in Katherine M. Jones, *The Plantation South* (Indianapolis, Ind.: Bobbs-Merrill, 1957), 204.

2. Edgar W. Martin, *The Standard of Living in 1860* (Chicago: University of Chicago Press, 1942), 57–64; Wilbur O. Atwater and Charles D. Woods, *Dietary Studies with Reference to the Food of the Negro in Alabama in 1895 and 1896*, United States Department of Agriculture Bulletin No. 38 (Washington, D.C.: United States Government Printing Office, 1897); Richard O. Cummings, *The American and His Food: A History of Food Habits in the United States* (Chicago: University of Chicago Press, 1941); Mar-

garet Cussler and Mary L. De Give, *"Twixt the Cup and the Lip"*: *Psychological and Socio-Cultural Factors Affecting Food Habits* (New York: Twayne, 1952); Dorothy Dickens, A *Study of Food Habits of People in Two Contrasting Areas of Mississippi*, Mississippi Agricultural Experiment Station Bulletin No. 245, 1927; and Rupert B. Vance, *Human Factors in Cotton Culture* (Chapel Hill: University of North Carolina Press,1929).

3. Thomas Hamilton, *Men and Manners in America*, 2d ed. (London: T. Cadell, 1834), vol. 2, 255, 258, and 262.

4. Harriet Martineau, *Retrospect of Western Travel* (London: Saunders and Otley, 1838), vol. 1, 212.

5. Frances A. Kemble, *Journal of a Residence on a Georgia Plantation in 1838–39*, ed. John A. Scott (New York: Knopf, 1961), 58.

6. Tyrone Power, *Impressions of America* (London: Richard Bently, 1836), vol. 2, 224.

7. Henry B. Whipple, *Bishop Whipple's Southern Diary, 1843–1844*, ed. Lester B. Shippee (Minneapolis: University of Minnesota Press, 1937), 103.

8. *Southern Cabinet of Agriculture, Horticulture, Rural and Domestic Economy* (1840), vol. 1, 125.

9. Frederick L. Olmsted, *Journey in the Seaboard Slave States* (New York: Mason Brothers, 1859), 411.

10. J. D. Anthony, "Cherokee County, Alabama, Reminiscences of Its Early Settlements, *Alabama Historical Quarterly* 8 (1946): 331; John S. Bassett, *The Southern Plantation Overseer as Revealed in His Letters* (Northhampton, Mass.: Smith College, 1925), 44–45; Martin B. Coyner, "John Harwell Cocke of Bromo: Agriculture and Slavery in the Ante-Bellum South," unpublished Ph.D. dissertation, University of Virginia, 1961, 408–9; George Powell, "A Description and History of Blount County," *Transactions of the Alabama Historical Society* (1855): 40–42; and Bayard Still, "The Westward Migration of a Planter Pioneer in 1796," *William and Mary College Quarterly Magazine* 21 (October 1941): 320.

11. Harriet Martineau, *Society in America*, 3d ed. (London: Saunders and Otley, 1837), 203.

12. C. D. Arfwedson, *The United States and Canada, in 1832, 1833, and 1834* (London: Richard Bentley, 1834), vol. 2, 415.

13. Arfwedson, *The United States and Canada, in 1832, 1833, and 1834*, 11.

14. William H. Wills, "A Southern Sulky Ride in 1837, from North Carolina to Alabama," *Southern History Society Publication* 7 (January 1903): 12.

15. James R. Creecy, *Scenes in the South* (Washington, D.C.: Thomas McGill, 1860), 84 and 106.

16. Bassett, *The Southern Plantation Overseer as Revealed in His Letters*, 74.

17. Francis M. Trollope, *Domestic Manners of the Americans* (London: Whittaker, Treacher, and Company, 1832), 238.

18. *Southern Cultivator* 13 (1855): 23.

19. *Southern Cultivator*: 23.

20. Frederick L. Olmsted, *A Journey in the Back Country* (New York: Mason Brothers, 1863), 161.

21. Emily Burke, *Reminiscences in Georgia* (Oberlin, Ohio: James M. Fitch, 1850), 233.

22. John C. Gunn, *Gunn's Domestic Medicine or Poor Man's Friend* (Philadelphia: G. V. Raymond, 1840), 182.

23. John S. Wilson, "Health Department," *Godey's Lady's Book* 60 (February 1860): 178.

24. See *Cotton Planter and Soil* 3 (1859): 306; *Southern Cultivator* 1 (1843): 172, 175, 195, and 208; *Southern Cultivator* 7 (1849): 114; Burke, *Reminiscences in Georgia*, 223; and Weymouth T. Jordan, *Herbs, Hoecakes and Husbandry: The Daybook of a Planter of the Old South* (Tallahassee: Florida State University Press, 1960), 45, 47–48, 52–54, for descriptions of the curing processes used.

25. Burke, *Reminiscences in Georgia*, 222.

26. *Southern Cultivator* 1 (1843): 174, and *Southern Cultivator* 17 (1859): 339.

27. Letter from Sarah Williams to Samuel Hicks of New Hartford, New York, December 10, 1853, in Sarah Hicks Williams Papers, File No. 3210, Southern Manuscripts Collection, University of North Carolina, Chapel Hill.

28. George G. Smith, Jr., *The History of Methodism in Georgia and Florida from 1785 to 1865* (Macon, Ga.: Burke and Company, 1877), 306.

29. George E. Brewer, "History of Coosa County," *Alabama Historical Quarterly* (Spring 1942): 127, and Ulrich B. Phillips, *Life and Labor in the Old South* (Boston: Little Brown, 1929), 92.

30. T. Lynn Smith and Lauren C. Post, "The Country Butchery: A Cooperative Institution," *Rural Sociology* 2 (September 1937): 335–37.

31. Ervin E. Williams, Journal for 1846, November 17, 1846 in Southern Manuscripts Collection, University of North Carolina, Chapel Hill.

32. Patent Office Report (1850), 287, and William P. Dale, "A Connecticut Yankee in Ante-Bellum Alabama," *Alabama Review* 6 (January 1953): 63.

33. *Soil of the South* 2 (1852): 294.

34. Louise Gladney, "History of Pleasant Hill Plantation 1811–1867,"

unpublished M.A. thesis, Louisiana State University, 1932, 45–46; William J. Dickey, Diaries, 1858–1859, Manuscript Collection, University of Georgia, Athens, Georgia; and Edward M. Steel, "A Pioneer Farmer in the Choctaw Purchase," *Journal of Mississippi History* 16 (October 1954): 235.

35. Susan Dabney Smedes, *A Southern Planter: Social Life in the Old South* (New York: James Pott and Company, 1900), 81 and *DeBow's Review* 30 (1861): 645.

36. Adam Hodgson, *Letters from North America* (London: Hurst, Robinson and Company, 1824), vol. 1, 21 and 31; and Martineau, *Society in America*, 306.

37. Olmsted, *A Journey in the Back Country*, 127.

38. Paul Ravesies, *Scenes and Settlers of Alabama* (Mobile, Ala.: n.p., 1885), 9.

39. Lewis C. Gray, *History of Agriculture in the Southern United States to 1860* (New York: Peter Smith, 1941), vol. 2, 832.

40. J. S. Buckingham, *The Slave States of America* (London: Fisher, Son, and Company, 1842) vol. 1, 404; Herbert A. Kellar, *Solon Robinson: Pioneer and Agriculturalist* (Indianapolis: Indiana Historical Bureau, 1936), vol. 2, 161; Benjamin M. Norman, *New Orleans and Environs* (New Orleans: Published by author, 1845), 56; Power, vol. 2, 250; and Kemble, 184.

41. Martineau, *Society in America*, 44.

42. Patent Office Report (1848), 516; Buckingham, vol. 1, 404; Kellar, vol. 1, 161; Norman, 56; Power, vol. 2, 250; Smedes, 82; and Francis and Theresa Pulszky, *White, Red, Black: Sketches of American Society* (New York: Redfield, 1853), vol. 2, 97.

43. Kellar, vol. 2, 161.

44. Patent Office Report (1849), 161.

45. Patent Office Report (1850), 365.

46. Gladney, 46; and Wendell H. Stephenson, "A Quarter-Century of a Mississippi Plantation," *Mississippi Valley Historical Review* 23 (December 1936): 367.

47. Kemble, 184.

48. Smedes, 82; and Elizabeth W. A. Pringle, *Chronicles of Chicora Wood* (Boston: Christopher Publishing House, 1940), 89.

49. Kolloch Plantation Books, vol. V, File No. 407, Southern Manuscripts Collection, University of North Carolina, Chapel Hill.

50. Martineau, *Society in America*, vol. 1, 306; Charles A. Clinton, *A Winter from Home* (New York: John F. Trow, 1852), 38; and Margaret H. Hall, *The Aristocratic Journey* (New York: G. P. Putnam's Sons, 1831), 209 and 221.

51. Olmsted, *A Journey in the Back Country*, 140.

52. Hamilton, vol. 2, 255–58; Martineau, vol. 1, 212; Fredrika Bremer, *The Homes of the New World: Impressions of America* (New York: Harper and Brother, 1853), vol. 1, 280 and 288; William F. Gray, *From Virginia to Texas, 1835* (Houston, Tex.: Gray, Dillaye and Company, 1909), 40 and 51; Frederick L. Olmsted, *The Cotton Kingdom* (New York: Mason Brothers, 1861), vol. 2, 86; Olmsted, *Journey in the Seaboard Slave States*, 565; and William H. Wills, *Publications of the Southern History Society* 6 (November 1902): 473 and 481.

53. Martineau, *Retrospect of Western Travel*, vol. 1, 212; and Hamilton, vol. 2, 255, 258, and 262.

54. Phillip H. Gosse, *Letters from Alabama* (London: Morgan and Chase, 1859), 128.

55. Everard G. Baker, Diaries, vol. I, 30 October, 1849, File No. 41, Southern Historical Collection, University of North Carolina, Chapel Hill.

56. Solomon Northup, *Twelve Years a Slave* (New York: Miller, Orton and Mulligan, 1855), 201.

57. David G. Harris, Farm Journals, 7 January, 1858, File No. M-982, Southern Historical Collection, University of North Carolina, Chapel Hill.

58. Clinton, 14; and Rosser H. Taylor, *Ante-Bellum South Carolina: A Social and Cultural History* (Chapel Hill: University of North Carolina, 1942), 15.

59. Diary of W. Thacker quoted in Taylor, 15.

60. Weymouth T. Jordan, *Hugh Davis and His Alabama Plantation* (University: University of Alabama Press, 1948), 126; and Joe G. Taylor, *Negro Slavery in Louisiana* (Baton Rouge: Louisiana Historical Association, 1963), 108.

61. Jordan, *Hugh Davis and His Alabama Plantation*, 126.

62. John Q. Anderson, "Dr. James Green Carson, Ante-Bellum Planter of Mississippi and Louisiana," *Journal of Mississippi History*, October 1956, 261.

63. Charles H. Stevenson, "Fisheries in the Ante-Bellum South," in *Economic History, 1607–1865*, ed. James C. Ballagh, vol. V in the South in the Building of the Nation (Richmond, Va.: Southern Historical Publication Society, 1909), 267.

64. Buckingham, Vol. 1, 157; John C. Butler, *Historical Record of Macon and Central Georgia* (Macon, Ga.: J. W. Burke Company, 1958), 162; and Martineau, *Retrospect of Western Travel*, Vol. 1, 217.

65. Grimes Family Papers, Box 2, File No. 3357, Southern Historical Manuscript Collection, University of North Carolina, Chapel Hill, and Edward Wood, Greenfield Fishery Records, File No. 1598, Southern Historical Manuscript Collection, University of North Carolina, Chapel Hill.

66. *DeBow's Review* 15 (1853): 70.

67. Olmsted, *A Journey in the Back Country*, 198, 200, and 240; Olmsted, *The Cotton Kingdom*, vol. 2, 86; and Olmsted, *Journey in the Seaboard Slave States*, 564.

68. Charles Lyell, *A Second Visit to the United States of North America* (New York: Harper and Brothers, 1849), vol. 1, 144.

69. Martineau, *Society in America*, vol. 1, 306.

70. Gosse, 46–47.

71. *DeBow's Review* 15 (1853): 70; David W. Mitchell, *Ten Years in the United States* (London: Smith, Elder and Company, 1862), 23; and A. De Puy Van Buren, *Jottings of a Year's Sojourn in the South* (Battle Creek, Mich.: By the author, 1859), 46.

72. Gosse, 46; Olmsted, *A Journey in the Back Country*, 242; Lyell, vol. 2, 34; and William E. Dodd, *The Cotton Kingdom* (New Haven, Conn.: Yale University Press, 1921), vol. 27 of *Chronicles of America*, 91.

73. Olmsted, *Journey in the Seaboard Slave States*, 478; and Charles Lanman, *Adventures in the Wilds of the United States and British American Provinces* (Philadelphia: John W. Moore, 1856), vol. 2, 137.

74. Hall, 245; Hamilton, vol. 2, 241; and Olmsted, *A Journey in the Back Country*, 161–62.

75. Lyell, vol. 1, 144.

76. Olmsted, *Journey in the Seaboard Slave States*, 478.

77. Bremer, vol. 1, 280.

78. Olmsted, *Journey in the Seaboard Slave States*, 454–55.

79. The process of canning in tins was in its infancy during the antebellum period, but other methods of keeping fruits preserved by sugar were well developed. Thus, while the true canning of vegetables and meats was essentially a postwar phenomena, there was an abundance of preserves, jellies, and jams. See Martin, 27–33; Cummings, 85; and Myrtie L. Candler, "Reminiscences of Life in Georgia During the 1850's and 1860's," *Georgia Historical Quarterly* 30 (June 1949): 118.

80. Olmsted, *A Journey in the Back Country*, 162; Olmsted, *The Cotton Kingdom*, vol. 2 86; Herbert Weaver, *Mississippi Farmers, 1850–1860* (Nashville: Vanderbilt University Press, 1945), 50; John F. H. Claiborne, "Trip through the Piney Woods," *Publications of the Mississippi Historical Society* 9 (1906): 522; and Bennie C. Mellown, *Memoirs of a Pre-Civil War Community* (Birmingham, Ala.: Birmingham Printing Company, 1950), 18.

81. Arfwedson, vol. 2, 11; and Taylor, 169.

82. Lyell, vol. 2, 158; Martineau, *Retrospect of Western Travel*, vol. 1, 221; Martineau, *Society in America*, vol. 1, 307; Olmsted, *Journey in the Seaboard Slave States*, 625; Timothy Flint, *Recollections of the Last Ten Years* (Bos-

ton: Cummings, Hilliard, and Company, 1826), 365; and James Stuart, *Three Years in North America* (New York: J. and J. Harper, 1833), vol. 2, 123.

83. United States Treasury Department, *A Report of the Commerce and Navigation of the United States for 1856*, House Executive Document Vol. 13, 34th Congress, 3d Session, 459–63.

84. Gosse, 47; Van Buren, 46; Lyell, vol. 2, 158; Mitchell, 23; and Martineau, *Retrospect of Western Travel*, vol. 1, 212.

85. Lewis E. Atherton, *The Southern Country Store, 1800–1860* (Baton Rouge: Louisiana State University Press, 1949), 78–79.

86. Wellington Vandiver, "Pioneer Talledega, Its Minutes and Memories," *Alabama Historical Quarterly* 16 (Spring 1954): 131.

87. Earnest C. Hynds, Jr., "Ante-Bellum Athens and Clarke County, Georgia" unpublished Ph.D. dissertation, University of Georgia, 1961, 258; and Atherton, 79–80.

88. Buckingham, vol. 1, 246, 251, and 287.

89. Hynds, 259; and John Hardy, *Selma: Her Institutions and Her Men* (Selma, Ala.: Bert Neville and Clarence DeBray, 1957), 117. For detail on the ice trade during the prerefrigeration period, see Richard O. Cummings, *The American Ice Harvest: A Historical Study in Technology, 1800–1918* (Berkeley: University of California Press, 1949).

90. Vandiver, "Pioneer Talladega, Its Minutes and Memories," 130–31.

91. "Modern Ice Cream, and the Philosophy of Its Manufacture," *Godey's Lady's Book* 60 (May 1860): 460–61; Martineau, *Society in America*, vol. 1, 307; Martineau, *Retrospect of Western Travel*, vol. 1, 221; and Lyell, vol. 2, 158.

92. John B. Grimball, Diaries, 18 October, 1832, Southern Manuscript Collection, University of North Carolina, Chapel Hill.

93. Grimball, 16 October, 1832.

94. Grimball, 7 July, 1832.

95. Van Buren, 46.

96. Mitchell, 23 and 37.

# 8

# Geophagy in a Mississippi County

## Donald E. Vermeer and Dennis A. Frate

Few dietary habits intertwine environment and culture more closely than geophagy, the deliberate consumption of earth. Although commonly considered strange and odd, geophagy in essence differs little from the use of water or rocksalt, both of which occur naturally and may enter into the diet directly and unaltered.

Geophagy has a worldwide distribution and cuts across ethnic, social, and economic lines.[1] It was a New World custom prior to European contact, and it has been reported among various Indian groups in both North and South America.[2] In the United States today, the custom is associated primarily with rural Black people in the South, but it has also been recorded within the White population of the same area.[3] It exists elsewhere in the United States among Whites and Blacks, children and adults, and in rural and urban populations.[4] Inasmuch as the custom of geophagy is recorded both from Europe and from the indigenous Indian population in the New World, Blacks could have acquired the practice from either or both, but geophagy is equally, or more, deeply ingrained in the African cultures that supplied the bulk of the slaves to the New World. Consequently it is not surprising that this custom continues so deeply set in the Black subculture in the United States today.[5] Its dominance and the depth to which it is imbedded in the culture and custom of the Black population in the United States support the notion that geophagy is a cultural trait that has persisted through two or more centuries following its importation from West Africa.

Reprinted by permission from the *Annals of the Association of American Geographers* 65 (1975):414–24.

An abundant literature reports widespread, early geophagy among slaves brought to the New World.[6] Mouthlocks (face masks) were used on slaves in the Caribbean and southern United States in attempts to suppress the eating of earths; owners thought clayeating was a cause of illness and death among slaves.[7]

Surprisingly few field studies have been made of geophagy in the rural South, despite its long tradition in that area and its spread by massive migration of Blacks into the urban centers of the North and West. Much of the data on geophagy have come through surveys conducted largely by medical, educational, and other institutions, and little consideration has been given the environmental and sociocultural matrices in which the practice operates.[8] We investigated geophagy within the Black community in rural Holmes County, Mississippi, as part of a large Health Research Project.[9]

## The Setting

The western third of Holmes County is part of the Mississippi–Yazoo River floodplain, popularly misnamed the Delta (fig. 8.1). A conspicuous north-south bluff with relief of eighty to one hundred feet (25 to 30 m) separates the floodplain from the undulating upland of the coastal plain to the east. The floodplain has relief of less than twenty feet (6 m). Bands of settlements linked by the principal roads stretch along its natural levees, but the poorly drained backswamps have few roads or settlements. The eastern upland is cut by a dense stream network that has created intricate dendritic patterns of ridges and valleys. Most of the upland has been cleared of its original woodland. Cotton cultivation, which dominated the upland until World War II, resulted in severe gully erosion. Since the end of the war, much of the former cropland has been converted into pasture or planted with loblolly pine plantations.

Soils correspond to the principal topographic units.[10] Alluvial soils cover the floodplain, with a narrow strip of colluvial soils at the base of the bluffs. The Yazoo fine sandy loams of the natural levees are more than 90 percent very fine sand and silts, and the Yazoo loams of the levees are about 80 percent silts and clays. Silt and clay fractions comprise more than 85 percent of the Wabash and Sharkey soils of the backswamps, which often have standing water. The Sharkey clays of the lowest parts of the backswamp cover three-quarters of the floodplain. Soil profiles are not well developed because of the recency of deposition, but all subsoils except those of the Yazoo fine sandy loams show a modest enrichment of clays.

Memphis silt loam and Richland silt loam soil types dominate the up-

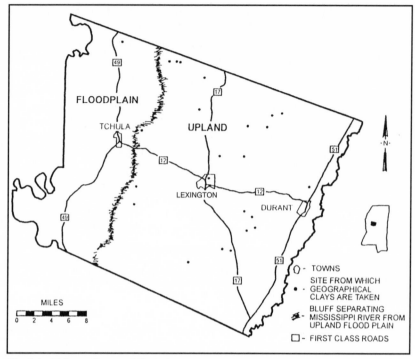

Fig. 8.1. Holmes County, Mississippi

land. Together they cover approximately 54 percent of the county. Both soils have been formed in situ from the mantle of loess, which thins from forty feet (12 m) along the bluffs to as little as four feet (1.2 m) along the eastern border of the county. In some areas prolonged cultivation has completely removed the loess mantle and exposed the underlying bedrock. The demarcation between soil and subsoil is seldom sharp, but within both the Memphis silt loam and the Richland silt loam, the percentage of clay increases with depth.

Quartz accounted for more than 75 percent by weight of fifteen geophagical earths, one from the floodplain, most from the upland, and some from unknown sites; samples were taken from the B soil horizon, the clay-enriched subsoil zone.[11] Clay minerals were present in lesser amounts; mica, chlorite, expandable clays such as montmorillonite, and feldspar were common. Montmorillonite was conspicuous in the sample from the floodplain.

Three samples, one from the floodplain and two from the upland, showed consistent chemical composition when analyzed by X-ray fluorescence. Silicon, aluminum, and iron were present in amounts greater than 5 percent by weight; titanium, potassium, calcium, and manganese were found in amounts of about one percent; and trace elements constituting about one-tenth of one percent by weight were cobalt, nickel, and copper.

## Social and Cultural Context

The rural population is predominantly Black.[12] Blacks traditionally provided much of the labor on the relatively large farms of the floodplain where cotton is still extensively raised; most of the floodplain farms are owned by Whites, but a few Blacks also own large farms on the floodplain. In contrast, most of the upland farms are small and owned by Blacks, but the upland also has a few large White-owned farms.[13]

Traditional social life revolves around named local "communities," groupings of perhaps two hundred to five hundred people commonly dominated by one or a few extended families, which center on the church and the burying grounds.[14] The local community plays a key role in perpetuation of folk notions about the practice of geophagy, and geophagical pits and their use become associated with specific communities. As a result, geophagical clays from many different sources become a characteristic of the practice of geophagy among Blacks in the county.

Selective male migration to urban areas in the North, especially Chicago, has left a residual Black population that is dominantly female in the age group responsible for the rearing of children and for the household; the thirty to forty-nine age group in 1970 showed twice as many females as males.[15] Children and young adults tend to be more demonstrative with and more subject to the authority of the mother than the father. The responsibilities of the father, even when resident, are most evident in the organization of outdoor work, on trips, in family religious observances, and in the family's public life.[16] Young children come strongly under female influence whether remaining at home or fostered to relatives. Strong female–child relationships have effects that persist into adulthood. These bonds are intimately involved in the transference of geophagy from mother to daughter and in its perpetuation within the community.

## The Practice of Geophagy

### Site and Substance

Geophagical clays come primarily form the upland. The only actively used site identified on the floodplain was in the backswamp area, and its soil was dominantly fine alluvial silts and clays; the pit was little more than the diameter of a hand and approximately eighteen inches (50 cm) deep. Although the floodplain is not a common source of geophagical substances today, a number of informants commented that floodplain clays were used more commonly in the past when Black residents lacked the mobility to obtain preferred clays from upland sites.

Clays from upland sites generally are obtained from roadcuts. A number of sites are near the main roads within a few miles of the bluff between the floodplain and the upland. Informants from the floodplain indicated they traveled to the bluff zone to obtain edible clays. Use of roadbank clays minimizes problems of transport. Roadcuts also expose potential geophagical clays for easy excavation.[17]

Clays are taken from the B soil horizon at depths ranging from eighteen inches (50 cm) to near four feet (130 cm) (fig. 8.2); clays are mined from greater depths in the deep loessal soils of the bluff zone than in the residual soils farther eastward. The use of the B horizon reflects an awareness of the concentration of clays in the subsoil through translocation from the A horizon.[18] Four sites were in the root zone beneath large trees; the single urban site was within the B horizon beneath the exposed roots of an oak

Fig. 8.2. Geophagical Pit in Mississippi Where Clays Are Being Excavated from a Zone about Two Feet below the Surface

tree within the White residential area of Lexington, the county seat. Clay accumulation beneath trees may be favored by the movement of clay particles down root channels into the subsoil. Although therapeutic qualities are sometimes ascribed to trees, no such association could be determined for the trees overlying the geophagical sites.

Excavation proceeds horizontally into the roadbank, following the clay-enriched subsoil horizon. Women principally gather clays, but an adult male may mine clays for his wife, or young children may aid their mother. Kitchen utensils appear to be the most common tools used for clay removal, and knife and spoon marks are commonly seen on the pitwalls. Impurities of root hairs and erratic rocks are discarded, and the clays are placed in a container and brought home. The amount of clay taken from a pit at any one time varies greatly. A small amount will suffice for a single person intending to return in a day or so, but a larger amount will be removed if it must last for a time or if it is also to supply others; clays are trafficked to former residents who have moved to urbanized areas in the North.[19]

Consumption and excavation appear heightened immediately following a rainfall. Informants note the pleasant smell of damp earth, "the smell of the good earth," which entices them to consume clays. If their supply is insufficient, effort will be made to obtain more.

Rather precise terminology identifies edible clays. The word "dirt" connotes an edible substance, but "clay-dirt" is inedible despite the fact that geophagical substances are dominantly clay.[20] Additional descriptive terms may be combined with the word "dirt" for greater specificity. Informants in the floodplain region refer to edible clays as "hill-dirt," thereby indicating the general source area of the clays. More precise designation of source may be given, as in "Franklin-dirt," to identify materials from the Franklin community. Modifying terms are all locational, thereby recognizing the numerous possible sources of clay, and underscoring the association of clay sources with certain communities or areas. Sites are local and serve small segments of the Black population within the county.[21]

Desirable characteristics of geophagical substances are sharply defined and consistent. Texture is the chief characteristic; good "dirt" must be fine, and gritty or sandy substances are shunned. Light grey and grey-white color is a second essential quality. Most of the edible clays in Holmes County are, in fact, light colored, which may have led to the criterion for selection of the suitable clay. Informants claim the taste of clays is sour, and sour taste is another criterion used in finding new sources of edible clays. All edible clays are chemically acid, and that quality may impart a sour taste to them.

## Preparation and Consumption

Clays are "baked" prior to consumption. Two-thirds of our respondents said they heated clays in a pan atop the stove or in an oven for two or three hours. Some informants claimed this process eliminated disease-bearing organisms. This practice may represent a carryover from the past when clays were obtained from the inside of mud chimneys. Although construction techniques and materials have eliminated chimney clays today, this established taste is at least partially satisfied through baking. Baking desiccates and hardens the clays, and gives them qualities comparable to those obtained from the insides of chimneys. A few informants also claimed that baking gave the clays a smoked flavor, a quality that would have been inherent in clays obtained from chimneys.[22] Approximately half of those who baked clays added vinegar, salt, or both, before baking; the amount added varied greatly. Both additives enhance the appreciated sour flavor, and this mechanism may also increase salt ingestion in a population significantly troubled by hypertension.[23]

Clay is consumed whenever the craving arises. Most practitioners ingest at random, but approximately one-third of our respondents associated geophagy with post mealtimes. Two basic meals are commonly eaten, one at midmorning and the other in late afternoon or early evening. A midday snack may be eaten, but little cooking is done for it. Thus, consumption occurs twice daily for practitioners whose geophagical habits parallel the meal pattern.

Individuals practicing geophagy claim craving for clays is more intense than for food. The craving intensifies when not appeased, and it may lead to discomfort and other side effects. One woman, who was unable to obtain clay from her usual source during an extended period of inclement weather, described the intensity of her craving in terms of headache, nausea, and abdominal cramps. Such symptoms may stem from physiological or psychological dependency, or both.

Although individual practitioners were asked to state their daily consumption of clay in familiar dietary items, such as peach seed, average-sized okra, or tomato, they commonly depicted the amount consumed by cupping one hand. We estimate daily consumption is about fifty grams, with a range from ten to one hundred fifty grams; the smaller amounts may be eaten at one time.

Questions pertaining to geophagy were included in a nutrition survey, a perinatal survey, and a health utilization survey conducted by the Health Research Project. The nutrition survey, the broadest and most comprehensive survey directed at the whole population, uncovered the practice of geophagy among women and children, but not among men or adolescents. These findings confirmed the data we had obtained from informants.[24]

Ten of fifty-six women were actively engaged in geophagy at the time of the survey, and one other woman claimed consumption of dry powdered milk. Twenty-two women had engaged in geophagy on a regular basis during the past, fourteen of them specifically during pregnancy. In short, more than half of the women surveyed indicated present or past earth eating on a regular basis, and nearly half of those admitting to the practice associated it with pregnancy.

The nutrition survey also revealed that 18 of 115 children were clay eaters; our data indicate no gender bias among them.[25] All children consuming clays were from the upland region of the county, and all had mothers who engaged in the practice; mothers provided information concerning geophagy. The absence of earth eating among children of the floodplain may be attributed to scarcity of sites and lesser availability of clays considered edible.

Our informants said that children learn the custom from their mothers, and not by personal exploration. The custom is transferred from one generation to the next when a mother pacifies a whining child by giving it clay to eat, or when a child eats clay in imitation of its mother.[26] Our data also indicate that children in Holmes County adopt the practice soon after the age of one year, but only two of the eighteen children were practicing geophagy after the age of four.[27] Reduction in earth eating at the age of four is explained by mothers' comments that they did not wish their children to become clay eaters at such an early age; this explanation was offered despite the fact the clays are deliberately given children in early years. The mother and other female authority figures attempt to suppress the practice when the mother can rationalize with the maturing child, and efforts are made to conceal clay from children. It is often hidden in the house, and in one case it was locked in the glove compartment of the automobile. The mother and other women in the household play a significant role in the initiation, continuation, and cessation of the practice during the formative years of the child. Social norms permit very young children to imitate the mother, and condone their appeasement by giving them clay. Society does not, however, condone the practice as the child matures, and overt effort is made to suppress it through rationalization and removal of the clays from sight and temptation.

The perinatal survey provided a specific means of assessing the incidence of geophagy during the period before and after delivery of a child, when it is most common.[28] Forty of 142 pregnant women admitted consumption of clays, and 27 more said they consumed other items, primarily laundry starch, but also baking soda, wheat flour, and dry powdered milk, which they considered replacements for clays. Nearly half of the women reached through the perinatal survey consumed clays or commercial substitutes.

Nineteen of the twenty-seven women using commercial products live on the floodplain, where desirable clays were difficult to obtain. The clay substitutes have similar color and texture, and the senses of sight and touch appear to be served equally by clays or one of the substitutes; it seems unlikely, however, that the sense of taste would be satisfied equally by clay and baking soda. The use of laundry starch, rather than cooking starch, may be related to its lump form and the ease of eating it directly from the box. It also has a chunky quality similar to clay.

The mean age of those consuming clay averages little more than twenty-five years, but those substituting commercial products averaged just under twenty-one years, suggesting that younger women are replacing traditional clays with purchased substitutes. Informants commented about the sanitary qualities of packaged, processed substitutes, but the unavailability of suitable clays in the floodplain area may induce substitution of commercial products that are comparable to sight and touch, if not to taste.

The health utilization survey data reflected an incidence of geophagy not greatly dissimilar from the other two surveys. Approximately one-quarter of the women admitted active consumption of clays, and an additional two-fifths said they had practiced geophagy regularly in the past but were not presently engaged in the practice.[29]

## Conclusion

Geophagy clearly is an integral part of the tradition of the Black population of Holmes County. This custom occurs commonly throughout the rural South, and it has been extended to urban areas throughout the country as a result of Black migration.[30] Geophagy is also practiced by Whites in the South.[31] The practice is strongly gender specific; it occurs chiefly among women, and to a lesser degree among young children of both sexes, but we have no evidence of it among men. The custom reaches its peak incidence among pregnant women, and adult females are primarily responsible for its transmission to young children. The practice is condoned for young children, but it appears suppressed about the age of four years. It resumes its strength as a female-related custom about puberty or at pregnancy.

At any one time, approximately 25 percent of adult Black females and 16 percent of the Black children of Holmes County are actively engaged in geophagy; 28 percent of pregnant women eat clay, and an additional 19 percent consume commercial substitutes such as laundry starch. Commercial substitutes appear to be gaining favor among younger practitioners, reflecting a continuation of the custom in other forms as traditional clays become increasingly unavailable and fall into disfavor. The incidence of geophagy among all groups probably is considerably higher than our data indicate because of reluctance to admit the practice.

Geophagy may be viewed as a physiological deficiency disorder, as an appetite aberration, or as a cultural practice that may in turn disturb physiological functions and appetite. Explanation of geophagy as stemming from a deficiency disorder ignores the very strong element of gender specificity in the practice and the occurrence of the custom at definite life stages. Geophagy may be deemed a deficiency disorder if one considered only pregnant women, but it is practiced by only about half of this group, and then not with every pregnancy. Furthermore, it is difficult to explain the shift to commercial substitutes if geophagy alleviates deficiency disorders; laundry starch supplies little besides calories whereas some clays may contribute essential micronutrients.[32] In addition, the custom takes place among children of both sexes long before puberty, and occurs among older women far beyond menopause. Specific deficiency disorders for each of these groups and ages would have to be shown before such an explanation can be invoked, and in some cultures men also are moderately involved in the practice.[33]

Part of the nutrition survey involved hematocrit determination for a sample of 368 women age seventeen years or more; the sample included 19 women who admitted geophagy.[34] Geophagy appears to have no bearing on hematocrit levels. Further evidence of the inability of deficiency disorder to explain the practice of geophagy comes from hemoglobin counts of 12 women, 5 of whom admitted geophagy.[35] Two women were anemic with a hemoglobin count less than twelve grams per milliliter, but neither practiced geophagy. The hemoglobin, hematocrit, and vitamin level data suggest that geophagy in Holmes County does not arise from specific deficiency disorder.[36]

Chemical analyses were made of clay samples from all sites we observed in Holmes County, plus samples from unknown sources given us by practitioners.[37] All samples are distinctly acid, perhaps thereby accounting for the "sour" taste ascribed to the clays by those consuming them. The geophagical samples supply no appreciable amounts of nutrients.[38] Two samples show unusually high amounts of potassium, calcium, and magnesium; one is from the only site on the floodplain, and the other was obtained from an informant. Although we are uncertain of its origin, it has chemical characteristics similar to the first, and probably is from the floodplain.

Floodplain clays are not preferred, and floodplain residents generally go to the upland for edible earths. X-ray diffraction of the floodplain sample revealed a high content of expandable clays, such as montmorillonite. The swelling clays would serve a very real function if geophagy in Holmes County, and especially in the floodplain region, were associated with appeasement of hunger or antidiarrheal purposes, but we have no evidence of such use.

Trace element determination of zinc and manganese was obtained from six samples. Mean concentrations of zinc in the clays approximate those in foods considered the best sources of that micronutrient; cow's milk contains 3 to 5 ppm zinc and human milk contains 1.34 ppm.[39] Zinc deficiencies have been related to various chronic diseases, retardation of healing of wounds and burns, and dwarfism.[40] Do clays given young children in Holmes County after cessation of breast or bottle feeding contribute significantly to micronutrient needs? Trace element determinations suggest this possibility, and only detailed investigation of serum levels of all trace elements over time and with controls will yield answers.

Zinc is also essential to vitamin A metabolism.[41] Deficient levels of caroteine and vitamin A are unusual in the Black population of Holmes County.[42] If zinc influence on vitamin A metabolism were significant in the Black population of the county, vitamin A deficiency should appear among all adult males and that portion of the women who do not practice geophagy. Vitamin A is not deficient among those groups, and zinc in geophagical clays appears to play no critical role in vitamin A metabolism in this population.

Geophagy has been proposed as both cause and effect of helminthic infection. Thirty-one percent of 116 children in the Holmes County floodplain and 17 percent of 108 children in the upland had roundworm.[43] Hookworm, *Trichuris*, and *Taenia* were rare. Geophagy has a 16 percent incidence among upland children, and is not practiced by floodplain children. Roundworm infection comes from eating contaminated earth, and it should be greater in the upland, but such is not the case. *Trichuris*, which also comes through ingestion of contaminated soil, should also have greater incidence in the upland, but it is rare in the whole population. Most clays are dug from depths of two to four feet (60 to 130 cm), and contamination by parasite eggs at those depths is unlikely. Further, baking desiccates the clays and still further reduced the possibility of parasite infection.

Clay eating to alleviate gastric pain from hookworm has been suggested to explain why slaves carried the practice of earth eating from Africa to the New World, but no association of geophagy with helminthic problems has been found.[44] It seems doubtful that captains of slaving ships, whose profit was in their cargo, would have permitted slaves to have brought clays aboard ship, and certainly not in quantities sufficient for a voyage of several weeks across the Atlantic. Geophagy appears to have been transferred to the Americas because it was so deeply imbedded in tradition that it was not modified by drastic relocation.[45] Relocation of rural Blacks from the South to the urban North has not terminated the practice. When kinfolk and friends fail to send clays from the rural birthplace, commercial substitutes, such as laundry starch, allow perpetuation of the practice in an altered form.

Explanation of geophagy within Holmes County on the basis of hunger also appears rather tenuous. The nutrition survey found that the population is not in ideal nutritional balance, but it faces no severe malnutrition problems.[46] If geophagy were related directly to hunger, the gender specificity of the practice would be difficult to explain, and hunger would have to be shown to exist with adult women and children only during certain periods of life. If hunger were the primary basis for the custom, it could also be argued that consumption of floodplain clays should be far greater than of the upland dirts. The expandable clays of the floodplain, when ingested, would give a feeling of satiety, and the floodplain sources would be more sought than those of the upland. Such is not the case. Voluntary caloric intake among pregnant women was found to decrease when clay or laundry starch was omitted from the diet, suggesting that geophagical substances, by themselves, in some manner stimulate the appetite. More realistically, however, the custom probably is so essential to emotional well-being that clay eating promotes contentment and increased caloric intake, whereas withdrawal of clays creates negative emotional responses and decreased caloric intake.[47]

Geophagy in the Black community of Holmes County represents a common custom arising from traditional values and attitudes, and it involves an awareness and exploitation of the environment. It does not appear to stem directly form either physiological or nutritional bases, yet it has implications for both. Our data give little evidence of the practice resulting in biological problems, but other studies have noted nutritional relationships, and even blockage and perforation of the colon with prolonged and excessive intake of clays.[48] The practice appears to have been transmitted directly from Africa to the New World; evidences of direct relation between the New and Old World practices come from the widespread occurrence of the custom in many West Africa groups, the use of mouthlocks (face masks) in the New World to preclude slaves from eating dirt, early reports of the cis-Atlantic practice and its assumed attendant illness (*Cachexia Africana*), and its dominance in the United States today in the Black population of the rural South. Regardless of modernizing influences, the custom appears destined to continue. It has defied severe social disruption, it has persisted despite drastic relocation of its practitioners through both time and space, and it occurs in altered form in modern urban settings.

## Notes

1. Berthold Laufer, "Geophagy," *Field Museum of Natural History, Publication 280*, Anthropology Series, 18 (1930): 99–198 and B. Anell and S. Lagercrantz, *Geophagical Customs*, Studia Ethnographica Upsaliensia, vol. 17 (Uppsala, Sweden: Almquist and Wiksells Boktryckeri, 1958).

2. Alexander von Humboldt, *Views of Nature: Or Contemplation on the Sublime Phenomena of Creation* (London: Henry G. Bohn, 1850), 142–46; John G. Bourke, "The Medicine-Men of the Apache," *Ninth Annual Report, Bureau of Ethnology* (Washington, D. C.: Smithsonian Institution, 1892), 537–40; and J. R. Swanton, *The Indians of the Southeastern United States*, Bureau of American Ethnology, Bulletin 137 (Washington, D. C.: Smithsonian Institution, 1946), 243 and 280.

3. The poorest rural White farmers in the antebellum South occupied commonly the sandy ridges of the plantation districts, the pine barrens of the coastal plains, and the sand hills along the fall line. They became known variously as "poor whites," "sand hillers," "red necks," "crackers," and "clay eaters." Charles Lyell, the famed geologist, described clay eaters in Alabama in 1846 as a most degenerate group in E. L. Roche, *Historic Sketches of the South* (New York: The Knickerbocker Press, 1914), 143. Other comments on clay eaters include A. N. J. Den Hollander, "The Tradition of Poor Whites," in *Culture in the South*, ed. W. T. Couch (Chapel Hill: University of North Carolina Press, 1935), 412–22; P. Lewinson, *Race, Class, and Party* (New York: Oxford University Press, 1932), 7; and Robert W. Twyman, "The Clay Eater: A New Look at an Old Southern Enigma," *Journal of Southern History* 37 (1971): 439–48.

4. H. A. Roselle, "Association of Laundry Starch and Clay Ingestion with Anemia in New York City," *Archives of Internal Medicine* 125 (1970): 57–61; W. M. Mitchell, "Pica in Adults," *California Medicine* 109 (1968): 156–58; and E. M. Layman et al., "Cultural Influences and Symptom Choice: Clay-Eating Customs in Relation to the Etiology of Pica," *The Psychological Record* 13 (1963): 249–57.

5. Anell and Lagercrantz, 79; Donald E. Vermeer, "Geophagy among the Tiv of Nigeria," *Annals of the Association of American Geographers* 56 (1966): 197–204; and Donald E. Vermeer, "Geophagy among the Ewe of

Ghana," *Ethnology* 10 (1971): 56–72. The Ewe clays find outlet through the vast market network of West Africa, and Vermeer has seen them in markets as far distant as Liberia, approximately a thousand miles from their source.

6. Anell and Lagercrantz, 48 ff.

7. Anell and Lagercrantz, 79.

8. Questionnaires and surveys have provided sound data on the frequency and prevalence of geophagy, but those data have not been set in the environmental and cultural contexts in which the practice occurs. See Dorothy Dickens and R. N. Ford, "Geophagy (Dirt Eating) among Mississippi Negro School Children," *American Sociological Review* 7 (1942): 59–65; A. N. Whiting, "Clay, Starch and Soot Eating Among Southern Rural Negroes in North Carolina," *Journal of Negro Education* 16 (1947): 610–12; and J. H. Ferguson and A. G. Keaton, "Studies of the Diets of Pregnant Women in Mississippi: The Ingestion of Clay and Laundry Starch," *New Orleans Medical and Surgical Journal* 102 (1950): 460–63.

9. The Milton Olive III Memorial Corporation, a Black community organization within Holmes County, was chartered in December 1967. The Health Research Project was funded in April 1969 by the National Center for Health Services Research and Development, United States Department of Health, Education, and Welfare.

10. W. J. Geib, "Soil Survey of Holmes County, Mississippi," *Field Operations of the Bureau of Soils, 1908* (Washington, D. C.: United States Department of Agriculture, 1911), 784–93. Holmes County has not had a modern soil survey.

11. Department of Geology, Louisiana State University, provided X-ray diffraction and X-ray fluorescence analyses of the samples.

12. In 1970, Blacks constituted 71 percent of the Holmes County population. In 1970, the Health Research Project conducted a census of the Black population as part of the health services and delivery efforts. That census indicated a Black population of 18,081 rather than the 15,260 reported by the United States Census; the data of the Health Research Project probably are more accurate and are used in this paper. The White population in 1970 numbered 7,345; the United States Census data for the White population probably were accurate, and we used them in this paper. The 1970 United States Census of Population found a decennial population loss of 16 percent for Holmes County; White population loss was little more than 3 percent (250 people), and thus the Black population loss was correspondingly much larger. More than 35,000 Blacks have left Holmes County since World War I, mainly for urban centers, and almost two-thirds of the living Black natives of the county are now resident elsewhere, primar-

ily in the Chicago area; (D. B. Shimkin, G. J. Louie, and Dennis A. Frate, *The Black Extended Family: A Basic Rural Institution and a Mechanism of Urban Adaptation* (The Hague, Netherlands: Mouton, 1976).

13. The county is rural, with individual homes dispersed along the roads. In 1970 only three places had more than 1,500 people: Lexington (2,753) and Durant (2,697) on the upland, and Tchula (1,721) on the floodplain. Our calculations indicate 79 percent of the rural population is Black.

14. Shimkin, Louie, and Frate.

15. In 1970, 48 percent of all Black households in the county were headed by females, a consequence of male migration to urban areas, but also of normally greater longevity of females than males.

16. Shimkin, Louie, and Frate.

17. Removal of clays in parts of Alabama has been so extensive and damaging that the highway department has posted signs requesting local residents not to dig on the road banks (M. V. Clayton, "A Study of Geophagy among Negroes in the Alabama Black Belt," unpublished M.A. thesis, University of Georgia, 1965, figures 1 and 2).

18. Geib, 791–93.

19. Movement of clays from the rural South to the urban North has been reported by Clayton, 28.

20. Similar precise terminology has been reported elsewhere in Mississippi (Dickins and Ford, 64).

21. In contrast, a site in Eweland in Ghana produces tons of edible clays that circulate throughout the market system of West Africa (Vermeer, "Geophagy among the Ewe of Ghana," 61).

22. Appreciation for dried, hardened clays has been noted in Alabama, and in at least one case, clays were deliberately placed in a chimney to acquire a smoked taste (Clayton, 30).

23. More than 25 percent of the Black population in the county was screened for hypertension, and 41 percent of the adults were found to have definite hypertension (E. Eckenfels et al., "An Exploratory Program for the Community Control of Hypertension in a Black, Poverty-stricken Rural Population," *Selected Studies in Medical Care and Medical Economics*, Annual Report, 1974, National Association of Blue Shield Plans, 164).

24. The nutrition survey randomly surveyed 500 of the 3,949 Black households in the county. The geophagy questionnaire was administered by one of the Black staff members of the project and by Frate to 50, or 10 percent, of the households. Within the 50 households, 229 individuals were interviewed: 56 women (members of established households, or those pregnant or who had borne children but were not part of independent households), 33 men (members of established households), 115 children (age

thirteen or less and members of households), and 25 adolescents (age thirteen or greater and not yet having established independent households, and young women not yet having borne children). Although the surveys had purposes other than investigation of geophagy, geophagy could be incorporated into each questionnaire without creating a disjunction in the overall thrust. The nutrition survey explored the nutritional status of the Black population by using twenty-four hour-recall of food intake and diet histories, and the geophagy questions could be logically added to this portion. The individual had to admit consumption of clay to be considered a practitioner of geophagy. Self-admission insures our data provide the minimum incidence of geophagy in this population. We believe some clay eaters did not wish to admit their involvement, and consequently the actual incidence of geophagy is greater than our data portray. Further, earth had to be eaten on a regular extended basis over a period of weeks, and those who had tasted clays at one time but did not continue the practice were excluded from our data. The word of a mother was accepted as evidence of participation by children less than thirteen years of age.

25. Absence of gender bias among children practicing geophagy has been noted elsewhere in Mississippi (Dickins and Ford, 63).

26. This mechanism of transmission of the practice has been noted among the Ewe of Ghana (Vermeer, "Geophagy among the Ewe of Ghana," 69).

27. Cessation of the practice about this age has also been recorded for Africa (Anell and Lagercrantz, 66).

28. The perinatal survey aimed at assessment of child and maternal care and well-being before, during, and after childbirth. The geophagy questionnaire was attached to the portion of the survey that pertained to dietary patterns and nutrition. It was administered by two Black midwives who had worked in the Black community for many years, and were trusted by expectant and postpartum mothers. There is good reason to believe the data reasonably portray the incidence of geophagy during pregnancy. Although the perinatal survey lasted two years, the geophagy portion of the questionnaire was included only during the ten months ending January 1971. Data were obtained on 142 pregnant women. Self-admission was the only basis for the data. Undoubtedly some practitioners did not admit consumption of earths, and these data are, therefore, minimum.

29. The health utilization survey began near the end of our fieldwork, and the sample is relatively small, but it provided an independent check on the reliability of data from the other surveys. The intent of the health utilization survey was to evaluate medical facility needs and use. The geophagy portion was appended to the questionnaire, which was administered jointly

by Frate and a Black member of the Health Research Project. The Health Research Project took a random sample of two hundred households. The geophagy questionnaire was administered to twenty households before fieldwork terminated. Data were obtained only from the upland region.

30. J. M. Hunter, "Geophagy in Africa and the United States: A Culture-Nutrition Hypothesis," *Geographical Review* 63 (1973): 192.

31. A 10 percent incidence of starch eating and a 7 percent incidence of clay eating have been reported among pregnant White women in Mississippi (Ferguson and Keaton, 461).

32. C. H. Edwards, "Effects of Clay and Cornstarch Intake on Women and Their Infants," *Journal of American Dietic Association* 44 (1964): 111.

33. Vermeer, "Geophagy among the Ewe of Ghana," 66.

34. We thank the University of Illinois Medical Center staff for the hematocrit data and the Department of Experimental Statistics, Louisiana State University, for analyses of these data.

35. We thank the Department of Food Sciences, University of Illinois, for the hemoglobin data and analyses.

36. Personal correspondence, K. E. Nelson, M.D., 11 September, 1973.

37. We thank the Department of Agronomy, Louisiana State University, for chemical analyses of the samples.

38. Macronutrient amounts in these samples vary little from those determined for Ewe clays in Ghana or for clays obtained from market retailers in Ghana (Vermeer, "Geophagy among the Ewe in Ghana," 68 and Hunter, 176).

39. J. A. Halsted, J. C. Smith, and M. I. Irwin, "A Conspectus of Research on Zinc Requirements of Man," *Journal of Nutrition* 104 (1974): 351.

40. W. A. Pories and W. H. Strain, *Zinc Deficiency in Delayed Healing and Chronic Diseases*, Geological Society of America Memoir No. 123 (Boulder, Colo.: Geological Society of America, 1971), and A. S. Pradad et al., "Biochemical Studies of Dwarfism, Hypogonadism and Anemia," *American Medical Association Archives of Internal Medicine* 111 (1963): 407–28.

41. J. C. Smith et al., "Zinc: A Trace Element Essential in Vitamin A Metabolism," *Science* 181 (1973): 954–55.

42. Unpublished data of Health Research Project

43. Unpublished data of Health Research Project

44. Hunter, 192; Roselle, 60; and Ferguson and Keaton, 462, note that hookworm incidence in the Black population is only one-twelfth that of the White population in Mississippi.

45. Vermeer, "Geophagy among the Ewe in Ghana," 71.

46. Unpublished data of Health Research Project. One of the major

health problems in the county is obesity; nutrition surveys revealed a mean weight of 165 pounds (75 kg) for 393 females seventeen years or older.

47. Edwards et al., 111.

48. J. R. Amerson and H. G. Jones, "Prolonged Kaolin (Clay) Ingestion: A Cause of Colon Perforation and Peritonitis," *Emory University Clinic Bulletin* 5 (1967): 11–15.

9

# "Mountain Moonshining" in East Tennessee

*Loyal Durand, Jr.*

For 160 years or more, a regional association has existed between the Appalachian hill lands and the illicit manufacture of corn whiskey— "mountain moonshine." From the time of the Whiskey Rebellion in western Pennsylvania, in September 1794 to the present day, the federal and state governments have wrestled with the problem, their concern stemming primarily from loss of taxes and, in the southern Appalachians, the existence of large blocks of dry or prohibition territory.[1] How much of the present illicit manufacture is the result of economic pressure, how much is a reflection of a traditional pattern of life in which a small still was as much a part of mountain occupance as the spinning wheel, and how much is attributable to increased federal and state taxes on legal beverages is difficult, if not impossible, to determine.

The industry has prevailed in many mountain and hill country settlements since the earliest days of the pioneer. The Appalachian mountaineer, under economic pressure, with a long-established way of life and a "mountain yeoman" complex, found that one of his crops, corn, was difficult to transport and of low value. By turning some of it into a beverage high in value per unit of weight and compact to transport, he could realize a greater profit. Furthermore, today a ready market is at hand, both in his home region and among neighboring "flatlanders." The jokes and cartoons about the Kentucky, Tennessee, Georgia, and other Appalachian moonshiners,

Reprinted by permission from *The Geographical Review* 46 (1956): 168–81.

probably regarded as such by distant persons, have a basis in fact. In 1955, the *weekly* manufacture of moonshine in the mountains of Tennessee alone was estimated to be about 25,000 gallons, and in the state about 32,000. In a single month (April 1955) 94 stills were destroyed by state and federal agents in East Tennessee alone, 23 of them in one day, and raids by county sheriffs brought the regional total to about 140.

Obviously, geographic distribution of the moonshine industry cannot be accurately mapped, but only the distribution of destroyed stills (fig. 9.1). What percentage these form of the total number is unknown, though enforcement officials have hazarded a guess. No doubt the percentage of captured stills is higher today than it was in the past; the airplane and the helicopter are efficient spotters of stills in the forests and woodlands, and large operations can often be detected by smoke and by the odor of the mash. Yet movement in difficult terrain is necessary for the capture of a still, and the agent must maneuver across hills and creeks, through dense brush, and along dead-end roads. The final rush may capture the still and the mash, but not the operators.

The routes and destinations of the whiskey are also matters of conjecture. What percentage is consumed locally, in regional cities, or in distant locali-

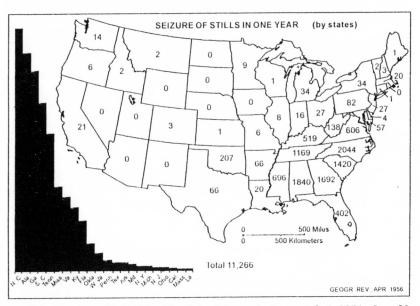

Fig. 9.1. Number of Stills Seized by Federal Agents by States (July 1, 1954—June 30, 1955)

ties is unknown. The estimated volume of production indicates an outflow of some magnitude. Highway patrols are familiar with some of the carriers, usually "souped up" cars capable of traveling ninety to a hundred miles an hour or more. Many of them are caught. Others, outdistancing or evading their pursuers, complete their runs and deliver their cargoes into outside channels of trade. The Tennessee State Alcohol Tax Division is aware that some illicit whiskey enters incognito into interstate commerce, and it attempts to stop the outflow into Michigan, Ohio, and Illinois.

### Estimates of Tennessee Moonshine Production

The moonshine industry of Tennessee is concentrated principally in the eastern third of the state. Although some of the raided stills are purely family enterprises for home consumption, there is not a single county in this Appalachian area without some illicit manufacture of whiskey. Commercial production, however, has apparently become the business of a few.

Officials of the Tennessee State Alcohol Tax Division of the Department of Finance and Taxation estimate a state moonshine production of about 1,664,000 gallons a year. If all of it is consumed within the state, the annual state tax loss, based on a tax of $2.00 a gallon, is $3,300,000.00. Obviously, much of this is a paper loss, since all but half a dozen counties out of the ninety-five in the state are dry. With a federal tax rate of $10.50 a gallon, the loss to the federal government is more than five times the state loss.

Federal agents of the Alcohol and Tobacco Tax Division of the Internal Revenue Service in the southern Appalachian region place the illicit whiskey production in the North Carolina Appalachians at probably five or more times the Tennessee production, in Georgia at three to four times more, in Alabama at three times, and in South Carolina at about the same; the Kentucky production is much smaller. If we assume that these official estimates are reasonably correct, and that the Tennessee output is a conservative million and a half gallons, we get the astounding total for the southern Appalachians of twenty-one million gallons or more a year.

### Chief Concentrations of Tennessee Moonshining

The state of Tennessee is divided for judicial purposes into three so-called Grand Divisions, East Tennessee, Middle Tennessee, and West Tennessee (fig. 9.2), and the inhabitants speak of themselves as being from these areas. Official estimates of weekly moonshine production in these

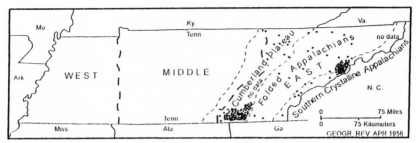

Fig. 9.2. Approximate Number of Stills Captured Each Month in East Tennessee and Location within the Physiographic Regions of the Southern Appalachians (Each Dot Represents One Still)

divisions are twenty-four thousand gallons in East Tennessee, six thousand in Middle Tennessee, and two thousand in West Tennessee. Middle Tennessee includes part of the hill lands of the state, particularly the western Cumberland Plateau, and much of the six-thousand-gallon estimate is for this physiographic region. In other words, most of the whiskey is distilled in the eastern, or hilly and mountainous, half of the state, whether or not production is administratively in East Tennessee. West Tennessee's coastal-plain terrain is generally flat; its views are unobstructed by hills or mountains. This is the cotton-producing and "Deep South" part of the state, and the attitudes of its rural inhabitants are quite different from those of the East.

Within the "most productive" East Tennessee region, two large centers of moonshine activity stand out, highest both in number of stills raided and in quantity of output.[2] One center lies in the true crystalline-rock mountains of the southern Appalachians, the other on the Cumberland Plateau (fig. 9.2). Each bears a relationship to market: the first is not far removed from Knoxville, and the second is close to Chattanooga—in fact, an area on the plateau within ten miles of Chattanooga is one of the most frequently raided in the state.

The mountains of the southern Appalachians lie along the eastern border of the state. Southern Cocke County (east of Knoxville) has long been recognized as the "capital of moonshining" in Tennessee. Federal and state agents capture an average of about forty stills a month in the county, and federal agents estimate that some 75 percent of the illicit whiskey of East Tennessee originates there. Stills are large, mostly five-hundred-gallon capacity (fig. 9.3); occasionally a still of one thousand gallons or more falls to the raiders. Inaccessible coves and valleys, steep mountain slopes, and river and creek sites are desired locations. From this center a large-still region extends northeast and southwest along the face and base of the mountains.

Fig. 9.3. A 500-Gallon Copper Still in the Mountains of the Tennessee–North Carolina Border

Thus, although an average of only four stills a month is captured in an adjacent county, they are usually of five-hundred-gallon size; in May 1955, a twelve-hundred-gallon still fell to government agents.

The Great Valley of East Tennessee lies between the southern Appalachians and the Cumberland Plateau. It is the physiographic region of the Folded Appalachians, the ridge-and-valley countryside. Every county in this region has some moonshining activity, based usually on locations along the ridges (fig. 9.4) rather than in the open agricultural valleys. Even Knox County, in which Knoxville is located, has yielded many small stills and an occasional large one, and during ten months in 1954–1955, the sheriff of Anderson County, in which Oak Ridge is located, captured thirty-five stills. Stills are small, commonly of fifty- to one hundred-gallon capacity, and production is for the home market, for home use, or for sale by the drink, in contrast with the true mountain area, where the production is "wholesale." The total number of these stills is unknown. During the preparation of the 59,000 acres of the Oak Ridge Reservation for the townsite and atomic plants, twenty-two stills were found, left behind by the rural population in

Fig. 9.4. Corn Whiskey Distilling Operation Occupying a Ridge-Top Site (Note Federal Agent after Raid)

the rather rapid evacuation of the area. Stills are hidden in the woodlands on the ridge sides and crests, and in rough karst country in the valleys and on lower slopes. Some of the karst country possesses relief of two hundred to four hundred feet and sinkhole pockets two hundred feet or more in depth. In much of this region, county sheriffs raid the stills and are important in the control; the small federal and state forces are compelled by circumstance to concentrate on the large operations in the mountains.

The Cumberland Mountains and Cumberland Plateau exhibit conditions of each of the aforementioned regions. The northern two-thirds is generally small-still country. Two of the roughest and least accessible counties, south of the Kentucky border in the Cumberland Mountains, probably have more stills that fall to the raiding forces. They average only about two "losses" a month. Southward, where the Cumberlands are flat topped and a true plateau, the size of still apparently increases. The largest are in the part of the plateau adjacent to Chattanooga, cut by the Tennessee River gorge and deep tributary valleys. Blocklike segments of the plateau are almost isolated, heavily wooded, and virtually inaccessible. Hamilton County, in which Chattanooga lies, "loses" some thirty stills a month; the next county to the west, Marion, about forty. In Marion County stills are located at escarpment bases, on slopes, in deep valleys, and on tabular outliers.

Suck Creek Mountain, a narrowed stretch of Walden Ridge (the part of the Cumberland Plateau between the Great Valley of East Tennessee and the long, linear Sequatchie Valley), is almost as notorious a moonshine area as southern Cocke County.

Illicit manufacture of corn whiskey continues westward on the Cumberland Plateau in Middle Tennessee. This part of the state, however, possesses its own "manufacturing district," apparently based on the Nashville market as well as on the hill-country location. Hickman, a hilly county in the Western Highland Rim, west of the Nashville Basin, is one of the five "most productive" moonshine areas in the state, on the evidence of raids and the experience of government agents. Neighboring counties of the rim share somewhat in the activity.

## Economic and Marketing Factors

To what extent is the corn-whiskey industry attributable to economic pressure in a region of low income where corn is a leading crop? Certainly the fact that this low-value bulk crop can be readily converted into a more valuable and more easily transported product has been influential, more so in the past than at present. Incomes have been increased, though the figures probably do not show. This circumstance combined with a traditional way of life has led some persons to engage in a more lucrative enterprise without particular trouble to their consciences.

Transportation has invaded the southern Appalachian hill lands rapidly, especially since World War I, and has opened the way to distant markets. Good roads, nearly all of them graveled and many of them paved, have been provided by the respective states. The moonshiner is able to dispose of his product several hundred miles from its region of manufacture, and "specialists" in production have appeared, who devote their full time to the activity. The increasing taxes on legally manufactured alcoholic beverages during recent years and the existence of dry territory throughout much of the adjoining region have provided the moonshiner with a special market situation, in which the customer (or consumer) seeks his goods and services and there is little or no need for him to employ "salesmen." The main problems are secrecy of manufacture in a secluded location, alertness toward the appearance of revenue agents, and transportation of the wares to market.

## The Human Element and Dispersion

The Scotch-Irish and American frontiersmen helped "transport" the corn-whiskey industry throughout the southern Appalachians during the early days of settlement. Their attitude toward corn whiskey was apparently different from that of the early New Englanders. As settlers from New England moved west by way of the northern routes, such as the Mohawk Valley, the whiskey still did not appear, at least not in any great numbers. However, literature is replete with references to the problem from central Pennsylvania southward, and history calls it to our attention through the governmental troubles during the Whiskey Rebellion. After the period of railroad and highway building, with the resulting improved accessibility of the northern Appalachians, the problem became less acute there; indeed, in many areas it disappeared. Government agents now find the illicit still in the Northeast mainly in urban areas, often in warehouses or dwellings, and operating in an entirely different manner and milieu from those of its southern hill-country counterpart.

How much of the present southern-Appalachian attitude is a carryover from past generations? How much is owing to the lack or difficulty of transportation in the hill and mountain lands? It must be remembered that, as late as 1900–1910, large areas of the southern Appalachians, even in the valleys of east Tennessee, were primarily in a stage of subsistence agriculture except near a few main railroad lines.[3] Undoubtedly there must have been a tradition of local whiskey making in certain mountain and hill-country locations, and these have acted as centers of dispersion. When a lumber company in northeastern Wisconsin decided to concentrate on selling its cutover lands to Kentucky mountaineers instead of specializing in immigrants (the usual target of the cutover-land salesman) and succeeded in bringing in large colonies of native Kentuckians, the moonshine still appeared with them.[4] Wisconsin suddenly, and for the first time, found itself confronted with an illegal moonshine industry. In the Cascade foothills of Washington, settlements of Cumberland Mountain people in the Cowlitz Valley introduced a moonshine industry there.[5] Many other such dispersal associations are known to exist.

## Some Reflections on the Future

The recent advent of improved transportation in the hill lands and the increased taxation of legal liquor pose other unanswerable questions. Are groups of outsiders or local "combines" moving in on the age-old corn-whiskey industry of the southern Appalachians? Is the hillsman moonshiner being reduced to the status of manufacturer alone, and is his product (aside from that destined for purely local consumption) being distributed by specialists—specialists in transportation, in distribution, and in sales? The evidence from raids indicates that the small moonshiner still grows his corn and produces corn whiskey, but many of the largest stills, those in the five-hundred-gallon class and above, use sugar, yeast, and similar ingredients as raw materials, and corn (or other grain) is not significant. Furthermore, the large operators possess no other apparent means of support; after a jail term they go back in "business." If specialization is increasing, in response to a combination of many factors, what will happen to the long-established way of life of the small mountain moonshiner? Subsistence farming in the hills and mountains of the southern Appalachians is on the way out. Each census records fewer true subsistence farms.[6] Perhaps "subsistence" manufacture of corn whiskey also is destined to go "commercial."

## Notes

1. Nearly all the area in and around the southern Appalachians is dry. Only a few counties in Kentucky and Tennessee permit the sale of whiskey or alcoholic beverages except beer. Some counties even exclude beer.

2. The federal government maintains enforcement offices at Knoxville, Chattanooga, Greeneville, and Johnson City.

3. Before 1870, practically all of East Tennessee had a self-sufficient economy. After this date, the Knoxville and Chattanooga areas developed rapidly as commercial and industrial centers. In 1903, the Tennessee legislature enacted a no-fence law; this marked the elimination of sheep for homespun woolen clothing. By 1900–1910, the exodus from the farms of East Tennessee to the textile mills of Knoxville and of the Carolinas was in full swing. See B. H. Luebke, "Problems Created by the Douglas Reservoir in East Tennessee," *Journal of the Tennessee Academy of Science* 29 (1954): 246–59.

4. These were the so-called Ky colonies of northeastern Wisconsin, mainly in southern Forest County and northeastern and eastern Langlade County.

5. C. L. White and G. T. Renner, *Human Geography* (New York and London: 1948), 379.

6. This is a result of a combination of factors: changed census definitions, present-day need for cash and the expansion of the burly-tobacco industry, and shift of the farm to a "part-time farm" basis, with the operator working in industry but residing on the land. See Loyal Durand, Jr., and E. T. Bird, "The Burly Tobacco Region of the Mountain South," *Economic Geography* 26 (1950): 274–300.

# Part III: Folk Music

Cultural geographers have begun to study various types of folk music during the past twenty-five years. See, for example, my anthology, *The Sounds of People and Places: A Geography of American Folk and Popular Music* (Rowman & Littlefield, 1994), which contains twenty chapters on various music genres ranging from bluegrass to zydeco. The two articles selected for this reader, however, were not included in the music volume because they represent some of the most recent research on folk music by geographers.

Folk music is often loosely applied to cover all traditional or aurally transmitted music, that is, music that is passed on by ear and performed by memory rather than by the written or printed musical score. Folk music must be heard before it can be retransmitted. Hence, the term "aural" is used rather than "oral." In addition to its aural transmission, two other criteria are required of genuine folk music. One is that the origin of the melody must be unknown to the performer. A second requirement is that the melody and lyrics exist in variant forms. As it is transmitted from one individual to another and diffused from one place to another, both conscious and unconscious modifications of the melody and lyrics occur. The melody and text of an authentic folk song, therefore, is in constant flux. Folk music, such as old-time fiddle tunes in the bluegrass repertoire, is an element of nonmaterial culture, whereas folk music instruments, such as the Cajun accordion, would be considered part of material culture.

Folk music is often used as a defining characteristic in the delimitation of *folklife regions*. In chapter 10, Cajun music is an ethnic-based folk music tradition associated with the French Acadians who migrated to southwest Louisiana from Canada during the eighteenth century. It remains one of the folk commonalties preserved in the Acadian French folklife region over time. The Cajun accordion is one of the three major instruments that make up the triumvirate of Cajun music along with the fiddle and *frottoir* (washboard). In all probability, German immigrants introduced the accordion to southwest Louisiana in the latter half of the nineteenth century. Because German factories converted to wartime production in the late 1930s, the importation of accordions was halted. Local Cajun craftsmen learned to build new accordions by restoring old ones, and have modified the instrument to suit their brand of folk music.

Under the *origin and diffusion* theme, the two music genres covered in part 3 are indigenous to North America. Although some questions remain

129

concerning the origins of bluegrass, Cajun music originated in the Acadia and Nova Scotia sections in Canada in the seventeenth century. Musicologists agree that the hearth of bluegrass is in the Upland South folklife region. Chapter 11 lends credibility to this thesis; however, it pinpoints western North Carolina as the specific origin in the Upland South. Regardless of origin, the diffusion of Cajun and bluegrass music has occurred throughout the twentieth century to become national and international in scope.

The theme of *folklife ecology* is approached in several ways for music. First is that these music genres may be performed in a natural setting, such as outdoor festivals featuring bluegrass and Cajun music. Second is that the natural environment provides materials used in the production of folk music instruments from various types of woods ranging from cedarwood for American Indian flutes to walnut and spruce for Appalachian dulcimers. Finally, the natural environment (climate and landforms) provides the basis for lyrics in folk music, such as "Stormy Weather" (jazz) and "Going Back to the Blue Ridge Mountains" (bluegrass).

*Folklife integration* examples are drawn from the interaction between music and religion as well as music and ethnicity. The folk melodies expressed in the Black and White spirituals of the Upland and Lowland South have exercised important influences in religious services. Bluegrass musicians, including Bill Monroe, the "father of bluegrass," began their musical careers singing gospel music in church. Many ethnic-based folk groups have generated their own folk music, including African Americans (blues and jazz) and German Americans (polka).

Many *folk landscapes* have been shaped by the presence of folk music. The impact of folk music in the landscape is seen in the emergence of folk music festivals ranging from blues festivals in Mississippi to Cajun music festivals in Louisiana. Facilities on the landscape are devoted entirely to folk music performances, including Cajun nightclubs in Mamou, Louisiana; Preservation Jazz Hall in New Orleans, Louisiana; and the New Ulm, Minnesota, Ballroom, specializing in old-time polka music.

The future of folk music in America in an authentic and unadulterated form is in question. Because of continued "crossovers" in the music field, pure folk music is constantly under pressure to retain its authenticity. It will only remain as a folklife trait if there are those rural and urban musicians who are willing to preserve the traditional melodies and lyrics from the past.

# 10

# The Cajun Accordion

## Malcolm L. Comeaux

The accordion has special meaning to the Cajuns of southwest Louisiana, and in this region it is the accordion that identifies the "Cajun" band. This was not always so. The fiddle was the traditional folk instrument of the Acadians in Canada, and it remained their main folk instrument for many years after their arrival in Louisiana. The accordion, therefore, is not an old traditional instrument with Cajuns, but it is now so widely accepted that it seems to have been always a part of Cajun music.

Acceptance of the accordion greatly changed Cajun music. Prior to the introduction of the accordion, there was much variety in the traditional music and dances of the Acadians, such as reels, jigs, polkas, mazurkas, contredanses, cotillions, quadrilles, and the like. These, however, were very difficult for the accordion player, though more easily done by the fiddler. With the accordion as the major instrument, many of these old songs and dance steps were no longer played, and they are remembered only by the oldest of musicians. Cajun music thus evolved around the accordion, and waltzes and two-steps were the major tunes played. Much, however, was lost to Cajun music.[1]

The basic idea behind the accordion is the concept of the "free reed." The free reed is a metal tongue almost exactly the same width as the slot in which it fits. It is fixed on one end, while the rest of it is free to vibrate to and fro through the slot. This is quite different from the typical European reed instrument, which has a "beating reed," as, for example, the

Reprinted by permission from the author. The article originally appeared in *Louisiana Review* 7 (1978): 117–28.

clarinet. The Chinese invented the concept of the free reed, and the first mention of a free reed instrument was in 1100 B. C.[2]

Instruments with free reeds began to make their appearance in Europe soon after European contact with the Far East. There is a report, for example, that a Persian mouth organ was played for King Louis XIV in 1648.[3] The popularity of free reed instruments, however, really began with the invention of the mouth organ and the accordion in the 1820s.

The accordion was invented in Berlin by Friedrich Buschmann in 1822, and the name for the instrument was patented in Vienna in 1829.[4] Throughout the 1800s, the principle of the free reed was used in Europe in the development of many new musical instruments. These instruments, however, were not entirely successful and created no lasting interest. The only instrument that was moderately successful was the accordion, and it is still commonly heard in the world of popular folk entertainment.

Popularity of the accordion has varied greatly since its introduction into Cajun Louisiana. The accordion was first brought into south Louisiana sometime in the latter half of the nineteenth century. It is not known exactly by whom, or when, why, or where it was introduced; but it was probably first brought to the Cajun area by German immigrants settling the prairie of southwest Louisiana in the 1880s.[5] Cajun musicians at first were not particularly attracted to the accordion, because the first accordions imported were in the keys of A and F. The fiddle, the traditional folk instrument of the Cajuns, could not be tuned to those keys.[6] Thus, the accordion could be played only as a solo instrument, and it did not receive much attention. Accordions in the keys of C and D began to be imported into south Louisiana from Germany about 1925. This permitted the coupling of the fiddle and the accordion, resulting in increased popularity of the accordion. In the 1930s, for some unexplained reason, the accordion declined in popularity, but this decline was short-lived; for, soon after World War II, it developed into the major folk instrument of the Cajun people. It is now an integral part of all Cajun bands in southwest Louisiana: no Cajun band is complete without one.

The type of accordion used in Cajun music is a variation of the diatonic accordion of the German style. This style differs from the Italian or Vienna-style accordion in that it is equipped with two bass keys; one or two rows of buttons on the treble side; and one, two, three, or four pull stops. The Italian or Vienna models have four or more bass buttons and one, two, or three rows of button keys on the treble side. The Cajun accordion used today has two bass keys, one row of buttons on the treble side, and four pull stops.

Cajun accordions have only one row of ten keys, and are in only one key.[7]

The most common key is that of C, although the keys of D, G, F, and A are sometimes found. The key of C is well suited to the tuning of the fiddle and guitar and often well suited to the range of a singer's voice. Each button has, like the harmonica, two tones of different pitch, one that will sound when the bellows is extended—draw tones—and the other when air is blown out of the bellows—blow tones. Each button admits wind to a reed assembly with two tongues, one mounted to sound when the bellows is pressed, and the other when the bellows is drawn. Blow tones produce the notes that make a C chord (C, E, and G in the key of C), while draw tones produce the intervening tones (D, F, A, and B in the key of C). Together the ten buttons suffice for a range of over two octaves.

In a Cajun accordion, the scale is tuned equal temperament with the exception of the thirds (in the key of C this is the E, and in the G scale it is the B). These two notes, E and B, are tuned to pure temperament, which in this case is 3.5 cycles per second less than equal temperament.[8] This works well in Cajun music because, for all practical purposes, there are no B and E chords when playing in C, F, and G. However, many persons, particularly older musicians, like the F note tuned to pure temperament (3.5 cycles per second sharp), but this is not advisable because F is a principal chord in the key of C, and a fundamental chord in the key of F.[9]

A unique feature of the accordion made for Cajun music is that the valve keys are exposed. Valve keys are arms that are connected to the buttons and allow air to enter or exit the bellows on the treble side. Being attached at the base, the valve keys open in such a way as to produce a wide angle at the top when the corresponding buttons are pressed. They are made of five-eighths-inch oak dowels that are cut in half, or simply purchased in that shape. Each valve key is either painted, as was done in earlier days, or decorated with metalic gold contact paper. These keys are connected to the key frame by small rods about an eighth of an inch thick. The rods are made of wire, often electrical motor wire, and are hammered into shape over a mold. The valve keys pivot on a thin wire, usually a bicycle spoke, that runs through the wood holding the buttons.

Most accordions used by Cajuns have four stops. These stops are on the top of the frame attached to the bellows on the treble side, and each is responsible for a type of sound produced by the instrument. For instance, when all stops are pushed in, no reeds will sound. The first two stops control middle octave reeds that are tuned identically, and this is called a "dry tune." This is different from imported accordions, which have the first two stops tuned slightly in variance to produce a vibrato effect, called a "wet tune." The third stop operates a set of reeds tuned one octave lower than that of one and two. The fourth stop operates another set of reeds tuned one octave higher than the set operated by the first two. Although described in seemingly technical terms, the use of these stops lends a variety to the accordion that could not otherwise be produced. With different combinations, a full rich sound, or a high or low tone, can be achieved. Cajun musicians usually play their instruments with all stops open.

Although the accordion manufactured in Germany has bass keys of the spoon variety, locally made ones are simply buttons. These two bass keys are responsible for sounding the chordal accompaniment. The lower key produces the fundamental bass tone (a C in a C chord), and the upper key the tonic major chord (a C chord in the key of C). Two different chords may be produced, the tonic or I chord (corresponding to a C chord in the key of C), and the dominant or V chord (corresponding to a G chord in the key of C). The former is produced when blowing air out of the bellows, and the latter when drawing air into the bellows.

This limitation of only two chords on the accordion fits in well with Cajun folk tunes. A C accordion can only produce a C and a G chord. If a song contains a C, F, and G chord progression, the G chord will have to be substituted for the F chord. This gives Cajun music its particular flavor—the discordant, sorrowful sound.

Another button found on the bass side, opposite the bass keys, is that of the "lung" button. When depressed it enables the player to quickly, easily, and silently draw air into the bellows.

Cajuns began repairing accordions during World War II when they were cut off from their suppliers of accordions and accordion parts. Broken accordions had to be repaired, and several musicians from necessity took it upon themselves to repair them. Most did it only as a hobby in their spare time, but for a few it grew to be a business. These craftsmen became very good at repairing accordions, and they soon began making the entire instrument. Locally made accordions were quickly recognized as superior to the imported models, and an industry had begun.

Sidney Brown, an accomplished musician from Lake Charles, was the first person to start repairing and making accordions, and he is still active in this business. When Cajuns began making accordions, they copied the old "Sterling" and "Monarch" brands. These were the two most popular makes in southwest Louisiana prior to World War II.[10] Cajun accordions still physically resemble the old German ones, but are very different from modern German diatonic accordions.

Almost all accordions used in Cajun country are today made by local artisans. The average locally made accordion costs about three times as much as an imported one, and the two usually have the same reeds and bellows; but no Cajun musician would choose to play an imported accordion, as locally made ones are better. One of the main advantages of the local accordion is its durability. As one Cajun musician said in a moment of exaggeration: "I can throw my accordion against a wall all day and still play for a dance that night." Locally made accordions are heavier than imported ones, but they are also quicker to respond, and consequently are easier to play. They are also more beautiful instruments, as they are hand-crafted. In the past, Cajun craftsmen sometimes made the entire instrument, and can still do so today; however, at present the bellows and reeds are usually not made, but are taken from new instruments imported from Germany. A few other parts of the German accordion may also be salvaged, depending on the accordion maker. For example, one maker also uses the buttons on the treble side and the knobs for the stops, another uses some of the wooden parts, and a third will also use the metal slides used for the stops. Most accordion makers, however, use only bellows and reeds, and discard the rest of the German accordion. The reeds and bellows taken from these inexpensive German accordions are not very good, and today a few high-quality reeds and bellows are being imported from Italy. One Cajun craftsman is now in the process of acquiring the equipment to produce good-quality reeds, so south Louisiana may soon be self-sufficient in the production of quality reeds.

The bellows are made of treated cardboard attached at the corners by sheepskin. The hide adds to the durability of the bellows in places in which they receive the most stress. Bellows can be patched, but most are simply discarded along with the locally made frames and replaced with new ones. The bellows are usually decorated with plastic tape to make a pretty design.

The interior of the accordion contains the sound producing reeds. Each note receives its sound from four reeds, providing that all stops are pulled. The material used for the reeds is tempered steel. Many musicians say the reeds made many years ago are better than modern ones, and therefore old reeds are used time and time again until they are broken. As a consequence, some new instruments will have old reeds in them. The reed assemblies are held in place with an airtight seal made of beeswax, or sometimes of beeswax mixed with wood resin. The finest Cajun accordions, however, have the reed assemblies screwed to the frame. The make of the reed is usually engraved in the form of letters or numbers on the frame holding it.

Tuning of the reeds is one of the more important processes in making an accordion. While some accordion makers tune by ear, others find that using a tuning machine makes the task easier and less nerve-racking. Most accordion makers testify that tuning was the hardest thing to learn about accordion making.[11] The actual process of tuning, the altering of the pitch of the reed, is accomplished in two ways. To make the pitch higher, the outer end of the reed is filed down a slight bit; while to lower the pitch, the inner half of the reed, that part near the fixed end, is filed down a slight bit.[12]

The wooden part through which the sound flows after it is made by the reed requires precision work. Two identical pieces of wood (often birch), each about one-sixteenth of an inch in thickness, are cut, the outer one usually having round holes, the other square holes. Both are cut from a pattern with a jigsaw. They are placed adjacent to each other with about a sixteenth of an inch between them. The space between the pieces is the place in which the slats for the stops fit. These three pieces must fit snugly enough to allow the stop slats to slide with only little resistance, and yet must be tight enough to prevent air leakage.

The wooden parts of the exterior of the accordion are of very high-quality wood. A hard wood, such as maple or gum, is used for the key mount due to its resistance to damage from fingernails. Many types of woods are used for the frames to which the bellows are attached, such as birch, magnolia, pine, and sometimes mahogany. These wooden parts, if made of particularly good wood, are stained and varnished or lacquered. Most, however, are simply painted with black enamel, and then decaled with floral designs and/ or the maker's name.

The buttons for keys are usually made from plastic dowels, though they can be salvaged from German accordions. The finest accordions have the buttons made of 45-caliber bullet jackets that are chromed locally. The bass buttons are made of chair glides.[13]

Many accordion makers are older men who enjoy making accordions and talking to customers. This business provides them a little extra money to supplement retirement incomes and, at the same time, affords pleasant visits with musicians. At present there is only one younger man making accordions as a serious business. These craftsmen are not found throughout the state, nor even throughout French Louisiana. They are concentrated in the prairie district of southwest Louisiana, with one in southeast Texas. This is the very area in which the accordion is popular (fig. 10.1). There are four major producers of accordions, each making twenty-five or more every year. The other accordion makers work only part time at this job, and each produces from three or four to perhaps twenty accordions a year. There are also two accordion makers in Canada, but they are only beginning.

Accordion makers cannot supply the demand for accordions, and are always turning away business. The demand is not just local, and most of the finest and most expensive accordions are sold to persons living elsewhere, especially in Canada. Accordions are not sold to the Acadians of Canada, for they, like their relatives along Bayou Lafourche, have not accepted that instrument in their folk music. Rather, they are sold to the French speakers

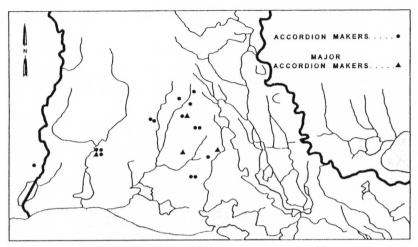

Fig. 10.1. Distribution of Accordion Makers in Southwest Louisiana and Southeast Texas

around Quebec and some to English speakers in the western provinces of Canada.

The price of the Cajun accordion varies greatly. The least expensive of the locally made ones today sells for about $350, and the most expensive for about $750. The average price is about $400. Accordions imported from Germany, the "Hohner" brand, retail for about $125, and they furnish parts for most Cajun accordions. Local musicians, however, are willing to pay the higher price of Cajun accordions to get what they consider the superior instrument.

In southwest Louisiana, accordion making is developing into an important industry, a dynamic and changing industry. In the future, better quality reeds and bellows will be imported or made locally, and there will be less use for parts taken from inexpensive new accordions. Local accordion makers fabricate a quality product, and the reputation of their instruments has spread greatly, resulting in many sales outside French Louisiana. French music is currently undergoing a strong revival, particularly on the prairies of southwest Louisiana, the very area where the accordion is popular. The accordion is now an integral part of Cajun music in southwest Louisiana, and the demand for this instrument will continue to grow.

## Notes

1. Gretchen Dewailly, "Mark Savoy: Skilled Craftsman Spends Time Manufacturing Accordions," *Opelousas Daily World* (16 March, 1976).

Most of this variety in the music came into Cajun culture long after the Cajuns arrived in Louisiana.

2. Curt Sachs, *The History of Musical Instruments* (New York: W. W. Norton, 1940), 184.

3. Sybil Marcuse, *A Survey of Musical Instruments* (New York: Harper & Row, 1975), 734.

4. Marcuse, 742, and Sachs, 466.

5. The first importer of accordions into the United States was the C. Bruno and Sons Company of New York. Most were retailed in southwest Louisiana by Jewish merchants (Personal interview, Mark Savoy, 17 October, 1976, Eunice, Louisiana).

6. This is because Cajuns tune their open fiddle strings to the pitch of the accordion, and to do thus with accordions pitched in A and F would have been difficult.

7. There is one exception. John E. Hébert of Lafayette, Louisiana, makes his accordions with only nine keys. He omits the top button, an E and G, because he says it is rarely used, and only when a musician is "showing off," so he feels it is not needed.

8. Equal temperament is the tuning system used for a piano, as opposed to pure temperament, which is accoustically pure or more simply, tuning by ear. See Willi Apel, *Harvard Dictionary of Music*, 2d ed. (Cambridge, Mass.: Belknap Press, 1969).

9. Personal interview, Mark Savoy, 15 October 1976, Eunice, Louisiana.

10. These brands have not been sold in Louisiana since World War II. The Sterling Company was ruined by Allied bombing and was never rebuilt.

11. John Hébert, the Lafayette accordion maker, said the man who taught him to tune the accordion did it by ear, and he ended up in a mental institution, supposedly driven to insanity from listening so intently while tuning.

12. Many Cajuns, to lower the pitch, add a bit of metal to the outer top end of the reed.

13. These are button-shaped pieces of chromed metal that have a screw or nail underneath. They are intended for use under chair legs so that they slide better.

# 11

# Western North Carolina:
# Culture Hearth of Bluegrass Music

## George O. Carney

Much has been written about the characteristics of bluegrass music and its historic origins, but, according to Bill C. Malone, noted country music historian, "few people know where it came from."[1] Most scholars indicate it originated somewhere in Appalachia as a form of mountain music, however, none have identified a particular source area. Others claim that it is rooted in the Pennyroyal Basin of western Kentucky, where Bill Monroe, the acknowledged "father of bluegrass," was born.[2] While in the 1950s, when bluegrass was named and recognized as a unique genre of American music, Ralph Rinzler, eminent folklorist, traced its geographic origins to the Bluegrass Region of central Kentucky.[3] Because of the unclear nature of its spatial origins, this overlooked and neglected aspect of bluegrass music bears examination from a cultural geography perspective.

Introduced by Carl Sauer and the Berkeley School, the culture hearth approach provides a useful conceptual framework for investigation of the source area for the bluegrass sound.[4] In defining culture hearth, Sauer explained that it is "the inquiry into the localization of culture origins."[5] This study contends that the culture hearth of the bluegrass sound was the mountain and piedmont sections of western North Carolina (fig. 11.1). Within this area were the bands and individual musicians who created and shaped the bluegrass sound and spawned a local music infrastructure. This network cultivated the exchange of music ideas and repertoires, generated

Reprinted by permission from the *Journal of Cultural Geography* 16 (1996): 65–87.

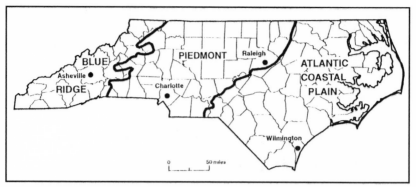

Fig. 11.1. Physical Regions of North Carolina

innovative vocal and instrumental techniques, and established outlets for performance opportunities.

## Definition of the Bluegrass Sound

In 1964, a groundbreaking graduate thesis in folklore identified three distinguishing traits of the bluegrass sound:

1. It is primarily an instrumental music consisting of musicians who play nonelectrified stringed instruments with the five-string banjo, fiddle, guitar, mandolin, and stand-up string bass as the standard ensemble.
2. Vocal harmonization may be as many as four parts expressed in either duets, trios, or quartets.
3. The defining criterion is the five-string banjo played in a lead capacity, emphasizing melodic over rhythmic aspects, and use of the three-finger roll, or "Scruggs Style" named after Earl Scruggs, a native of western North Carolina.[6]

Rosenberg suggested three additional characteristics that give the sound its final form—vocal tone, tempo, and repertoire.[7] First, bluegrass is recognizable for its high-pitched singing, often referred to as "the high lonesome sound," a contrast to other substyles of country music. Second, its average tempo is faster than other forms of country music, usually in duple meter, that is, 2/4 or 4/4 time, frequently described as "folk music in overdrive." Finally, the repertoire of secular vocals resembles that of the brother duets of the 1930s, based on lyrics dealing with home, family, and male-female relationships. The sacred vocal repertoire is represented by a wide spectrum of songs ranging from old spirituals to modern gospel. But, according to Rosenberg, it is the instrumental repertoire that is the most important component of the bluegrass sound demonstrating the virtuosity of the musicians, and the sound's linkage to the fiddle, banjo, and guitar-dominated rural string bands of the 1920s and 1930s.

## Human Innovators and Place Incubators

Norm Cohen, country music historian, reports in a study on country music pioneers that the most significant precursor to the bluegrass sound was Charlie Poole and the North Carolina Ramblers, who first recorded in 1925.[8] Poole, originally from Alamance County, established his string band in the Spray-Leaksville area in Rockingham County, where he worked in a textile mill (fig. 11.2). At the mill, he met fellow workers, Posey Rorer, a fiddler, and Norman Woodlief, a guitarist, both local musicians. The Ramblers differed from other string bands in the South, which relegated the banjo and guitar to minor accompanying roles. Their banjo-fiddle-guitar combination featured finger-style banjo, a bluesy fiddle lead, and the flowing melodic guitar runs, which became the basic ingredients of the bluegrass sound.[9]

Poole died in 1931, but his legacy was perpetuated by other string bands of western North Carolina in the 1930s and 1940s. Bill C. Malone, author of *Country Music, U.S.A.*, states that "the most influential of the old-time string bands was a group from Buncombe County, North Carolina, known as Mainer's Mountaineers" (fig. 11.2).[10] J. E. and Wade Mainer's group was

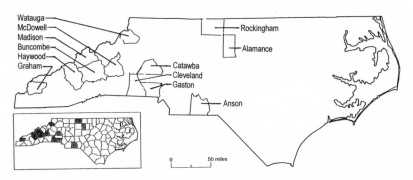

Fig. 11.2. County Origins of Precursors to Bluegrass

the most important transitional organization of the period because it preserved the heritage of traditional country material while at the same time anticipated many of the stylistic features of the bluegrass sound. The Mainers experimented with vocal harmonies that were later reflected in bluegrass singing and featured the full retinue of instruments of the modern bluegrass sound—five-string banjo, fiddle, guitar, mandolin, and string bass. Furthermore, it was Wade Mainer, with his distinctive two-finger style, who maintained the banjo tradition as an important aspect of the bluegrass sound. Bob Artis, bluegrass scholar, asserts that this was the banjo style that Bill Monroe tried to emulate when he hired his first banjoist in 1942.[11] Finally, the Mainers, during the 1930s, provided a training ground for a number of instrumentalists who were progenitors to the bluegrass sound, including Wiley and Zeke Morris, Dewitt "Snuffy" Jenkins, and Clyde Moody.[12] Bluegrass scholars conclude that the Mainers were the first bona fide singing band, the direct predecessor of the bluegrass sound.[13]

A musical phenomenon that became associated with western North Carolina in the 1930s was the brother acts featuring tight vocal duet harmonies. The brother acts were forerunners of the bluegrass vocal sound. Perhaps the most notable of these duos was the Morris Brothers (Wiley and Zeke), natives of Old Fort in McDowell County (fig. 11.2). Among their many contributions to the bluegrass sound were such compositions as "Salty Dog Blues," a classic in the modern bluegrass vocal repertoire, and they were the first employers of Earl Scruggs and Don Reno, the seminal bluegrass banjoists.[14]

Bill and Earl Bolick of Hickory in Catawba County (fig. 11.2) were better known as "The Blue Sky Boys." This appellation was given to them because of their roots in the area where the piedmont meets the mountains in western North Carolina. Their absolute, consummate perfection of the vocal duet is widely imitated by today's bluegrass singers, and their songs have been extensively preserved in the bluegrass repertoire.[15]

A host of additional western North Carolina groups influenced the bluegrass sound. Among these were the Callahan Brothers from Madison County; the Briarhoppers, who hailed from Graham County; Roy Hall and the Blue Ridge Entertainers from Haywood County; the East Hickory String Band and the Good Coffee Boys from Catawba County; the Blue Ridge Hillbillies from Buncombe County; and the Aristocratic Pigs from Anson and Gaston Counties (fig 11.2).[16]

Equally as important as the bands in the creation and evolution of the bluegrass sound were the individual musicians who hailed from western North Carolina. The most significant of these was a cadre of finger-picking banjoists from Rutherford and Cleveland Counties (fig. 11.3). The over-

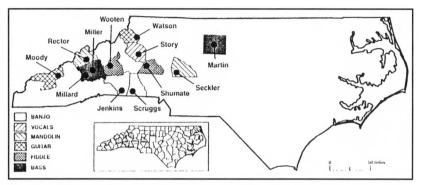

Fig. 11.3. Bluegrass Innovators (Instrumental and Vocal)

whelming credit for the most distinctive instrumental element in bluegrass is given to the Jenkins Family of the Harris community. Snuffy, Hoke, Verne, and Oren Jenkins are singled out by bluegrass scholars as the proto- typical bluegrass banjoists because of their popularization of the three- finger roll.[17] The most influential of the family was Snuffy because of his influence on such premier banjoists as Don Reno and Ralph Stanley. Both trace their lineage to him as apprentices under his tutelage.[18] In addition to the Jenkins Family, the bluegrass literature suggests that neighboring banjo- ists in the Harris area, including Smith Hammett, Rex Brooks, and Mack Woolbright, also played a vital role in the development of the three-finger picking style.[19]

It was the Scruggs clan from the Flint Hill–Boiling Springs area in Cleve- land County, however, who introduced this unique component of the blue- grass sound to the world and personalized the three-finger roll known as the "Scruggs Style" (fig 11.3). Junie and Horace Scruggs provided the inspi- ration for their younger brother, Earl, who was to become the "master of bluegrass," according to bluegrass scholars.[20] After stints with the Morris Brothers and Carl Story, fellow North Carolinians, Earl joined Bill Monroe and the Bluegrass Boys in 1945 upon the recommendation of Jim Shumate, Monroe's fiddler and a friend of Scruggs from back home. Earl's introduc- tion of the three-finger roll provided the key element to form the quintes- sential bluegrass sound from 1945 to 1948. After leaving the Bluegrass Boys, Earl teamed with Lester Flatt to assemble the most commercially successful band, the Foggy Mountain Boys, in the genre's history. The popularity of Flatt and Scruggs was based on their musical score for the film *Bonnie and Clyde*, featuring "Foggy Mountain Breakdown" as well as the "Ballad of Jed Clampett," the theme for the popular television series, *The Beverly Hillbill-*

*ies.*[21] Besides the three-finger roll, Scruggs added a second innovative technique that characterized bluegrass banjo—Scruggs tuning. Scruggs's adjustment of the tuning pegs at various intervals in a melody allowed him to move from one key to another. This was made famous with his banjo compositions such as "Flint Hill Special," "Earl's Breakdown," and "Foggy Mountain Chimes."[22] As Robert Shelton, music critic for the *New York Times*, concludes: "Scruggs bears the same relationship to the five-string banjo that Paganini does to the violin."[23]

Regarding the fiddle innovators in bluegrass, Art Wooten was the first fiddler with the Bluegrass Boys from 1938 to 1940. A native of Marion in McDowell County (fig. 11.3), Wooten brought to the band a short-bow, hoedown style that broadened the background of Monroe's music and first charted the course of bluegrass fiddling.[24]

Jim Shumate carried on the bluegrass fiddling tradition established by Wooten. Coming from the western North Carolina community of Hickory in Catawba County (fig. 11.3), Shumate's breakdown style was a major contributor to the Bluegrass Boys in the mid-1940s, to Flatt and Scruggs in 1948 as their first fiddler, and to the Stanley Brothers in 1949. Shumate's role in shaping the bluegrass sound was significant for two additional reasons. First, had it not been for Shumate's friendship with Scruggs, the classic sound may never have developed because it was he who recommended Scruggs to Monroe in 1945. Second, Shumate's hometown of Hickory was the launching pad for Flatt and Scruggs in 1948 when he arranged for their first radio appearance on WHKY.[25]

The mandolin in the hands of Bill Monroe became a principal instrument in the bluegrass sound; however, two western North Carolinians demonstrated virtuosity on the instrument and helped define its role in bluegrass. A native of China Grove in Rowan County (fig. 11.3), Curly Seckler was a key figure in a series of bluegrass groups, including Charlie Monroe's Kentucky Partners, the Stanley Brothers, Jim and Jesse, and, most notably, Flatt and Scruggs on all their Mercury and Columbia recordings.[26] With the latter, Seckler played a simple chord rhythm on the second and fourth beats that contrasted with the bass notes on the first and third beats. This, according to Rosenberg, gave the Flatt and Scruggs band "a distinctive bounce."[27] Red Rector, described by *Bluegrass Unlimited* magazine as one of the mandolin's leading stylists, was a native of Marshall in Madison County.[28] His mandolin wizardry gave the instrument an aggressive, percussive role in the high-powered, strident bluegrass sound.

The guitar did not emerge decisively as a lead instrument in the bluegrass ensemble until guitarists adopted the use of the flat pick. It was Arthel "Doc" Watson from Deep Gap in Watauga County (fig. 11.3) who was as responsible as any one entertainer for generating a vogue for lead guitar picking in bluegrass.[29] Clyde Moody, however, set the stage for bluegrass guitarists. A native of Cherokee in Swain County (fig. 11.3), Moody introduced a bluesy-style guitar using thumb and index finger picks. As a member of the Bluegrass Boys from 1940 to 1945, he laid the groundwork for the flat-picking technique perfected by Watson.[30]

Other individual western North Carolinians who provided valuable input to the bluegrass sound included John Miller of Asheville and Tommy Millard of Canton (Buncombe County), both of whom played spoons, bones, and jug as the rhythm section for the first Bluegrass Boys in the late 1930s.[31] Wilma Martin of Greensboro (Guilford County), who played bass for Charlie Monroe's Kentucky Partners, was one of the first women in bluegrass.[32] And, Carl Story from Lenoir (Caldwell County), whose otherworldly falsetto voice rivaled Monroe's for "the high, lonesome sound" vocals, was dubbed the "Father of Bluegrass Gospel" (fig 11.3).[33]

The aforementioned groups and individual musicians represent only a handful of the almost ninety musicians born in North Carolina who helped fashion the modern bluegrass sound from 1925 to 1965 (fig. 11.4).

## Social Institutions

The innovative bands and creative individuals from the various western North Carolina communities would have made little impact had it not been for the myriad social institutions of the region that provided performance opportunities, repertoire exchanges, and professional exposure for the musicians to gain regional prominence and national recognition. The most

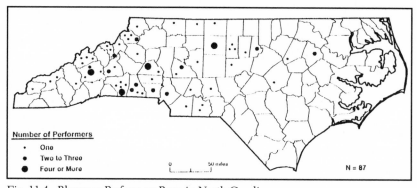

Fig. 11.4. Bluegrass Performers Born in North Carolina

influential of these institutions were the homes, schools, and churches within the immediate neighborhoods of the artists involved.

The home served as the first performance place, consisting of picking and singing sessions on the front and back porch after a day's work, the Sunday afternoon family gatherings in the parlor, and at house "warmins" and barn "raisins" for the newly arrived neighbor. Only when the musicians performed outside the home did they consider themselves embarking upon a possible musical career. Small social functions, often held as fund-raisers in the community, established the musician as a local favorite. These included pie suppers, cake walks, and play parties held in nearby one-room schools and churches. These events were just a step away from performing at home; however, they often led to a professional career. Performance outlets beyond the musician's neighborhood included the regional fiddle contests, music festivals, radio station air-play, and recording studios.

## Fiddle Contests

The early contests in western North Carolina were usually held in conjunction with county fairs or similar events such as Old Settlers Days. Fiddling was recognized as both an "old-time" art and a Southern music phenomenon. Old-time fiddle tunes were genuine folk music because authorship had been lost or forgotten over the years. Many were of British origin such as "Soldier's Joy," "Irish Washerwoman," and "Patty on the Turnpike," while others were of American derivation including "Flop-Eared Mule," "Cumberland Gap," and "Cripple Creek." Organized and promoted by local civic groups and schools, these events attracted every grade of fiddler from novice to professional.

The Old-Time Fiddler's Convention at Union Grove ranks as the "granddaddy" of them all for the southeastern United States. Established in 1924, it is one of the two oldest events of this type in the nation; the other is at Galax, Virginia. Fiddler Henry Van Noy, while serving as the Union Grove School principal, created the idea as a fund-raising project.[34] Held on Easter weekend for seventy-two consecutive years, the Union Grove event, as well as thirty other fiddle contests in North Carolina (fig. 11.5), provided numerous bluegrass fiddlers the performance opportunity to ply their fiddling wares.[35] As described by Bill Monroe, the fiddle was the "kingpin of bluegrass music." He has incorporated old-time fiddle tunes into the basic instrumental repertory of the bluegrass sound. Prominent among the bluegrass fiddlers who participated in the fiddle contest circuit in western North Carolina was Chubby Anthony of Lincolnton in Lincoln County. Anthony

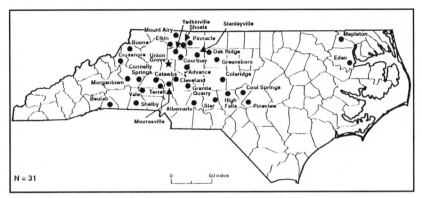

Fig. 11.5. Old-Time Fiddle Contests

competed in fiddle contests at Morganton, Mooresville, and Shelby; and eventually won the North Carolina Fiddling Championship in Greensboro in 1949.[36] Along with fiddlers, these contests have opened doors to other bluegrass instrumentalists such as the aforementioned "Doc" Watson, who was discovered at Union Grove as guitar accompanist to old-time fiddler Clarence Ashley.

## Music Festivals

Bascam Lamar Lunsford, old-time banjoist, avid collector of folk music, and composer of "Good Old Mountain Dew," was one of the major figures in the folk festival movement in the country. A native of Asheville and an attorney by trade, Lunsford was organizer and promoter of three folk festivals in his hometown that prominently featured music affecting the bluegrass sound. The oldest of the Lunsford festivals is the Mountain Folk Festival begun in 1928, followed by the Rhododendron Festival in 1933. Shindig-on-the-Green, a weekly Saturday night affair, has been held on the grounds of the Buncombe County Courthouse since the 1950s. Lunsford also initiated the Mountain Music and Dance Festival in Mars Hill in 1967 (fig. 11.6). Many bluegrass performers, such as the Callahan Brothers and Red Smiley, began their careers as amateurs participating in these events.[37]

As a predecessor to the outdoor bluegrass festival, the earlier folk music festivals paved the way for individuals like Carlton Haney. A native of Rockingham County, Haney was the first of the bluegrass festival promoters. He had been immersed with bluegrass since childhood and, with a sense of business acumen, became Bill Monroe's manager in 1953–54 after quitting

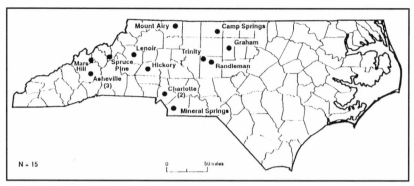

Fig. 11.6.  Festivals/Oprys/Jamborees

his factory job. After Monroe, Haney managed Don Reno, Red Smiley, and the Tennessee Cut-Ups for ten years. He then sponsored a forerunner to the bluegrass festival concept at the Surrey County Fair at Mount Airy in 1964 (fig. 11.6) with Monroe and the Bluegrass Boys and the Tennessee Cut-Ups as headliners. Based on this trial success, he launched the outdoor bluegrass festival movement in 1965 with the first at Fincastle, Virginia, and a second later that year at Camp Springs (fig. 11.6). These two Haney-promoted festivals provided the groundwork for a phenomenon that has diffused throughout the country, with more than five hundred held annually from coast to coast.[38]

## Radio—Barn Dances and Farm Programs

The beginnings of a legitimate professional career for local performers came with access to the new medium of the 1920s—radio. The oldest radio station in North Carolina was WBT in Charlotte, which went on the air in 1921 (fig. 11.7). Thereafter, the phenomenon diffused down the urban hierarchy to reach the small towns throughout western North Carolina during the 1920s and 1930s. In many of these locations, it was possible for locally popular musicians to obtain a fifteen-minute live program. Although nonsalaried, radio coverage resulted in an expansion of the performer's activity. These broadcasts led to a demand by the listeners for an opportunity to see as well as hear the performers. From a limited local following in a circumscribed area, the performers augmented their popularity through radio broadcasts and public appearances. The radio programs allowed the performers to promote public appearances, thus complementing each. As their territorial popularity expanded, sponsors were secured to pay the radio

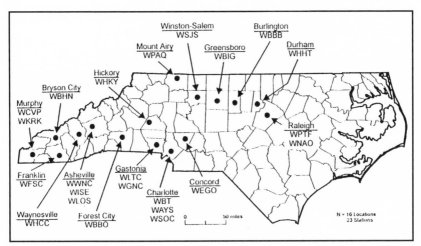

Fig. 11.7. Radio Stations Programming Bluegrass

station for the time during which the bluegrass musicians were on the airwaves.[39]

The first of the major radio programs sponsored by a national company was the Crazy Water Crystals Barn Dance, which began on WBT in Charlotte in 1934.[40] Ten bluegrass-oriented groups appeared on the Crazy Barn Dance in the 1930s. During the next two decades, twenty-three stations in sixteen North Carolina locations followed WBT's lead in programming the bluegrass sound (fig. 11.7). In addition to WBT, Charlotte boasted two other bluegrass-oriented stations, WSOC and WAYS.

Asheville also possessed three stations—WWNC, WISE, and WLOS—offering the bluegrass sound (fig. 11.7). WWNC (Wonderful Western North Carolina) introduced two regionally popular programs including "Mountain Music Time" featuring the Monroe Brothers, and the Western North Carolina Farm Hour, which scheduled eleven bluegrass acts during the 1930s, the most of any of the western North Carolina stations.

Additional western North Carolina stations that promoted the bluegrass sound during this period were WPTF in Raleigh, with nine acts featuring the Monroe Brothers' noontime program in 1937; WLTC in Gastonia, with five acts including Earl Scruggs's first appearance on radio in 1934; and WHKY in Hickory, with five acts featuring Flatt and Scruggs's inaugural performance on radio in 1948. As their local popularity was enhanced, performers moved to different stations in the region, thereby expanding their radio coverage as well as their personal appearance schedule where they made the most money. The most active of the bluegrass groups was Mainer's Mountaineers, who appeared on four stations.

## The Phonograph Record

Finally, the phonograph record was the ultimate medium for documenting and preserving performances. Although slow to accept early country music, a number of recording companies issued some string band music during the 1920s including Columbia, Edison, Paramount, and Gennett. Most notable were the one hundred recordings by Charlie Poole and the North Carolina Ramblers.[41] The Great Depression, however, caused a precipitous decline in sales, leading to bankrupt companies and forcing many of the performers to curtail recording, including many of the pioneer bluegrass groups who had exhibited little commercial appeal.

As an alternative, some of the major record companies established a cheaper subsidiary line. The first of the majors to do so was Victor with its Bluebird label devoted to blues and hillbilly talent and leased to Montgomery Ward for mail-order sales. Decca and ARC, the other two majors with subsidiary labels, focused their attention on the Southwest, signing new singing cowboy and western swing acts. Victor, on the other hand, concentrated its efforts in the Southeast. It took advantage of the network of performers on radio and those who had achieved popularity on the personal appearance circuit. Successful radio and personal appearances were seen as a key to successful records, and performers were contracted after they had proven themselves.[42]

With a southeastern focus, Victor selected Charlotte as the node for its only recording sessions in the 1930s (fig. 11.1). Bluebird's studio on the second floor of the Southern Radio Building in Charlotte was the center of activity for recruiting the major bluegrass talent of western North Carolina.[43] The acts included the Monroe Brothers, whose first venture into recording in 1936 consisted of ten songs, including such bluegrass classics as "Rollin' in My Sweetbaby's Arms," "Nine Pound Hammer," and "New River Train,"[44]; the Morris Brothers, whose recording of "Salty Dog Blues" became the most requested number in bluegrass history; and Mainer's Mountaineers, whose recording of "Maple on the Hill" was a regional favorite.[45]

## Conclusion

Musicologists have documented the origin of several American music genres to a local area.[46] It is apparent from the preceding evidence that the genesis of bluegrass is similar in nature. The locally based bluegrass subculture of western North Carolina was the culture hearth for the distinctive elements of the bluegrass sound. While many of the notable professional bluegrass musicians were born in eastern Tennessee, eastern Kentucky, and southwestern Virginia, it is clear that the defining characteristics, outlined by Smith and Rosenberg, were created and shaped by the piedmont pickers and mountain musicians of western North Carolina, including the three-finger roll on the banjo; the flat-picking technique on the guitar; the bluesy, hoedown style on the fiddle; and the tight vocal harmony of bluegrass singing.[47] Moreover, the network of social institutions (homes, schools, churches, music festivals, and fiddle contests) in western North Carolina resulted in a music infrastructure that gave these innovative musicians an opportunity to produce a locally based sound that achieved national recognition.

Finally, cultural geographers are obligated to investigate the source areas of culture traits, innovations, and ideas, including music, in the Sauerian culture hearth tradition. Similarly, music geographers, a developing group within cultural geography, are compelled to assist our sister disciplines in musicology and folklore in unraveling geography-based inquiries such as the question Malone posed concerning the matter of "where bluegrass came from."

## Notes

1. Bill C. Malone, *Country Music, U. S. A.* (Austin: University of Texas Press, 1985), 323.

2. Neil Rosenberg, *Bluegrass: A History* (Urbana: University of Illinois Press, 1985), 13, 111.

3. Ralph Rinzler, liner notes to *American Banjo Scruggs Style*, Folkways FA 2314, 1957.

4. R. J. Johnston, ed., *The Dictionary of Human Geography* (Oxford, U. K.: Basil Blackwell, 1986), 88.

5. Carl O. Sauer, "Foreword to Historical Geography," *Annals of the Association of American Geographers* 31 (1941): 12.

6. L. Mayne Smith, "Bluegrass Music and Musicians," unpublished M.A. thesis, Indiana University, 1964.

7. Rosenberg, *Bluegrass: A History*, 7.

8. Norm Cohen, "Early Pioneers," in *Stars of Country Music: Uncle Dave Macon to Johnny Rodriguez*, eds. Bill C. Malone and Judith McCulloh (Urbana: University of Illinois Press, 1975), 24–27.

9. Kenny Rorrer, "Leaving Home: Charlie Poole's Early Years," *Journal of Country Music* 9 (1981): 82–86, and Kenny Rorrer, *Rambling Blues: The Life and Songs of Charlie Poole* (London: Old Time Music, 1982).

10. Malone, 122.

11. Bob Artis, *Bluegrass* (New York: Hawthorne Books, 1975).

12. Ivan M. Tribe and John W. Morris, "J. E. and Wade Mainer," *Bluegrass Unlimited* 10 (1975): 12–21.

13. Malone, 122; Artis, 17.

14. Wayne Erbsen, "Jim Shumate: Bluegrass Fiddler Supreme," *Bluegrass Unlimited* 13 (1979): 14–25.

15. Ed Davis, "Blue Sky Boys Story on the Famous Bolick Brothers Who Pioneered the Ole Time Harmony Sound in the Late 30s and 40s," *Muleskinner News* 6 (1975): 5–13.

16. Malone, 110, 114, and 124; Ivan M. Tribe, "The Briarhoppers: Carolina Musicians," *Bluegrass Unlimited* 12 (1978): 31–38; and Pat Ahrens-Striblin, "The Aristocratic Pigs: An Early Carolina String Band," *Old Time Country* 6 (1990): 8–10.

17. Rinzler, liner notes to *American Banjo Scruggs Style*.

18. Tony Trischka, "Snuffy Jenkins," *Bluegrass Unlimited* 12 (1977): 20–21.

19. Liner notes to *Mountain Music, Bluegrass Style*, Folkways FA 2318; liner notes to *Early Bluegrass*, RCA Victor Vintage Series LPV-569; and liner notes to *Hills & Home: Thirty Years of Bluegrass*, New World Records NW 225.

20. Rosenberg, *Bluegrass: A History*, 73; Artis, 24–25; and Cantwell, 101.

21. Rosenberg, *Bluegrass: A History*, 259–65.

22. Robert Shelton, "Folk Joins Jazz at Newport," the *New York Times*, 19 July, 1959.

23. Robert Shelton, *The Country Music Story* (Indianapolis, Ind.: Bobbs-Merrill, 1966), 140.

24. James Rooney, *Bossmen: Bill Monroe and Muddy Waters* (New York: Hayden Book Company, 1971), 32–33.

25. Erbsen, 14–25.

26. Barry Silver, "Curly Seckler: From Foggy Mountain to Nashville Grass," *Bluegrass Unlimited* 14 (1979): 10–16.

27. Neil Rosenberg, "Lester Flatt and Earl Scruggs," in *Stars of Country Music: Uncle Dave Macon to Johnny Rodriguez*, eds. Bill C. Malone and Judith McCulloh (Urbana: University of Illinois Press, 1975), 262.

28. Ivan M. Tribe, "Red Rector: Mandolin Virtuoso," *Bluegrass Unlimited* 10 (1975): 12–19.

29. Don Rhodes, "Doc Watson," *Bluegrass Unlimited* 12 (1978): 10–13.

30. Artis, 45.

31. Rooney, 32.

32. Ivan M. Tribe, "Charlie Monroe," *Bluegrass Unlimited* 10 (1975): 12–19.

33. Ivan M. Tribe, "Carl Story: Bluegrass Pioneer," *Bluegrass Unlimited* 9 (1975): 8–14; Don Rhodes, "Carl Story," *Pickin'* 4 (1978): 6–15.

34. Richard K. Spottswood, "Union Grove 1971," *Bluegrass Unlimited* 5 (1971): 9; Charles Mathis, "Union Grove '75," *Bluegrass Unlimited* 9 (1975): 9.

35. Audrey A. Kaiman, "The Southern Fiddling Convention: A Study," *Tennessee Folklore Society Bulletin* 31 (1965): 7–16.

36. Don Rhodes, "Making That Fiddle Sing! Chubby Anthony," *Bluegrass Unlimited* 13 (1979): 30–33.

37. Malone, 57, 110, and 336.

38. Fred Bartenstein, "The Carlton Haney Story," *Muleskinner News* 2 (1971): 8–10, 18–21; George O. Carney, "Bluegrass Grows All Around: The Spatial Dimensions of a Country Music Style," *Journal of Geography* 73 (1974): 40–46.

39. Rosenberg, *Bluegrass: A History*, 23–24, 95–96.

40. Crazy Water Crystals was a regionally based commercial product in the southeastern United States known for its cathartic qualities as a purgative or laxative. Similar type medicines, such as Texas Crystals, were sold in the Great Plains states. Patent medicines often sponsored country music radio programs in the 1930s and 1940s. See also Malone, 98.

41. Cohen, 25.

42. Malone, 94.

43. Ralph Rinzler, "Bill Monroe," in *Stars of Country Music: Uncle Dave Macon to Johnny Rodriguez*, eds. Bill C. Malone and Judith McCulloh (Urbana: University of Illinois Press, 1975), 210.

44. Brad McCuen, "Monroe Brothers Discography," *Bluegrass Unlimited* 4 (1969): 8–9.

45. Malone, 123; Rosenberg, *Bluegrass: A History*, 27.

46. Examples include rockabilly in Memphis, Motown in Detroit, jazz in New Orleans, urban blues in the south side of Chicago, bebop in New York City's 52nd Street, rap in the Bronx, and grunge in Seattle.

47. Carney, 35.

# Part IV: Folk Sports and Games

Play is a form of expressive behavior common among all human beings and manifested overtly in all cultures, including folk culture. Play is defined by two main criteria. First, it is voluntary, that is, it does not directly satisfy any biological need for survival. Second, it is generally considered nonproductive in any tangible sense (disregarding professional athletes). It does contribute substantially to the physical, social, and psychological growth and development of the individual. If play does not involve competition, it is considered recreation. Games and sports, however, differ from recreation because they include competition between two individuals or two teams, but also include competition between an individual and an animal (e.g., rodeo and bullfighting), a person and the natural environment (e.g., mountain climbing), an individual and an ideal standard (e.g., shooting par in golf or running the four-minute mile), and competition between animals supervised by humans (e.g., foxhunting and cockfighting—two of the folk sports covered in part 4).

According to Paul Weiss, a sports philosopher, "sport" means to "disport," that is, to divert and amuse. This may be in the form of either direct participation or as a spectator. Hence, sports and games are aspects of folklife by which humans divert themselves from labor.

Sports and games have become a major research arena for cultural geographers, although little research has been published from the folk perspective. See, for example, Karl B. Raitz (ed.), *The Theater of Sport* (John Hopkins University Press, 1995) for a collection of thirteen original essays, eleven authored by cultural geographers, covering a myriad of sports ranging from climbing to rodeo.

Folklife scholars are more interested in the variations and informal changes made in sports and games rather than the formal rules and policies of governing bodies associated with organized versions. The folklife slant on sports and games has focused on oral traditions (superstitions like not touching the third-base foul line after baseball pitchers complete an inning, and rituals associated with college football homecomings); informal variations of sports (H-O-R-S-E in basketball and "Workup" in baseball); sport-derived aphorisms ("bush league"); sports lingo and nicknames ("hot corner" and "Dizzy" Dean in baseball); and sports heroes (Babe Ruth).

In chapter 14, the cow pasture baseball reading relates the local characters and stories associated with a loosely organized form of this sport in the

Missouri Ozarks. It exemplifies the *folklife region* of the Ozarks, a section of the Upland South, where baseball was a major pastime for local folks who had little money for uniforms and equipment.

The *origin and diffusion* theme is represented in chapter 12, in which the sport of foxhunting originated in seventeenth-century England and diffused to the American colonies in the 1730s when hounds were used to pursue foxes.

Under the *folklife ecology* theme, all three sports in part 4 take place in a pastoral setting provided by the natural environment. For example, a hilltop site is chosen by foxhunters because the sounds of the hunting hounds can be heard over longer distances.

The *integration of sports with other folklife traits* is portrayed in chapter 14, in which Sunday baseball in the Ozarks was a violation of the religious codes of several local folks. Lingo depicts the relationship between sports and language. For example, the sport of cockfighting in chapter 13 uses a variety of terms unknown to the outsider, such as "pits" (arenas), "cockers" (name for cockfighters), "gaffs" (steel points attached to the legs of the cocks), also called "slashers" or "bayonets," and "butcher" (a strain of gamecock known for aggression).

The *folk landscape* theme is illustrated in all three sports as the natural environment is transformed into a folk-sport landscape with human activities, including the cow pasture baseball field, cockfighting arenas, and foxhunting pens and clubhouses.

Although sports and games have become increasingly organized and modern communication technology has affected folk traditions, it appears that superstitions and rituals, lingo and nicknames, and informal variants will persist in contemporary society.

# 12

# American Foxhunting:
# Landscape Ensemble and Gratification

## *Karl B. Raitz*

Nunnely Ballew was a hill farmer on the Big South Fork of the Cumberland River who lived to hunt fox in Harriette Arnow's *Hunters Horn*. He sacrificed the health and well-being of his children and wife so that he could buy canned dog food for his hound, Zing. The dog, not youngsters or spouse, became the center of the family's attention and a source of respect from the neighbors. Arnow helps us imagine the scene: "Late November's gentle misty rains made a fog across the hills and brought a grayness and stillness to the bright noisy leaves. The good hunting weather, the dog food, eggs, fresh milk, and scraps of meat from a just killed pig all gave new life to old Zing. This fall, as on other falls, he was the pride and wonder of Little Smokey Creek Country."[1]

Many hard-core foxhunters would recognize the yearning of Nunn Ballew. Among members of the hunting fraternity, the best hunter is the person with the best hound. The hound that leads the hunt reflects the wisdom of its master. Wisdom in selecting appropriate breeding lines and wisdom in training the dog so that it learns the way of red foxes on dark nights. Stories are told of spending $8,000 for a dog or, during the Great Depression of the 1930s, trading a cow and a calf for a prized hound.

American foxhunting is thought to have originated in south central Kentucky a hundred years ago or more.[2] It differed from English-style foxhunt-

Reprinted by permission from *Sport Place: An International Journal of Sports Geography* 2 (1988): 2–13.

ing in a number of ways. Although a special breed of dog was used for hunting, the hunters did not follow the dogs (*hounds* is the preferred term) on horses as did the English-style hunters. In fact, the American hunters made no effort to follow the hunt other than to listen to the barks of the pack and follow their progress in the imagination. The men who hunted were often gentry or urban professionals whose fortunes vanished with the end of the Civil War, but who continued their interests in horses, hounds, and hunting. Some of the early American hunters were Southern yeoman farmers of English, Irish, or Scottish ancestry who hunted their own land and that of their neighbors. The preferred place for hunting was rolling-hill land with wooded creek bottoms. Hounds would pursue the red fox (sometimes called the *dog fox*), often at night, and a group of hunters would gather at a vantage point, a hill or ridge top, build a fire, talk, eat, and listen to the dogs (fig. 12.1). In the morning the dogs would be gathered together and returned home.

## Changing Patterns of American Foxhunting

There were 239 foxhound kennels officially registered by the *International Fox Hunters Stud Book* in 1966 (fig. 12.2).[3] Registered kennels may represent a reasonably accurate estimate of the distribution of foxhunters because the expense and effort of breeding a dog pack, purchasing quality hounds for breeding, and submitting annual registration information to a centralized administrative office requires a commitment of time and money. A registered kennel is likely to be more intensely involved than

Fig. 12.1. Hounds in Pursuit of the Red Fox

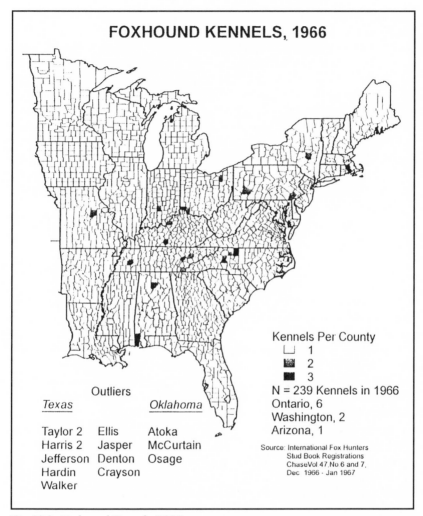

**FOXHOUND KENNELS, 1966**

Kennels Per County
⊔ 1
▨ 2
■ 3
N = 239 Kennels in 1966
Ontario, 6
Washington, 2
Arizona, 1

Source: International Fox Hunters
Stud Book Registrations
ChaseVol 47.No 6 and 7,
Dec 1966 - Jan 1967

Outliers

*Texas*

Taylor 2   Ellis
Harris 2   Jasper
Jefferson  Denton
Hardin     Crayson
Walker

*Oklahoma*

Atoka
McCurtain
Osage

Fig. 12.2.  Foxhound Kennels (1966)

the individual with a hound or two whose job or ambition may affect the seriousness of his commitment to hunting. Moreover, a kennel may well represent the presence of a cluster of avid hunters where one person has influenced others to buy hounds and take up the sport. The distribution of kennels exhibits two general location types. A few kennels are found near large cities: Boston, Philadelphia, Cincinnati, Louisville, and Houston. These probably represent kennels that provide hounds for English-style hunting, where the hunters ride blooded horses in pursuit of the pack, which may be following a fox or a drag (a scented bundle of cloth) across land leased for the purpose. The remaining kennels, including six in Ontario, are likely owned by American-style hunters. Kennels are found in twenty-three eastern states, most are east of the Great Plains and south of the Great Lakes. Few kennels are found within fifty miles of the Atlantic or Gulf coasts (with a notable exception at Mobile) and most seem associated with rolling, wooded topography.[4] North Carolina had the largest number of kennels, of which twenty-one were found in the Piedmont and the Blue Ridge. Seventeen of Tennessee's kennels were in the eastern Ridge and Valley counties in the foothills of the Smoky Mountains. Other concentrations were in south Kentucky's Pennsylvanian and Mississippian plateau lands (hardscrabble sandstone hills in the west and coal-bearing ridges in the east), West Virginia's Ohio and Big Sandy Rivers counties, and in the Appalachian counties of Ohio. Marginal hill lands did not necessarily harbor foxhunters. The Missouri Ozarks, and the Boston and Quachita Mountains of Arkansas had only scattered kennels as did the tier of Gulf states from Louisiana east to Georgia and Florida. The reputation (or stereotype) that men in these states have as avid hunters (Louisiana auto license plates proclaim that state to be a *Sportsman's Paradise*) does not appear to include hunting fox with hounds.

A small increase in the number of kennels by 1976 (now 257) brought some rather substantial adjustments in the distribution (fig.12.3).[5] Registered kennels in the three core areas (North Carolina, Tennessee, and Kentucky) had thinned somewhat. Kentucky kennels increased in number in the Bluegrass counties while fading elsewhere. The Piedmont of the Carolinas had also declined. Notable increases occurred in eastern Virginia where thirteen new kennels were registered in Caroline and Hanover counties north of Richmond. But most impressive was the expansion in Florida. With only four kennels in 1966, there were now forty-five. Clusters of five or more per county appeared in Duval County (Jacksonville) and Volusia County (between the St. Johns River and Daytona Beach). Some of the activity in each area may have been initiated by an increase in popularity of English-style foxhunting. But, by and large, the increase can be attributed to a rapid growth in popularity of American-style hunting. Especially interesting is the observation that this growth of registered kennels did not take place in the hilly uplands where one imagines a land of farmers, blessed with plenty of spare time in the fall, winter, and early spring months, which might present the opportunity to pursue the plentiful game of the uplands. The new kennels instead appeared on the coastal plain, many of them on the fringe of urban areas. This seems to be the first suggestion that foxhunt-

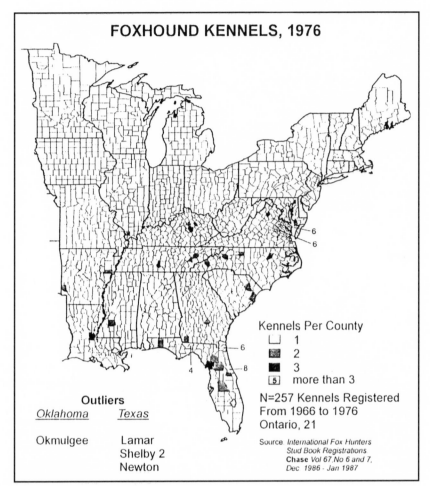

**FOXHOUND KENNELS, 1976**

Kennels Per County
⊔  1
▨  2
■  3
⑤  more than 3

Outliers

Oklahoma    Texas

Okmulgee    Lamar
            Shelby 2
            Newton

N=257 Kennels Registered
From 1966 to 1976
Ontario, 21

Source: *International Fox Hunters*
*Stud Book Registrations*
**Chase** *Vol 67.No 6 and 7,*
*Dec. 1986 - Jan 1987*

Fig. 12.3.  Foxhound Kennels (1976)

ing is no longer exclusively a sport for rural folk, but may well be attracting town and city people as well.

Between 1976 and 1986 the number of registered kennels increased by about two and one-half times to 638 (fig. 12.4).[6] Most growth occurred in a few rapidly developing clusters. Some clusters, such as east Tennessee, eastern Virginia, and West Virginia's Ohio and Big Sandy Rivers country, had a long tradition of foxhunting. Other clusters, such as the Carolina Coastal Plain, the southeast Georgia swamplands, the western Florida Panhandle, and especially north and south Mississippi and adjacent Louisiana

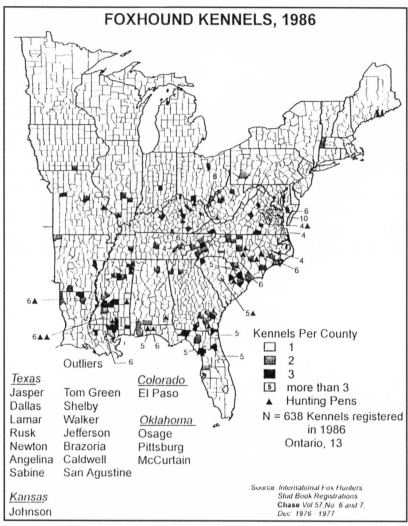

Fig. 12.4. Foxhound Kennels (1986)

parishes, are areas that had not seen organized hunts and registered hunting dogs before the mid-1970s. This increase in the number of registered kennels is largely caused by the growth in popularity of the sport among young men. The clustering of kennels in adjacent counties is largely the result of two major factors: first, the increased popularity of hunting in pens, and second, the demonstration effect of a successful dog breeder whose hounds command stud fees of $100 or more and who can sell puppies for hundreds, perhaps thousands of dollars each.

Pens are wire-fence enclosures that contain 100 to as much as a 1,000 acres of land (remember 640 acres equals one square mile). The fence's wire mesh is small enough that foxes released into the enclosure cannot escape. Although expensive to build, the pens are popular for a number of reasons. Foxes (or coyotes or wolves) will always be present for the hounds and hunter, a prospect that is not usually the case in the "wild." The fence also contains the hound's hunting range. The dogs are thus protected from the many hazards of this sport such as highway traffic, barbed wire fences, leg-hold traps, or irate landowners with guns. Not only are expensive hounds safe, but they never get lost and are easily called back to the starting point. Hounds following a fox while hunting open land run for miles and become scattered or lost. Pens are especially popular with two different types of hunters. Men with "city" jobs are constrained in their hunting because they do not have time to search for lost dogs, nor do they have time for unproductive hunts. Hunters who are less physically active may also prefer the pens because they do not have to traverse rough, inaccessible ground on foot to locate stray dogs.

Pens often include a "clubhouse," where the hunters can sit and listen to the hounds, cook a meal, and talk or sleep while enjoying shelter from rain or mosquitoes. The major drawback to pen hunting is that the environmental setting is constant. It varies only with the season. The most important aspect of the foxhunting landscape ensemble thus becomes predictable and less stimulating. Other parts of the hunting experience must be enhanced to maintain interest and enthusiasm. The "clubhouse," initially a concession to weather extremes, is an important part of that enrichment. Friends and neighbors gather in the clubhouse and enrich this simplified hunting environment by enhancing the fellowship setting. This seems to be one of the most important factors underlying the growth of the kennel clusters.

The demonstration effect of breeders influencing friends and neighbors to take up the sport and thereby produce clusters of kennels and hunters is also important. An individual hunter may breed forty hounds a year or more and sell up to two hundred pups. Some sell for several hundred dollars each. His success encourages friends who, though they are neither dog lovers nor avid hunters, might see the sport as a way to have fun while supplementing their income. Informants argue that this is the case, and certainly the patterns on figures 12.2, 12.3, and 12.4 support the contention.

There is no list or other objective data source for foxhunting pens. The thirty-three pens tabulated here are based on an examination of *The Chase* and *Hunter's Horn* (the two organs of American foxhunting), to locate advertisements and other references about pens. This brief list cannot be considered exhaustive, authoritative, or even representative, yet the pattern shows general agreement with the map of 1986 kennel clusters with some notable exceptions. The largest contiguous area with no fox pens is in southern Appalachia. Although there are numerous registered kennels in north Georgia, the western Carolinas, east Tennessee, and western Virginia, the area seems to be without pens. Intuitively, this pattern is to be expected. Much of this land is hilly or mountainous with farmland confined to valley bottoms, and large expanses of woodland with few hazards for uninterrupted hunting. If one assumes that many hunters in this area are farmers, with work schedules more flexible than those who punch a time clock, then a fox pen would not offer significant advantage and would unnecessarily restrict the hunting environment for the participants.

Many hunters have written letters to *The Chase* and *Hunter's Horn* complaining of the increasing difficulty of hunting in farming areas or places with high rural-population densities. Farmers erect fences or otherwise restrict hunting to prevent disturbing poultry or livestock or simply avoid the cacophony of twenty or more barking dogs at 3:00 A.M.[7] Although a great deal of land has been taken out of agricultural production by timber companies in the past three decades, this land is usually available for hunting through lease arrangements with the corporate owners.[8] Traditional farming areas are even less likely to be accessible to hunting in the future, and the pen may offer the best solution for more and more areas.

## Foxhunters

The stereotype of the foxhunter (and this likely applies to those who hunt a variety of waterfowl and upland game as well) may not be far removed from the image one might have gotten from reading Harriette Arnow's *Hunter's Horn* above. Updated, this image would likely include a redneck good ol' boy who chewed tobacco, drove a pickup with a gun rack, loved country music, and probably did not hold a regular job. In part to assess the merits of this stereotype, and in part to try to bring together something more than vague impressions, a group of kennel owners were surveyed as to their personal characteristics. A brief questionnaire was sent to a 25 percent sample of the 638 kennel operators who were registered with the *International Fox Hunters Stud Book* in January 1987. The sample was weighed by the proportion of kennels in each state. One hundred and sixty-four questionnaires were distributed and 104 were returned for a response rate of about 62 percent. The three-page survey included questions establishing social and economic status, preferred hunting environments, travel to hunts, and a preference scale for various hunting-related activities.

The typical foxhunter-kennel owner was 55 years old (the range was 19 to 81), had hunted for 40 years (range from 4 to 70) and had owned a kennel for 26.5 years (range from 1 to 60). Almost 75 percent held jobs. Almost two-thirds of those not working were retired and one-third (or 5.9 percent of the entire group) were unemployed. The employment profile of those with jobs was of considerable interest. Blue-collar-unskilled, that is garbagemen, day laborers, and other service jobs, comprised 6.9 percent of this group. Blue-collar-skilled, including farmers, mechanics, plumbers, and related occupations, comprised 27.7 percent of the total. White-collar workers, individuals with office jobs or their own businesses, were surprisingly 31.7 percent of the whole. Finally, white-collar-professionals, those whose jobs required specialized training and education, including engineers, lawyers, doctors, and judges, comprised the remaining 13.9 percent. Most attempts to describe cultural character in terms of categories are not terribly successful and this one is no exception. Consider, for example, that the farmers in the blue-collar-skilled category include the poor tenant in North Carolina who raises tobacco for cash, and the wealthy gentleman farmer in Kentucky's Inner Bluegrass who has a classical education from a traditional Virginia university, a stable of fine thoroughbreds, and an appreciation for Seneca and Shakespeare. If this classification has merit, it is interesting that 93 percent of the respondents did not match the stereotype. A note of caution is in order. Even though 99 percent of the respondents said that their kennels were a hobby, and not a business or a primary source of income, it is quite likely that a sample of registered kennels is not wholly representative of all kennel owners because the mere act of registration implies that a person has an awareness of the business aspect of hound breeding and has read hunting-related literature. It is entirely possible (though unlikely) that the majority of foxhunters who are not registered are also less informed and might occupy the bottom two employment categories.

Most hunters hunted year round. During the warm months of late spring and summer, 85 to 89 percent hunted each month. During the rest of the year, 90 percent or more hunted at least once each month, with a peak in October, when 98 percent hunted. Most states do not have a season that limits running foxes with hounds. Limitations are otherwise imposed during the trapping or gun seasons for other game because fox hounds are frequently caught in leg-hold traps or shot by other hunters. In addition to informal, impromptu hunting in fields or pens, many hunters, especially those interested in selling dogs at a profit, will attend organized hunting competitions. The competition usually has two parts. After hounds are officially entered, a bench competition is held in which dogs in different age and sex categories are judged for conformation and desirable hunting qualities (much as livestock are judged at county fairs). The second competition is actual field hunting. Judges walk, ride horses, or drive to observation points, and the entire pack (it may be well over a hundred hounds) is "cast" or released at a point where fox scent is likely to be picked up or a fox has been released. The hounds are painted with large block numbers, and judges record performance in hunting, training, speed and driving, and endurance categories. After several hours, the hunt is stopped, scores are totaled and winners announced. Winning an organized competition not only bestows prestige on the owner, it also adds credibility to one's breeding stock and allows the owner to increase stud fees and dog prices. Hunt competitions are held at national, state, and local levels. The serious competitor may travel to several competitions each year. Ninety-one of the sample group had traveled to a hunt competition during the past year. The mean number of organized hunts attended was 10.5 (the maximum number was 97). These hunters traveled an average 3,101 miles to attend (the maximum was 20,000). The highest mileage was accumulated by those who are popular judges and are hired to supervise the event and lend credibility to the results. Hunt competitions have a direct influence on the more frequent informal, unorganized hunts. In order to be properly conditioned and trained, hounds must be hunted frequently. This helps keep the hound's interest peaked and allows the owner to cull out the poor quality animal before it is an embarrassment at an organized hunt where judges and colleagues are present.

One assumes that place and environment are key elements in the experience and enjoyment of hunting. In hunting and fishing activities, where game is taken for consumption or trophy purposes, it might be argued that many participate for the "thrill of the kill" or simply as a practical way to supplement the family diet.[9] That motivation is not present in foxhunting. The fox is rarely killed. In fact, hunters want the fox to survive to run another day. It cannot even be argued that this type of hunting is popular because of the thrill of the chase, as the chase is done entirely by the hounds. The "hunters" rarely move from a central point where they listen to the hound. Therefore, we must look for other reasons why people enjoy foxhunting.

It could be that the foxhunt ensemble—place, environment, and related activities—is the principal appeal to the hunter. Place, here, is the physical and cultural context of the race. It may be a state forest in northern Mississippi or open farm fields and large wood lots in eastern North Carolina. It may include a clubhouse or farm buildings but may simply be a hilltop clearing in the woods. Environment refers to weather conditions, as well as seasonal and diurnal character. Related activities are those that are directly or tangentially a part of the hunt. The greater the number of activities, the greater the potential for a rich hunting experience.

Let us examine briefly the role of place and environment in the foxhunt. Participants in leisure and sport activities should seek out the most enjoyable experience available to them. One would not expect to find that people will sacrifice their valued leisure hours to activities that do not stimulate them or provide satisfaction. One way to measure the level of satisfaction in foxhunting is to compare the place of residence and the place where hunting is thought to be best. Most types of hunting are environment specific in part because of the natural cover required by the game animal. But within that environmental niche are areas that provide good or poor hunting opportunities. A question concerning the state with the best hunting brought answers from 84 of the 104 respondents. When the state of residence is compared to the state where the best hunting is perceived to be, the relationship appears to be quite direct where the states with the most hunters in the sample also received the highest number of preference votes. But these summary numbers are deceiving. Only forty-eight of the eighty-five respondents (56.6 percent) said that their own state had the best foxhunting, whereas thirty-seven (43.5 percent) thought hunting better in another state. Clearly the most favored state for hunting is North Carolina, with thirteen citations for best hunting over the number of respondents from the state. Kentucky had three and Mississippi had one, respectively. Among the highest negative states, in absolute terms, Virginia and Louisiana both had four fewer citations for best hunting than the number of respondents in each state. Georgia had five and Tennessee six. The reasons most frequently listed for poor hunting conditions were fencing of rural land, frequent roads (cars kill hunting dogs quite frequently), and lack of appropriate cover.

Respondents were asked to list the environment they most preferred for hunting to refine the assessment of appropriate hunting places a step further. Again, the environments of residence were also the most preferred environments. Most hunters travel relatively short distances to hunt (recall that it is the organized competitive hunts that draw hunters from longer distances). Consequently, one would expect the majority of hunting activities to be close to the residence. About 80 percent of the respondents preferred the environment they lived in for hunting. The remaining 20 percent preferred to hunt elsewhere. The two most preferred environmental types were wooded, rolling hills and flat to rolling open farmland. The others had slightly fewer citations as preferred places to hunt than number of residents. Both the wooded hills and rolling open farmland seem to offer a combination of the best conditions for fox habitat, the best conditions for hounds to pick up and follow a scent, and the most aesthetic environment for hunters to find a hilltop or other vantage point from which to listen to the chase.

An open-ended question asking respondents to describe the best environmental conditions for hunting was included to provide the most detailed information about preferred hunting environments. Perhaps because the question was open-ended, the response was not as complete or detailed as I had wished. Nevertheless, the results allowed the construction of an environmental profile of those conditions that hunters would find most desirable. Cool temperature was the modal characteristic. Other preferred qualities included clear skies; humidity, mist, or fog; nighttime; and cloudy skies. Many of the responses were very specific. A respondent from western Kentucky said the best conditions were "the second night following a rain [with a] south-west wind." Another respondent from central Kentucky summarized the preferences of many hunters in the following manner: "Crisp, cool fall morning, particularly after a rain, when the mist and fog is heavy at dawn, [temperatures are] in the high 40's or low 50's, warming as the day blooms." Not only is the character of the environment an important influence in whether hounds can "raise" a fox, but it also influences the hunter's aesthetic gratification from the experience. Invariably the most memorable hunts are described in the context of the character of the environment where the hunt took place.

Anticipation of a good hunt and memories of hunts past are also important parts of the enjoyment of the hunt. The two most important activities found by the questionnaire, rated as "Enjoy Very Much" by more than 95 percent of the respondents, were visiting during hunts, and hunting with friends. In addition to listening to hounds striving after the fox and perhaps catching a glimpse of a "crossing" (the fox, pursued by the pack, breaks from cover close enough to the gathered hunters so that they can see it), the most enjoyable aspect of the hunt is the fellowship with friends. This is the time for small talk, exchange of family news, and storytelling. Especially valued is the well-told story of memorable past hunts and anecdotes about friends or well-known hunters. Some measure of prestige accrues to the person with the best experiences and the most diligent hounds. When several hunters come together, their dogs are often combined into a common pack. Each dog's voice can be recognized by its owner and becomes a measure of whose hound is in the lead. Owners take great pride, as did Nunnely Ballew, in a hound with superior tracking ability and stamina.

Visiting other hunting environments is of considerable interest (81 percent rated this as "Enjoy Very Much"). This strongly suggests that hunting in other environments is an enriching experience. It is a conscious way of adding variation to the hunting landscape ensemble. Just as travel to a distant college town to watch one's team play an away football game introduces a new landscape ensemble and dimension into one's experience, the distant hunt offers new challenges to the hounds and introduces new adventures into the hunter's repertoire.

About two-thirds of the respondents gave the highest rating to the competitive aspects of hunting, although only 37 percent throughly enjoyed bench competitions. This relatively low rating seems related to the unexpectedly low value placed on activities that center on the hounds. The comparatively low ratings plus the broad spread of the ratings for caring for hounds, breeding hounds, and selling hounds strongly suggests that this aspect of hunting is not central to the overall enjoyment of the hunting experience.

## The Foxhunting Ensemble and Gratification

Americans experience sporting events in special places that are often designed specifically for that activity and little else. The ballpark, golf course, racetrack, and even the high school gym are all common examples. The sporting event does not simply occur at such places in isolation. The sport place is part of a set of material and nonmaterial elements that make up a landscape ensemble that is the integral part of the sport experience.[10] I have argued elsewhere that the landscape ensemble is an important factor in sport participation.[11] All landscapes stimulate. Complex landscapes with much variation and detail are more interesting and lead to higher levels of gratification in the sport experience, increasing the likelihood that the experience will be repeated. A simple landscape ensemble might be an asphalt inner-city school yard with a lone basketball hoop and white lines painted on the tarmac to delineate the court. A game played here is usually pure recreation. This is little to attract spectators. A more complex ensemble can be found on college and university campuses where often the largest building is the basketball arena. Students and alumni attend games in a noisy and colorful setting. Pregame activities may include "pep rallies" and "tailgating." A band, cheerleaders, and a student cheering section add excitement. The after-game festivities of private parties and other activities elsewhere on campus are also a part of this experience. The game played on the bare school yard and the hardwood college floor are essentially the same. Of course, the college game is much more sophisticated, but the reason why one game is attended by thousands of spectators and the other is ignored is not simply the skill of the players. It is because the total sport experience of the college game is played out in a stimulating environment, an ensemble of elements that are intended to entertain.

Field sports such as hunting may provide the best examples of the interrelationship of landscape and sport experience gratification. Most hunting activities have little formal structure. The ensemble provides virtually the entire context for the sport. A successful hunt could mean bagging the limit. Good shooting could be interpreted as a good sporting experience. These may be the determining factors for the few, but most hunters expect more from the experience than simply killing wild game. American foxhunting reduces these influences to their basics. The hunt becomes a communion between the hunters, their distant dogs, and the environmental ensemble. Pen hunting simplifies this milieu further and the role of the ensemble and other "hunt" elements becomes even easier to assess.

## Conclusion

The foxhunting ensemble is composed of a number of supporting, interrelated activities that are indispensable to the enjoyment of the hunt experience. The ensemble has social (visiting, storytelling) as well as environmental (topographic, vegetative, weather, and diurnal) dimensions. The memorable hunt comes not from the speed of the kill or the size of the game, but from the complex interaction of place, people, and related activities. Respect is afforded the crafty fox who leads a long and complex chase. Prestige is rewarded to the hunter whose hounds exhibit the best qualities of the committed hunter: trail wit, endurance, and gameness. The removal of any of these ensemble elements would appreciably diminish the hunter's gratification, perhaps to the point where hunting would stop.

This chapter represents one small step toward understanding better the geography of folk sport in America. As Fred Kniffen pointed out almost forty years ago, there is an exceedingly scant harvest of facts regarding the distribution and origins of these activities and yet they have thousands of devotees and often their own regional and national organizations and journals.[12]

## Notes

1. Harriette S. Arnow, *Hunter's Horn* (Lexington: University Press of Kentucky, 1986).

2. Roger Longrigg, *The History of Foxhunting* (New York: Clarkson N. Potter, 1975).

3. *The Chase* 47 (1966–67), Supplement.

4. Carlton P. Barnes and Frederick Marschner, *Natural Land-Use Areas of the United States* (Washington, D.C.: United States Department of Agriculture, Bureau of Agricultural Economics, 1933).

5. *The Chase* 57 (1976–77), Supplement.

6. *The Chase* 67 (1986–87), Supplement.

7. E. Makey, "On the Road Again," *The Chase* 67 (1987): 17.

8. Alexander Mackay-Smith, *The American Foxhound, 1747–1967* (Milwood, Va.: American Foxhound Club, 1968).

9. J. Hautaluoma and P. J. Brown, "Attributes of the Deer Hunting Experience: A Cluster-Analytic Study," *Journal of Leisure Research* 10 (1978): 272.

10. Mackay-Smith, *The American Foxhound, 1747–1967*.

11. Karl B. Raitz, "Perception of Sports Landscapes and Gratification in the Sport Experience," *Sport Place: An International Journal of Sports Geography* 1 (1987): 5–19.

12. Fred B. Kniffen, "The Deer-Hunt Complex of Louisiana," *Journal of American Folklore* 62 (1949): 187–88.

# 13

# Cockfighting in the Piney Woods: Gameness in the New South

## Fred Hawley

Going to a cockfight does not require much preparation. No special deportment or dress code is enforced. No one will comment on your beat-up old Ford pickup. However, one does have to know the *right* people to get in. One must also have the right stuff, gameness, in order to stay in. The right people may be a cockfighter, a gambler, or just a cockfighting fan. Whoever gets you in, however, it is best to go to one's first cockfight in the company of a regular at the pit. While cockfighting is more widely practiced throughout the American South than generally realized by city folk, do not plan an outing to a pit unless you know someone and they know you.

The route to the cockfight is simple, yet obscure. Simply jump in your truck in any of a thousand Sun Belt communities, drive through the suburbs, and leave the city and interstates behind. The roads will be quiet with only George Jones's or some radio preacher's wailing to disturb the serenity of the drive. This journey from the workaday urban milieu through Danté-esque concentric zones of ever-decreasing economic and social development represents a symbolic rite of passage that in a sense represents a departure from *real time* and *real space* as one enters the symbolically anachronistic world of the cockpit. For the deracinated blue-collar, rural-oriented, urban-residing good old boy, it is also a return to one's roots.

Reprinted by permission from *Sport Place: An International Journal of Sports Geography* 1 (1987): 18–26.

## The Cockpit

The prototypical brush pit is in a remote rural location, usually not readily identifiable by the uninitiated. Sometimes it is identified with signs proclaiming the "Elder Mt. Game Club" or the "Spring Valley Sport Club," but usually it is unmarked. An entrance or membership fee is collected either at the gate or the arena. These fees are relatively standardized at $5.00, but may range up to $20.00. At many pits the ticket will be stapled to the spectator's collar. Security at the gate is usually provided by one or more adolescent males, perhaps with CB radio walkie-talkies. Entrance is only possible if you are known, with someone who is known or have been vouched for by someone familiar with the management. The arena usually is located down a red dirt or graveled road some distance from the main road in a large shed, small barnlike enclosure, or perhaps a Quonset hut (called "Kiwanis huts," by some cockers), where the action takes place. A cluster of men and boys drinking beers among a wide variety of cars, vans, and trucks of varying vintage parked around this edifice signal the newly arrived visitor that there is more than an old chicken house up here in the woods. These days the distinct aroma of marijuana may also be detected as one passes a closed car or two. Most pickups have rifle racks and some bear whimsical or combative bumper stickers, and others even have pictures of license tags emblazoned with gamecocks. Some pickups have special boxes for chickens, while some cars are pulling trailers with small cages or boxes built into them. Fathers and sons will be seen in the parking lot carrying birds in wooden boxes or metal cages to be weighed in, tagged, matched, and held until their moment of truth. Dress is decidedly casual at most pits, but usually not abjectly sloppy. Denims predominate and new overalls and western wear are *de riguer*. Some of the participants and spectators wear clothing, hats, and jewelry emblazoned with chickens in combative postures. These items are widely advertised in the cockfighting press. Baseball hats are the dominant form of headgear; no urban cowboys these! Since cockfights are often held on Sunday, the more *respectable* elements show up after church is over at noon and dressed in polyester jumpsuits and vinyl shoes. For all, spectators and participants alike, comfort and utility seem to be the deciding factors in one's attire.

The cockpit itself often may be a shoddy shedlike affair barely affording adequate protection from the elements (I have experienced the most intense extremes of cold and heat in my life in such an aluminum shed in south Georgia) or it may be heated, air-conditioned, and insulated (Fig. 13.1). Most have at least rudimentary bleacher seating around the circumference of the pit. The pit itself is usually a sixteen- or eighteen-foot circular

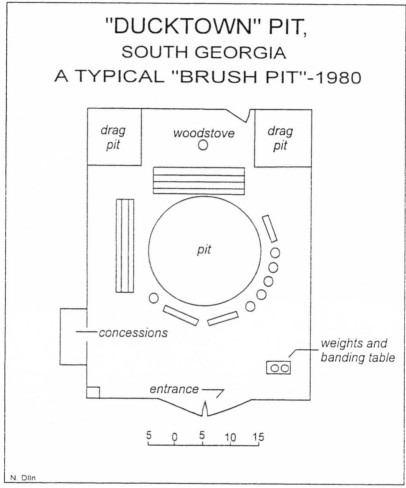

Fig. 13.1. Plan of the Ducktown Pit in South Georgia

area surrounded by a wood, metal, or chicken-wire-covered plastic sheet wall about twenty inches high.

Most cockpits have a primitive concession stand serving hot food, though few sell or allow beer to be consumed on the premises. The pits that sell or allow alcohol to be used openly are thought to be somewhat less savory by more committed cockers. Alcohol and other intoxicating substances *are* consumed by spectators in the parking lot, however, much like pro-football game tailgate parties. Overt drunkenness is prohibited at most cockpits, and obviously intoxicated participants are escorted to their cars or trucks by the pit owner or by his own friends. Notorious drunks or rowdies are seen as sources of potential law enforcement problems and are barred from the pits.

## The Cockfight

Participants must match cocks by weight in derbies. In a derby, the entry whose birds win the most fights wins the day. For example, in the extremely complex process of matching, six owners enter four birds each. This would create twenty-four possible matches. In this system each man pits each of his four birds once, therefore, he would fight only four matches at the most. The man whose birds win a majority of the matches will carry the day and the purse. Purse size is determined by entry fees. If six individuals paid a $50.00 entry fee, the prize money would total $300.00 (including the victor's entry fee). In the case of a tie, the "money" is split among the winners. These occur fairly frequently. In the matching process, the fowl must weigh within two ounces of each other, as higher weight is a considerable advantage in cockfighting.

Those cocks thought unworthy, too untested, or too immature (stags) for a derby are fought in hack fights, which characteristically take place without weigh-ins. These might by viewed as a warm-up act in a nightclub or rock concert. Betting also takes place in these events, but usually involves only the principals, their families, retainers, and serious gamblers. The ambience at this stage is still relaxed and somewhat desultory.

Finally the main events begin. The first principal entries are matched and begin the elaborate preparations of heeling, that is, tying the sharpened metal spurs, or gaffs, on their chickens. They then weigh their cocks, check band numbers to ensure against substitutions, remove the bands, and bill the birds in the pit itself (fig. 13.2). Billing is the act of holding the birds in the pitters' arms while standing about eighteen inches apart, thus allowing the birds to peck at each other. Betting, having commenced at the weigh-in, reaches a crescendo of shouts and frenzy that continues after the fight is under way. After a few vicious pecks, the birds are pitted from scores, that is, they are set down on lines eight feet apart and released by their handlers or pitters at the command, *"Pit!"* The birds attack each other with little thought of safety or tactics—it is a bravery born of instinct (fig. 13.3). They attack viciously with both beak and spurs, both leaping in the air and circling frantically. When the spurs of the birds become entangled in the other's flesh or feathers, the referee will call, *"Handle!"* At this point the pitters quickly, but gingerly, separate the birds causing the birds as little

Fig. 13.2. Billing the Cocks Before a Derby

damage as possible. This process is carefully screened by the referee for *unnecessary roughness*. The cocks are accorded a twenty-second rest or count at the conclusion of which they are again pitted at the eight-foot line. Betting can continue all the while this process repeats itself. The handlers try to revive the weakened birds by various seemingly bizarre methods: taking the bleeding bird's head into his mouth to warm it and drain blood from its lungs; he may breathe on its back; he may toss the bird in the air or make threatening motions at it. He may allow the bird to pace around his own corner like a boxer. In any case, at the command, *"Pit!"* the birds return to the twenty-two inch, or short, lines and the fighting and rest periods continue until one bird receives three tens and one twenty count, the one who fought or pecked last (thus showing the most gameness) being the victor. If the fight is not resolved expeditiously, the fight is moved to the drag pits to continue while another fight begins anew in the main area. Most cock pits have at least two such drag pits because cockfights can last from less than a minute to as long as several hours. The serious betters with big money on a specific fight will move to the drag pit to follow the progress or demise of their favorite. At the conclusion of the fight all bets are settled immediately. It is viewed as the interested individual's responsibility to see

Fig. 13.3. Two Cocks Engaged in Battle

that he receives his winnings, though notorious welchers, like fighters or rowdies, may be barred from specific pits. Novices are warned that they need to collect their winnings as soon as possible. In order to keep track of their wagers, many heavy betters keep a tab or list of the amount bet and the individual with whom the bet was made. Betting is generally a one-on-one affair and is almost universal among spectators and participants alike.

Some women and young children may be present as interested and active spectators, although this varies greatly from pit to pit. Women occasionally even pit cocks at powderpuff derbies, though these bizarre spectacles are a rarity. Betting loudly and competitively, those women who are in attendance may be wives and daughters or paramours of cockers.

When it becomes obvious that one party will win a derby, the remaining matches may be called off and the winner receives his purse. More hack fights or *mains*, informal fights that are not derbies, occur between individuals as the greater part of the crowd collects its side bets and leaves. Some cockers leave the arena to quiet their birds for the trip home. Many cockers travel long distances to pit their birds, sometimes driving all night to a pit or a home in another state.

While some of the spectators are clearly at cockfights primarily to gamble, these are a distinct minority. Deals and side bets are constantly being made as people coming and going from the arena swirl around the negotiators. Some cockers feel it is bad form to sell a cock, but will trade or give a cock to another cocker for the promise of one of the progeny of his cock when it is bred with a different type of hen. Cockers also trade information and gaffs, tiestrings and conditioning information, gossip, and generally palaver. It should be noted that these casual conversations form the bases of networks of obligation and reciprocity that span miles, national boundaries, and even generations. Sons of cockers hold the sons of other cockers responsible for fulfilling deals made by their fathers. Those who welch, or do not fulfill their obligation, are viewed with great disfavor. At one pit, several new acquaintances took me aside to warn me about the reputed sharp operator. The owner of another cockpit told me that he would see to it that all welchers would be barred from his pit until they made restitution to the aggrieved party. This is a society that puts a premium on a man's word and sense of responsibility. Proven cheaters are seldom given a second chance unless they repent and are ostracized by being banned from the pits. The concept of personal honor and masculinity are inextricably linked to the concept of gameness.

## Gameness

Cockfighting is part of a formerly legitimate, but presently archaic, cultural pattern that emphasizes certain values epitomized by the characteristic behavior of the ideal gamecock in combat, that is, *gameness*, a quality of unquestioning, instinctual bravery or will to fight when fighting is obviously unproductive, or indeed, counterproductive. The romantic (almost Byronic) valuation of this trait among members of the cocking fraternity is in stark contrast to the rationalistic institutionalizing spirit of the age. Like members of the plantation gentry, the cockers value the *beau geste*. This identification with the antebellum aristocracy is especially evident in cocking ideology. The gamecock with his gaffs or slashers is the *beau sabreur* presenting for his devotees a veritable mythic totem of bravery. It should be noted that should this seem peculiar, the ancient Greeks (recalling Themistocles), Romans, and Britons held the game fowl in such regard.

Sir Thomas Wyatt, the English poet, expounded thusly on the value of gameness to a Spanish visitor in 1539:

> There is nothing more serious, more useful or more worthy of praise in any well constituted republic. . . . Leaving aside the diversion which the contest affords, I say that there is not a single prince or a captain one might find among the spectators who, contemplating how fervently these little animals seek victory at the expense of their own lives and with no profit in view, even if he were a cowardly nature, would not recover a positive strength of spirit to vanquish his foe or to die bravely whenever it is necessary to fight for one's children sake, for religion, for one's sacred places, or for the honour and salvation of one's country.[1]

These self-same arguments are widely heard today, though not stated nearly so eloquently. Indeed, the union of poetry and cockfighting would seem incongruous to almost all cockfighters and cognoscenti of the sport.

Many cockers wear caps, shirts, and jackets and carry wallets emblazoned with a combative chicken. In any case, the valued gameness of the gamecock is based on toughness, bravery in the face of physical threat. Furthermore, as one might expect, most cocking devotees place a premium on masculinity, strength, and endurance, and derogate such effete areas as academe, art, and literature. One cocker asked me sarcastically if I could really look at myself in the mirror, stealing as I did the taxpayer's money by teaching at a state university.

It would be difficult to overstress the importance of this particular value for the average cocker. Since cockers identify with their birds quite thoroughly, a bird's degree of gameness may reflect on the bravery and masculinity of the bird's owner. In one pit I saw a bird *chicken out* of a fight by jumping out of the pit on two successive pittings. The owner, crestfallen, forfeited the match with a great deal of bitterness and blamed the loss on the referee.

"It wasn't the bird's fault," he was heard to say.

The referee, unfazed, loudly retorted, "If you can't fight game roosters you ought to go home."

This body blow almost precipitated a fracas, which was immediately mediated by third parties.

## Speaking of Gameness

The cocker is a proud, easily affronted, even pugnacious individual. When disputes arise among such game persons when money, pride, and honor are being wagered, it necessitates strong group mores concerning social control. Disputants are effectively ostracized if they refuse the mediation, which is almost invariably proffered. Thus, an interesting tension exists between individualistic gameness and the needs of collective solidarity on the other. Cockers are cognizant of these countervailing forces and become, as I have observed, physically agitated if disputes among their number are observed by outsiders. Thus, it can be said that the cocker who would be true to the imperatives of his fraternity must walk a fine line inside and outside of the metaphorical pit.

## Conclusion

After the cockfight, the return to real world concern is anticlimactic. The pitting of one's character, reputation, and self-esteem against those of others is elating yet enervating. One often departs from the precincts of the cockpit in almost reverential quiet and contemplation. Pickups and old cars roar to life and leave in clouds of fine red dust. Although some bantering does occur, most conversations are subdued and focused upon mundane themes. The spectacular public juxtaposition of life and death occurs so infrequently in our homogenized society, that its occurrence occasions considerable ambivalence from even experienced cockers. Cockfighting, not for the overly introspective and faint of heart, is a not unalloyed pleasure, even for the enthusiast.[2]

## Notes

1. Quote by Sir Thomas Wyatt in R. Graziani, "Sir William Wyatt at a Cockfight, 1539," *The Review of English Studies* 27 (1976): 299–303.
2. This article is based on my Ph.D. dissertation, "Organized Cockfighting: A Deviant Recreational Subculture," completed at Florida State University in 1982.

# 14

# Cow Pasture Baseball:
# Images of a Folk Sport Place

*George O. Carney*

I grew up in "Cardinal Country," about ninety miles north of Springfield, Missouri (capital of the Ozarks). I did not realize I lived in the "Redbird Region" until I was old enough (about eight) to get a haircut from a professional barber in the nearest town of Calhoun (approximately six miles north of our 320-acre farm where I spent the first eighteen years of my life with my parents, Josh and Aubertine). We were a struggling, "dirt poor" farm family and "crock haircuts" were in order during my formative years in that life of marginal poverty. That first trip was more important than I ever imagined.

My first recollection of following the Cardinals was during a Saturday afternoon haircut in Jim Martin's barbershop in Calhoun. It was a weekly ritual for farm families to make the trek to the nearest hamlet (economic geographers would call it a central place) to buy groceries, sell our eggs and cream, visit with relatives (my Grandpa lived there), and "get your ears lowered" as my Dad used to say. Mr. Martin's shop was located on the west side of the town square sandwiched between the post office and Snare's Grocery. Two chairs lined the south side of the room; however, he never had a partner that I recall. Nestled among all the hair tonics and other toiletries used to make his customers "smell good" was an old table model Philco radio. From it blared Harry Caray, the "voice" of the Cardinals. Day-

Reprinted by permission from *Sport Place: An International Journal of Sports Geography* 4 (1990): 22–32

time baseball was still in vogue in 1950 and "Jimmy," as Mr. Martin was known to adults, always had his Philco tuned to the Saturday afternoon broadcasts. Harry, long-time announcer for the "Birds," reigned as "King of the Cardinals-dominated Ozarks," and I was to become a serf in his "kingdom." "It was a beautiful day for baseball," proclaimed Harry over KDRO (Sedalia), a station about forty miles northeast of Calhoun. He had that broadcasting knack to make the sport "come alive" and stir the imaginative processes in your mind. The radio airwaves became my box seat along the third-base dugout. It seemed like I was always there when Harry would shout, "It might be, it could be, it is, a home run." I agonized with Harry when the Redbirds did poorly and, conversely, cheered with him in the thrill of victory. I can remember many a night falling asleep in my bed with the radio, next to my ear, tuned to KDRO. And when my parents awoke me at 6:00 A.M. (the appointed hour for milking the cows), they would find the radio still screeching static—long after the conclusion of the Cardinal broadcast.

A third influence in the evolution of my baseball fever was the Eaton "clan" who attended the same church I did. Going to Sunday School and "preachin'" (could only afford a minister to come on second and fourth Sundays of the month—he or she usually pastored another rural church on the first and third Sundays) was another weekly ritual for farm families. Our family attended the Mt. Gilead Church. It was a one-room, clapboard-covered, Southern Baptist type—plain, simple, unadorned—not even a steeple.

The Eatons were one of the two major clans making up the Mt. Gilead congregation (clans in the Ozarks were large families who lived in the same community). Grandpa and Grandma Eaton (known affectionately as the "old he" and the "old she") had six kids and oodles of grandkids. The other clan was the Russells (George and Mary Jane) who were turkey farmers known for forty-five-minute prayers. I vividly remember those long prayers because all I could think about was Mom's fried chicken Sunday dinner while Mrs. Russell called on the Almighty to bring rain for the crops or whatever was on her mind that particular week. She never prayed for the Cardinals to win or anything important like that.

The men of the church always gathered on the church steps prior to the Sunday services (some even skipped because they believed churchgoing was for the women) and talked baseball. The Eaton boys (sons of the "old he" and "she") were all die-hard Cardinal followers. It was the highlight of the week for a young boy to be able to talk about the pennant chances for the Cardinals, Stan Musial's batting average, and Vinegar Bend Mizell's potential as a twenty-game winner. Jack, one of the Eatons, introduced me to

*The Sporting News*, the St. Louis-based publication that became my "Bible" of baseball. He would bring his old, dog-eared copies for me until I earned enough money "buckin' hay bales" to pay for my own subscription. Endless hours were spent in my room compiling "stats" on the Cardinals, especially the up-and-comers in their farm system from Triple A to Class D.

Those cultural stimuli created a yearning in me to play baseball. There were no Little Leagues for country boys, and my Dad was never much of an athlete. Despite these drawbacks, I harassed my parents for a new base-ball glove. Finally, for my twelfth birthday, they gave me a Rawlings Stan Musial model. After the chores were done each evening, I would throw the hard ball against the rock foundation of our farmhouse to practice my "grounders." On several occasions, I misjudged the foundation and the lower weatherboard would crack from the impact of the ball. Dad and Mom would smile and replace the board. It was the only way I had to practice because of my only-child status. Once in a while, Dad would play catch with me over the dairy-barn fence in between milking "Old Bessie" and "Susie."

That summer of 1954 after my twelfth birthday in March, I begged my Dad to organize a team. Several boys in the Bronaugh community were about my age—Bronaugh was the one-room school I attended until the seventh grade. And there were more boys in the Thrush community—it was east of Mt. Gilead Church. Thrush was a general store (another central place) located on a hill overlooking Pridgin Holler. It used to be on the Missouri highway map with a population of four—Charley and Violet Hearn, the proprietors, and their two kids, Willard and Joann.

My Dad possessed what we would call today "organizational skills." We also were blessed with two telephones that my Grandpa Carney had in-stalled in our farmhouse. We, therefore, had access to two different ex-changes. So I began to contact the boys at school and Dad got on the "horn" to those in the Thrush neighborhood. We combined the boys from two different communities to form the Thrush baseball team.

We had to have a place to play. Dad again came to the rescue. He se-lected an open space on the north forty of our 320-acre farm. The diamond was to be shaped from pasture land north of Minor Creek, which flowed between our house and the "ball field." We had a herd of pure-bred Here-ford cattle that roamed and grazed that forty, but the area was free of trees and brush, and was level. It was the ideal place for baseball—the field was beautifully suited to its natural environment. It was a pastoral setting with no astroturf, no asphalt parking lots, no triple-decker stands, no vendors crying "cold beer," and no fences, except the barbed wire that enclosed the north forty acreage. A bank of timber lay to the south and east of the dia-mond and a clump of trees to the north served as hitting background for

the batters. And the rabbits, squirrels, and cows were the nonpaying spectators. There was a simple beauty and harmony with nature to the whole
scene—a visible expression of Ozarks culture on the natural landscape. One
might call it a folk sport place. It was one of the rare places where that
natural and cultural landscapes blended with each other without much disturbance to either. Karl Raitz has described these unique sport places as
those that embody a "meaning and importance based on personal experience."[1] For me, the cow pasture baseball field of my youth will always remain as one of those special places in my memory (fig. 14.1).

Dad carefully selected four young hickory trees from the timber that grew
to the east of the site. With skillful hands, he prepared the poles one spring
weekend. We bought some chicken wire from the local hardware in Calhoun and set to work crafting the necessary "backstop." Bases were "gunnysacks" (formerly used to hold chicken mash) filled with a straw and dirt
mixture. Instead of loose dirt around the bases, the ever-present "cow
patty" provided the needed sliding material.

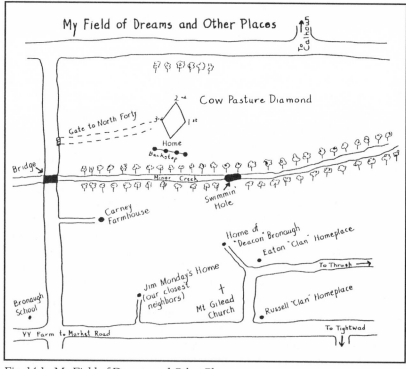

Fig. 14.1. My Field of Dreams and Other Places

Those were the basics—no batter's box, no chalked foul lines, no pitcher's mound—we were ready for competition. In terms of equipment, all the boys had gloves of some description and we had one bat used by all. It was a Hillerich and Bradsby Louisville Slugger 33-inch Stan Musial model.

Dad was coach. He was a P.R. man and long on organization, but not too astute as a coach. His philosophy was that everyone could pitch and play the position they liked. We rarely practiced because most of the team worked in the fields during the week (plowing, cultivating, and buckin' hay bales). Usually our only practice was a little warm-up before a game. We were never certain if nine boys would show at game time—1:30 on Sunday afternoons following church and dinner—but Dad was always on the phone rounding up players.

We finally scheduled our first game with the Tightwad boys. Now Tightwad was a "one-horse" town about ten miles south of the Bronaugh–Mt. Gilead–Thrush communities—a little further into the Ozarks. It was located on Missouri Highway 7 and boasted a population of twenty-five counting cats, dogs, and a few soreheads (fig. 14.2). The Tightwad team already had a field and an established reputation of being pretty fair country players. They had played some games, so to us they were veterans.

When they arrived in their pickups and stepped on our cow pasture field, I was in awe. They were older, bigger boys, some of whom sported uniforms

Fig. 14.2. Tightwad, Missouri (Baseball Field to Right of the Town Sign)

with sponsorships on the back of their jerseys like "Tightwad Tavern" and "W. E. Parks Grocery." They had the Terry Brothers (Larry and Gary), both of whom could throw "heat," and the Cochran Twins (Jim and John) who could knock the cover off the ball. One of the Cochran boys even had a first baseman's glove and the other a catcher's mitt. Our team was lucky to have a new baseball for the game and that was only if we had made it to town on Saturday before the game. I don't remember the score of the first Thrush-Tightwad encounter, but if there had been a ten-run rule, I believe it would have been invoked on that long Sunday afternoon on Carney's cow pasture. But we scheduled another game at their field because it did not matter what the score was—we were finally realizing a dream.

It became the topic of conversation in the three communities—the boys talked about it at school, the parents discussed it at church, and the senior citizens sat around the pot-bellied stove at Thrush store and mulled it over on Monday morning. We had created a community spirit and—as John Rooney has called it—pride in place.[2] Up for grabs was "bragging rights" between the two communities. And the more times we challenged Tightwad, the more people came to watch—bringing their lawn chairs, blankets, and water jugs filled with iced tea or lemonade. And there was always that glimmer of hope that one, just one of us might make it to the "big show." After all, the Ozarks had produced the likes of the Dean Brothers, Bill Virdon, and Jerry Lumpe (the latter betrayed the entire Ozarks by signing with those dreaded Yankees from back East).

But the community pride was not embraced by all. Dad was chastised by several of his fellow churchmen. "Brother" Carney, who was Sunday School superintendent, was promoting an "un-Christianlike act" by playing ball on Sundays. One staunch deacon by the name of Fitzhugh Bronaugh took my Dad to task before church one muggy Sunday morning. "What are you teaching those boys, Josh," he sermonized. "Don't you know that Sunday is the Lord's Day?" My Dad, who was also known for his mediating abilities, comforted the deacon, but took his remarks with a "grain of salt." Perhaps Dad recognized that Mr. Bronaugh, albeit a sanctimonious churchgoer, was also known as the community "sorehead." Ironically, the next Sunday, Deacon Bronaugh apologized to Dad. He had started thinking what a hypocrite he was. He had to admit to being the first in his household to turn on the radio after church to listen to the Cardinals (he wasn't all bad). He reckoned that playing ball on the Sabbath wasn't too much different from listening to it. As a matter of fact, he began attending some of our Sunday afternoon games.

The Thrush team consisted of several rather colorful characters who sported interesting backgrounds (fig. 14.3). The Fields Brothers (Jackie and

Fig. 14.3. Thrush Baseball Team

Everett) came from a family of thirteen kids. Big families were still considered important by some Ozark parents, to work in the fields and perform domestic duties. Our "wild thing" in those days was a lanky righthander named Dennis Bonnewitz, who stood 6'4". "Bonney," as we called him, was just as likely to hit the batter as throw a strike. For those opponents who didn't attend church before the game, he carried out some missionary work by putting the "fear of God" in most hitters who stepped up to the cow pasture plate. John Gordon, fleet of foot and a pretty fair outfielder, lived in a log cabin with a dirt floor. There were no fences in the outfield, so John had to run down many a ball hit over the outfielder's heads. It was a gregarious assortment of individuals, and camaraderie ran high when we gathered for those Sunday afternoon occasions. We never kept batting averages or won-loss records—we were just content to be able to play our beloved national pastime.

The highlight of the first summer of getting to play baseball was my first trip to St. Louis to witness a "big league" game (fig. 14.4). One of the Eaton "clan" (Big Ed, who was a gentle giant) agreed to take his nephew and me to the River City. We boarded the Missouri Pacific passenger train in Warrensburg one hot July Sunday morning and arrived at the Union Station in St. Louis about two hours before game time. Not wanting to spend money on cab fare, the elder Eaton hailed down a milk truck at an

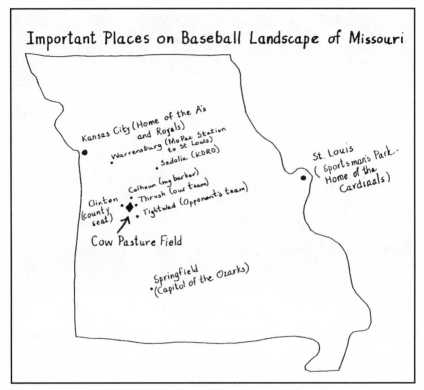

Fig. 14.4.  Important Places on the Baseball Landscape of Missouri

intersection near the station. The driver happily delivered us to Sportsman's Park. It was a "beautiful day for baseball"—Harry's radio descriptions had come true for the farm boys from Thrush. The Cardinals were wallowing in sixth place and going nowhere in the late-season pennant race. They were pitted against the New York Giants (who went on to win the N.L. pennant that year) that sultry St. Louis Sunday in 1954. The Giants had a center fielder by the name of Willie Mays making those famous basket catches. Don Mueller, the N.L. batting leader, was in right field, and Johnny Antonelli, on his way to a twenty-game season, was on the mound. But those weren't the players I came to see. My heroes were Stan "The Man" Musial, Harvey Haddix, Ray Jablonski, Rip Repulski, Albert "Red" Schoendienst, Wally Moon, and the McDaniel Brothers (Lindy and Von). Musial, a consistent .300 hitter, went on that year to hit thirty-five home runs, drive in 126 runs, and chalk up 359 total bases. Haddix, the crafty, diminutive left-hander who had won twenty games the year before, was selected for the All-

Star Game, as was the Polish tandem of Jablonski at third and Repulski in the outfield. Wally Moon was named Rookie of the Year in 1954 and the old Redhead was also an All-Star nominee. And with the young McDaniel boys showing potential on the mound, the future for the Cards looked promising. I was always optimistic—even if the Cards finished near the bottom of the N.L. that year. I was just happy to finally see my baseball gladiators in person—Harry Caray's play-by-play accounts had not disappointed me. And I was one of the 1,039,695 fans to pass through the turnstiles at Sportsman's Park in 1954. The Cardinals lost that first pilgrimage to my "mecca" of baseball, but it didn't matter because another one of my childhood dreams had become a reality.

The next summer I played in a Babe Ruth League at Calhoun. The high school baseball coach organized the team in an attempt to develop a minifarm team for his high school roster. But it wasn't the same—we played on real diamonds in places like Leeton, Lincoln, Green Ridge, and Windsor and, in some cases, under the lights. We had uniforms, catcher's mitts and chest protectors, knee pads, batting helmets, and cleats. We even had to have practices twice a week. I don't remember much about those games except that I got home late, and the coach and parents began to take the game I loved too seriously.

My baseball playing days finally ended the next summer when I tried out for the American Legion team in the county seat town of Clinton. It was the only Legion team in the county so all the farm boys as well as the "city slickers" who thought they could play ball attended spring tryouts. But I was a scrawny 130-pounder with a weak arm who sprayed the ball around and never averaged more than .250. I couldn't compete with those bigger, stronger farm boys from all over the county who could throw out a runner from deep short, hit a ball so far over the Legion Park fence that it looked like a "pea," or throw "aspirins" at seventy-five m.p.h. So I hung up my Stan Musial-model glove and laid my Louisville slugger in the garage. There were too many "naturals."

Thirty-five years later, I still have that glove and bat—they gather dust in my attic in an Oklahoma home. That isn't all that has changed. Cardinal Country has shrunk because of what they call "competitive forces."[3] KDRO discontinued the Cardinal broadcasts when the Athletics moved from Philadelphia to Kansas City in 1969. Now the Texas Rangers also intrude into the Redbird region. And, worse yet, my beloved Harry Caray has departed. After a brief stint with the White Sox, he has become a "living legend" broadcasting for those arch-rivals, the Chicago Cubs. There's a feeling of nostalgia every time I hear Harry sing "Take Me Out to the Ball Game" over WGN cable channel. Unfortunately, I didn't raise my eldest son right—he's a Cubbie fan!

So many of the familiar places no longer exist on the cultural landscape of my home turf. Mt. Gilead Church continually lost members as folks moved to town. It was torn down about fifteen years ago and on its site stands the Henry County Foxhunter's Association pavilion. They gather there on the weekends to visit, eat, and listen to the hounds bay on the trail. Bronaugh School was razed several years ago after it was consolidated into the Calhoun School District. All that's left is the old coal shed and the privy. I still recall Mrs. Jessie (one of the Eaton girls), our teacher, trudging to that old coal house to bring in the needed fuel to stoke the furnace on those chilly Ozark mornings.

Thrush General Store is now a shell. Charley and Violet are gone—he died from a heart attack a few years back and she recently passed away in a rest home where Alzheimer's disease took its toll. Willard went on to M.U. Law School and is now assistant D.A. for Jackson County (Kansas City), and Joann works in a local bank.

Went by Tightwad over the last spring break. It's had a population explosion—latest Missouri highway map lists it at fifty-six—partially due to the Truman Lake traffic that passes by on Highway 7. Tightwad now boasts having the Bank of Tightwad (written up in the *Wall Street Journal* and Kansas City *Star* when it opened its doors about five years ago). Seems everybody wanted to open up an account so they could have checks bearing "Bank of Tightwad" on them. Also has the Tightwad Opry, a country music show to entice those city slickers to listen to some Ozark hillbilly music on the weekends while they're boating and fishing in the Truman Lake area. But the Tightwad baseball field is gone—some would call it "progress"— having been replaced by the Linger Longer Cafe, which specializes in Ozark BBQ.

Finally, the cow pasture field is gone. Dad sold out to "the Corps" (U.S. Army Corps of Engineers) in 1970 when they dammed the Osage River to make the Harry S. Truman Lake. The cattle had eventually worn down the backstop—it made a perfect place for them to scratch their backs. Our ball field is now a wildlife refuge for those hunters who come from Kansas City. Deer and quail now roam where the cattle once did. Minor Creek, where we used to swim after the Sunday afternoon games, is today a fisherman's paradise. And my cow pasture coach is gone. Died a couple of years ago from leukemia. The doctors say it was from overexposure to DDT, that banned pesticide he once used to spray those cattle who grazed over our ball field.

As I write this piece, it's springtime and my baseball juices are beginning to awaken after a long, cold winter of "hot stove" chats and baseball withdrawal. It's the time of year when I begin to scour the newsstands for baseball magazines, renew my subscription to *The Sporting News* and *Redbird Review*, take my youngest son to baseball card shows that I observe with more than passing interest, and lock in my car radio to WBBZ (Ponca City, Oklahoma), which has carried the Cardinal games for thirty-two consecutive years. Living in Oklahoma is not all bad. I get back to St. Louis once in a while for a game. I took my bride there for our honeymoon—and two Cardinals games. More recently I returned with my two teenage boys to indoctrinate them to "big league" baseball.

But the visits to home are not the same. The days of cow pasture baseball in the Missouri hills are only memories—geographers would call them place images. But those images of that folk sport place are as vivid, clear, and unfaded as if they had happened yesterday. The gratification and appreciation of those sport experiences on the cow pasture field of thirty-five years ago still live with me today—it has become my field of dreams.

## Notes

1. Karl B. Raitz, "Perception of Sport Landscapes and Gratification in the Sport Experience," *Sport Place: An International Journal of Sports Geography* 1 (1987): 14.

2. John F. Rooney, Jr., *A Geography of American Sport: From Cabin Creek to Anaheim* (Reading, Mass.: Addison-Wesley, 1974), 16.

3. Rooney, *A Geography of American Sport*, 8.

# Part V: Folk Religion and Cemeteries

Folklife scholar Don Yoder has defined folk religion as "unofficial religion," a spiritual experience that exists separate from the theological and liturgical religion of the mainline established churches. It lies at the opposite end of mainline denominations that are characterized by formal administrative structures, a professionally trained clergy, and a systemized complex of dogma and doctrine. Their worship services are highly structured and follow liturgical patterns associated with the seasons of the religious year.

Folk religion is at the other end of the religious spectrum. It is comprised of religious groups in which oral tradition and customary example play a much more important role. These churches are often unaffiliated with a national organization and tend to be led by lay ministers whose preparation for their vocation is by personal spiritual experience rather than a formal religious education. The worship services are informal and do not follow a predictable liturgy printed in a service book. Moreover, their services, often led by charismatic personalities, follow a traditional pattern of hymn-singing accompanied by a variety of musical instruments (often tambourines, guitars, and drums are used), exhortation, testimonials, glossolalia (speaking in tongues), and ecstatic movements of believers filled with the spirit. Finally, the services are often characterized with scriptural literalism, the rhythmic chant of the preacher, and a highly charged emotional atmosphere.

Folk religion is another nonmaterial element of folklife, while folk cemeteries are visible elements of material culture. Folk religion as well as folk cemeteries are folklife traits that reveal a highly regionalized character. For example, the Upland South folk cemetery discussed in chapter 16 is a folklife trait that helps delineate the Upland South as a distinctive *folklife region*. As a unique type of burial ground widely dispersed across the Upland South, it is characterized by hilltop location, scraped ground, mounded graves, east-west grave orientation, creative decorations, preferred species of vegetation, the use of graveshelters, and cults of piety (an organized event to commemorate the deceased).

The *origin and diffusion* of many of these Upland South folk cemetery characteristics can be traced to European origins, especially the northwestern and Mediterranean areas. Burial customs of European origin include the mounding of graves, the use of shells, the use of gravestones, and the use of evergreens for vegetation.

In terms of the *folklife integration* theme, the Amish in chapter 15 as a folk religious group have retained a diet of traditional foodways, including shoo-fly pie, chow-chow, and green tomato pie. Additionally, the Amish serve as examples for another intermixing of folklife traits—religion and music. Music in the Amish service is entirely a cappela because musical instruments are considered ostentatious and contrary to the spirit of humility. Moreover, the Amish have adhered faithfully to the singing of sixteenth-century hymns from the *Ausbund*, a hymnbook that appears as poetry without musical notations.

The Amish also clearly demonstrate the *folklife ecology* theme, especially in their use of soils. For the Amish, soil holds a spiritual significance (Genesis 2:15) because they believe that care of the soil is on behalf of God (Psalms 24) and to damage the earth is to disregard God's calling.

Finally, the Navajo traditional burial practices provide an exceptional example of a folklife trait's impact on shaping the *folk landscape* (chapter 17). The Navajo grave was often a rock crevice or gully and was covered by a high mound of earth that included rocks, branches, and poles. Traditionally, some of the deceased's favorite possessions were buried with the body, and food and water were placed by the grave. In some cases, the deceased's saddle was slashed and left on top of the burial mound. Finally, broken dishes were placed on top of the graves to serve as a marker, as no gravestones were used.

Many practices and customs associated with folk religion remain intact, including the old-style rhythmic-inspired preaching found in folk churches, but also among "televangelists," traditional "Decoration Day" services honoring the graves of the dead, and sacred ordinances (baptism by triple immersion, foot washing, and fire and snake handling). Folk religion has proved a tough and enduring expression of tradition in the midst of the modern world.

# 15

# The Amish and Their Land

## *Maurice A. Mook and John A. Hostetler*

The Old Order Amish people have been the subject of newspaper and magazine articles for half a century, but their way of life and the religious beliefs on which they base their life are still little known and still less well understood. During recent years, their beliefs, attitudes, and customs have been less distorted, leered at, and carpingly criticized than formerly. But the group is still usually presented to us as a picturesque people, practicing an economy and living a social life doomed to extinction in the modern world. They have been, however, a part of our history for nearly three hundred years and have been a steadily increasing group since their arrival in America.

It will be our purpose here to present these people as realistically as possible, and to treat their farming practices and manner of living matter-of-factly as another variant of modern rural America. In order to do this, the Old Order Amish of the Kishacoquillas Valley, in central Pennsylvania, are selected for description. Fortunately they call their valley "Big Valley," a phrase we too may accept as more descriptive, if less euphonious, than the Indian appellation.

The Amish originated in Europe in the late seventeenth century as a religious group that withdrew from the Anabaptists, or Swiss Brethren (now known as Mennonites), who had separated from the Zwinglian Church, which had earlier split from the Catholic Church. They were an extreme left-wing offshoot of the Protestant Reformation, believing that the reformers had not gone far enough in divesting the Christian Church of features

Reprinted by permission from *Landscape* 6 (1957): 21–29.

that had developed since the time of Christ and the Apostles. They were thus reformers of the Reformation.

They were politically also a divergent group, adamantly insisting upon the principle of strict separation of church and state. They were also pacifistic, as were other schismatic sects that split from state-established churches in central Europe in the sixteenth and seventeenth centuries.

From the standpoint of established churches, whether Catholic or Protestant, these people and their forebears were heretics, and from the standpoint of the state they were not good citizens. They were therefore severely persecuted by both the church and the state. Instead of eliminating them, persecution spread the group from their origin in Switzerland to Alsace and the Palatinate. Dispossession of their property, political oppression, and religious persecution made them soft prospects for William Penn, who offered his Sylvania as a haven and a refuge for such Europeans. From the early eighteenth century to the Revolutionary War, from four to five hundred Amish people, coming both individually and in family groups, migrated to Pennsylvania through the port of Philadelphia.

They first settled in present Berks, Chester, and Lancaster counties in southeastern Pennsylvania. Later in the century some joined the trans-Alleghenian migration, establishing a colony in present Somerset County in southwestern Pennsylvania in 1767, and arriving in Big Valley, in present Mifflin County, in the early 1790s. These three areas of Pennsylvania—southeastern, central, and southwestern—have been continuously occupied by Amish peoples since the eighteenth century, where their communities remain the largest, as well as oldest, sectarian settlements in the state at the present time.

There are at present eight other Amish colonies in Pennsylvania, all established since 1800, six of them during the past several years. Their largest present settlements are in eastern Ohio and northern Indiana, with the "mother colony" in southeastern Pennsylvania their oldest, richest, and third largest New World community. They no longer exist as a separate people in Europe, having there coalesced with Mennonites or joined other churches. In America, however, they now inhabit some twenty states of the United States and also a province of Canada. There are now more Amish churches, more Amish communities, and more individual members of these churches and communities than ever before in the two and a half centuries of their New World history. Due to their large families, and in spite of the fact that they never proselytize, they have been steadily growing in numbers, and there are currently no signs of decrease in their rate of growth.

The religious beliefs of the Amish so pervasively permeate their economic and social life that their communities are among the best examples of "sectarian societies" in the Western world. Each aspect of their life is so determined by basic beliefs that it is impossible to understand their farming practices and economic life, or any other part of their culture, without a knowledge of their religion.

Among their most important religious principles are the following:

1. They are "primitive Christians," which means to them that both work and worship would be plain and simple, as in the days of early Christianity.

2. Life in all its principles should be four-squarely based upon the Bible. By this Bible standard, if a thing is scriptural it is good, and if it is nonscriptural it is bad. They assiduously search their German Bible for those verses that charter their customs and vindicate their lifeways. Their outlook is fundamentalist and they interpret the Bible literally.

3. One of the Bible's most fundamental teachings, as they see it, is "be not conformed to this world" (Romans 12:2). They emphasize that they should be "a peculiar people" (Titus 2:14), "not unequally yoked together with unbelievers" (II Corinthians 6:14). They see nonconformity to the world, separation from it, and the principle of the "unequal yoke" as three separate principles, which we shall here treat as a single emphasis. This explains their policy of strict social separation from others; their "clannishness," as some of their neighbors call it; and their objection to joining organizations other than their own church. It is also the basis of their plain clothes, their long hair, their rejection of automobiles and electricity, their use of the Pennsylvania German dialect in everyday speech, their practice of worshiping in homes and barns rather than in "church houses"; and of worshiping every other Sunday, instead of once a week as "English" do. ("English" is an Amish term for non-Amish, irrespective of nationality or race.) These and dozens of other practices, regardless of their historic origin, are now regarded by them as marks of their nonconformity to, and as symbols of their separation from, the world.

4. Their belief that the church should be independent of the state and that warfare is incontrovertibly un-Christian and unscriptural has been clung to by the Amish more consistently than by most peace churches. In this connection, and characteristically, they emphasize New Testament rather than Old Testament teaching. They feel that government is necessary, but worldly and essentially evil, so their attitude is that the less they have to do with it the better off they are. This leads to their opposition to holding public office and results in political apathy. However, they maintain their registration as voters, so they may vote if a local issue (such as roads or schools) that affects them demands their participation; otherwise they take little interest in government or politics.

They pay their taxes, though they know that much government revenue goes for military preparedness. They are law-abiding, except where laws conflict with their religious principles. They pay taxes for the support of public schools, although they will not permit their children to attend public school beyond the eighth grade. They employ lawyers in civil matters, but never carry criminal cases to our courts of law. They claim that they go to jail "for conscience rather than for crime." They refuse to fight, and some even refuse to participate in special projects for noncombatants, for this would throw them into association with non-Amish people and thus violate their principles of separation and the unequal yoke. During wartime they do not regard their farming as a productive contribution to the war effort, and, therefore, see no inconsistency in accepting agricultural deferment.

All of the foregoing are testimonies of the Amish as a corporate group; there are, of course, individual deviations from their corporate principles. For example, Amish young men occasionally volunteer for military service; strictly, however, they are not yet Amish, for they have not yet joined the church. They are subject to the draft in their late teens, but they usually join church in their early twenties. There were undoubtedly fewer deviations from the peace principle among the Amish during our two most recent wars than among most nonresistant churches.

5. A fifth basic belief is that the church must be kept pure, and this is done by both "ordnung" and "meidung." Ordnung are rules designed to govern the conduct of church members, and meidung is the avoidance or shunning practice by which the church controls its errant members. The severity of the meidung varies among Amish congregations, but, in general, if a man is in the meidung he is not only excommunicated from his church, but is shunned in domestic and community relations by his former fellow communicants. In extreme cases, his wife may refuse to sleep with him; neither she nor their children are permitted to eat with him (for St. Paul said "with such do not eat," I Corinthians 5:11); they may do good turns for him but may receive no favors, goods, or services from him. He is, as has been indelicately stated, "on ice at home and in hot water in the community."

With the strictest congregations the ban is for life, or until the excommunicated one "confesses fault" before the assembled members, gives evidence of his penitence, and promises to mend his ways. The case is then considered by all members of the church at a meeting following a regular Sunday worship service. If he is forgiven, he is returned to the fellowship of the church; but if he continues under the ban he might as well "cut his hair," "go English" (both are Amish phrases), give up his plain clothes, leave the farm, and lose himself in the English world. While there are no data on the number of "meidunged" members of Amish congregations, there is adequate evidence as to the efficiency of the practice as an agency by which nonconformity and separation are maintained in Amish society.

6. A motivation of most interest in the present connection is the firm conviction of the Amish people that to assure their persistence as nonconforming, separate, and nonresistant people, they *"must"* maintain a strictly rural way of life. Here again they find Biblical bases for their adamant rurality: were not the cities of Sodom and Gomorrah noted for their sinfulness? Did not God interfere with plans for the building of the first city? Was not Christ Himself crucified in a city? Did not Judah and Israel dwell safely with "every man under his vine and under his fig tree"? Moreover, farming is not only the work and life the Amish people know best; it is the only way of life they have ever known. They also are convinced that when their children turn cityward they will be lost to disbelief.

Therefore, the church requires that every able-bodied man shall farm, or pursue an occupation closely related to farming in a rural environment. Every girl is asked when she joins church if she is willing to be a farmer's wife, and a preacher's wife, if need be. She will be married soon after joining church and she may have to be a preacher's wife, for their ministers are chosen by lot, and anyone's husband may be "hit by the lot," as the Amish phrase has it. There are no full-time nonfarming specialists among the Amish, save for a few carpenters, perhaps a stone mason, a blacksmith, or a harness-maker in each local community; and in smaller communities even these are part-time occupations. Even their bishops, preachers, and deacons—all of whom serve without pay—are full-time farmers, and should be good ones.

Living in cities or large towns is proscribed by the church. Amish farmers do not even retire to rural towns, as is elsewhere the practice in rural America. The farmer and his wife retire to a separate small house on the family farm, or to an apartment of separate rooms in the large house on the farm. Here the old folks have their privacy, yet with many of their married children living near them on neighboring farms. Such retired couples may have a horse and buggy, a small vegetable garden, a cow, and some chickens; and their children see to it that they are sustained and in comfort "until death do them part." The "grossdawdy (or grossmutter) house" for retired old people is one of the most enviable institutions of the Amish people.

Although they are but one of several "plain church" groups in rural Pennsylvania, the Amish have had more than their share of the exuberant publicity recently accorded the Plain People. In the 1950s, they were the subjects of a popular Broadway musical show—the tuneful and amusing, but ethnologically atrociously inaccurate "Plain and Fancy." Three novels have fictionalized their life; a half-dozen juvenile books have presented Amish children for "English" children; two teenage books deal with their culture; and they have been the subject of a series of popular pamphlets that are sold in bookstores, drugstores, tobacco shops, railroad stations, bus terminals, and turnpike rest stations extending from Philadelphia to the Middle West. These, on the whole, sympathetic, although patronizing, treatments extol Amish virtues and give the impression that they are the best farmers in America. The Lancaster County Amish, who are usually the subjects of these eulogies, are, indeed, among the most successful farmers of our eastern states. They are atypical of the Amish in other aspects of their culture. The Lancaster County Amish, for example, are commercial farmers who intensively cultivate a few cash crops, such as tobacco and tomatoes, on farms that average less than fifty acres in size. The Big Valley Amish of Mifflin County, on the other hand, practice general family-type farming, with some attention to dairying, on farms of larger size. For this reason, also, the Big Valley Amish are here chosen as a more typical group of this interesting people.

Big Valley, located not more than forty miles from the geographical center of Pennsylvania, extends northeasterly for some thirty-five miles and averages four miles in width. The rich farmlands of the valley are here and there interspersed with a gently sloping hill. Pride is supposed to be a sin to the Amish people, but they are proud of their valley. It is beautifully located, its soil is rich, and it has been their home since 1790. And home to them is much more than a mere physical fact. One of them once said that "it looks as though God carved that valley out of the mountains and made it for the enjoyment and employment of man." On top of Stone Mountain an Amishman once claimed that, as he looked over the valley, he was impressed with three ideas—"order, sufficiency, and peace." These are three qualities in high esteem among these people, and they realize that Big Valley has been of real assistance to them in their quest of their utopia.

The valley floor is a rich limestone plain, as is also eastern Lancaster County, the home of the better-known Pennsylvania Amish settlement. There is a saying that an Amishman "can smell limestone for a hundred miles." They prefer limestone soil, but as they have had to disperse across the eastern and middle western states in search of more land for more farms, they have not always been able to obtain it. They are locally well known, however, for their maintenance of the fertility of good soil and for their improvement of poor soil. This they do by rotating crops, by the use of legume crops, and by generous applications of fertilizer.

They now use commercial fertilizers. They have long used lime, but their main reliance is upon manure. Most Amish churches prohibit the use of tractors in the field (or the use of any rubber-tired vehicle on the farm), and an Amish rationalization of this is that "tractors make no manure" (fig. 15.1). Not the least value of the former Amish practice of steer fattening, and of their present emphasis on the stall feeding of stock, is that the manure is not spread over pastures, but remains at hand to be put on the right field at the right time.

According to some agricultural historians, Pennsylvania German farmers were the first to introduce crop rotation in this country. As a Pennsylvania German people, the Amish are careful to rotate crops and have always done so, as far as the record goes. In Big Valley, the rotation is a four- to six-year cycle; clover mixed with timothy, or alfalfa for one to several years, followed in order by corn, oats, and wheat. The first few years of the cycle may vary: alfalfa may be planted for several years, to build up nitrogen in the soil, or clover with a little timothy may be planted in the fall, followed by clover and alfalfa in the spring. Corn may be planted for two years, the second year for ensilage, which is then followed with oats and wheat. Unlike the pattern among the Amish of Lancaster County where farming has been commercialized, Big Valley crops are not grown primarily for a cash return. Although no longer as self-sufficient as formerly, the Amish of Big Valley try to grow what they eat and eat what they grow. Here an Amish farmer is considered a poor farmer if he sells feed crops. They sell peas, beans, and sweet corn to a local cannery, but the main emphasis is on food for the farmer's family and food for his stock.

In this connection, the vegetable garden is to be neither ignored nor

Fig. 15.1. Teams of Horses in an Amish Field

neglected. Gardening is women's and children's work, although the man will start the garden by spading the plot. A large and varied garden is the housewife's pride and joy, and accordingly it is never inconspicuously placed out behind or beside the barn, but is right up near, even in front of, the house, where it will be handy for the womenfolk and easy for all to see. Gardens are watched with much interest by all members of the Amish community. For one thing, a good garden is a source of prestige for the women of the house. It is also much prized as a good place to teach growing children the value of work.

Another feature of the Big Valley Amish farm as a productive unit is the persistence of the orchard. While most Pennsylvania farmers have given fruitgrowing over to commercial orchardists, the Big Valley Amish farmer still produces apples, peaches, pears, and cherries. Whereas the Lancaster County Amish have reduced their pastures, wood lots and orchards, in order to increase the acreage devoted to cash-commercial drops, the Big Valley Amish have resisted this tendency. Big Valley Amish cellars are still well stocked with jars of homegrown canned goods, both fruits and vegetables, and fall canning is one of the women's busiest seasons. Apples and potatoes are also stored for the winter, for potatoes are consumed in quantity and there must be plenty of apples for apple butter and for "schnitz" and pies, both of which are great favorites among the Amish for dinner after preaching and for other special occasions.

The principal cash "crop" of the Big Valley Amish is fluid milk. The "Reedsville Cheese House—Swiss Cheese Our Specialty" is Amish owned and operated, with its cheese-maker imported from Switzerland. (Amish cheese plants are a characteristic feature of their more conservative communities in the United States.) When the Amish sell their milk to their own plant, they do no have to deliver their product on Sunday, and moreover, they do not violate their principle of not being "yoked" in an economic transaction with the "English." Their Sunday milk is consumed by the family and churned into butter. Buttermilk is thus a recurrently available drink, whether one likes it or not.

An essential aspect of the Amish effort to make their rural life as self-sufficient as possible is their cooperation and mutual aid activities. This is also a refreshing contrast to the strife and competition so often evident in the livelihood activities of other Americans. Amishmen are never on the relief roles of our welfare and assistance agencies. If an Amish family comes to grief through crop failure, disease among stock, a barn burning, individual illness, or any other "act of God," relatives, neighbors, even all the members of the congregational community come to the rescue. One of the main functions of the deacon of the church—whose title is "Armen Diener (minister to the poor)"—is to see that those in need receive help when they need it. Twice a year, or more often if need be, the members of the church contribute to the Armen Dieners' fund—a fund that is never audited for the members of the church have full confidence in their custodian. Families also help each other during harvesting, silo-filling, when a family moves from one community or church district to another, and on all occasions when a group larger than the family itself is needed to get work done with dispatch. If a person is sick or when death visits a family, neighbors, relatives, and friends help so that all farm work and housekeeping duties go on uninterruptedly.

The Amish do not believe in life or property insurance, for such, they feel, might be an attempt to thwart the will of God. Buying insurance from an outside source would also violate the principle of the unequal yoke. For the former reason they also oppose the use of lightning rods on the house or barn. If a barn burns, many of the members of the community, as well as members of neighboring or even remotely removed Amish communities, converge on the site to raise a barn in a day. Collections are taken, even members may be assessed, roughly according to one's own property evaluation, for contributions toward buying the materials for a new barn. These materials must all be at hand, properly prepared and orderly arranged, for a barn-raising "frolic." The frolic is a social festivity, as well as a productive enterprise: a large meal is served and there is opportunity for their principal recreational activity—visiting—on such occasions. Not only do the men cooperate in raising the structure, but the women and girls of the congregation and of "fellowshiping" congregations assist in providing, preparing, and serving the collective meal at these large work parties.

Other examples of "frolics" are quilting and sewing bees, corn-husking bees, butchering, apple-butter boiling, apple "schnitzing" parties, threshing, and log and wood cutting. Some of these are for men, some for women, some for children, and others are occasions when all work together. Such occasions necessitate less work and draw fewer people in cooperation than a barn raising, but they show the same combination of work and conviviality. In this connection, it is of interest that the Pennsylvania "Dutch" (German) dialect of the Amish contains no word that precisely expresses the concept of cooperation; the nearest synonym is "frolic," deriving from the German *fröhlich*, meaning gay, jolly, playful. Although it may be averred that some of these festivities are primarily recreational or social in nature, usually a large amount of work is accomplished and sometimes, as at a barn raising, an astounding amount of labor goes into the collective effort. It would be difficult, indeed, to separate the economic and social aspects of these collective enterprises.

The Amish farm is also distinctive in certain material cultural properties. Although they much prefer to live close together, non-Amish farms often adjoin those owned by members of the sect. There are, in fact, few examples of all-Amish rural communities in the United States; even in Big Valley, where the Amish have been buying farms for a century and a half, the juxtaposition of Amish and non-Amish farms is a characteristic distribution. It is possible, however, to identify an Amish homestead by certain visible characteristics; and in some places, as in Big Valley, it is possible to determine the particular church or congregation to which an Amish family belongs by such characteristics as whether the barn is painted, how the roof projects over the gable end of the house, and the color of buggy tops. For example, the dwellings of the most conservative Amish people in the Valley (the so-called Nebraska Amish) have roofs that project very little beyond the gable ends of the house; also their buggy tops are white, while the buggy tops of another church are yellow, and those of two other churches are black (in Lancaster County they are gray). Sectarian variation is thus seen not only in beliefs, but extends to houses, barns, buggies, clothing, and other material properties.

Apart from cultural variations within the group, Amish farms in general show certain characteristics that easily distinguish them from those of the non-Amish. Electric wires do not extend from the road to an Amish house or barn (unless the farm is rented from English owners); Amish barns are larger than those of most non-Amish owners; houses are also larger and less architecturally compact, or there may be two dwellings on the farm; fences near the house and barn are whitewashed, but gates are painted a solid color, usually red (the "blue gate" legend of the English, to whom the blue gate is a sign of a marriageable Amish daughter on the farm, is a myth); and there are other architectural and ecological marks of peculiarity. It should be noted that if the farm is rented from an English owner, its buildings and improvements will be English, not Amish. It is necessary to say this, because there is a high incidence of tenancy among Amish farmers. Each aspires to own his own farm, for ownership is the top rung in the Amish agricultural ladder. This is impossible for all, however, especially inasmuch as land prices increase in areas long occupied by large Amish communities. Providing a suitable farm for all newly married Amish young people is one of their most persistent and still unsolved economic problems.

All of the Pennsylvania Amish, and most Amish elsewhere, are "Pennsylvania German" in ethnic affiliation (although less than 5 percent of Pennsylvania Germans are Amish or otherwise sectarian), and, as such, they brought to America a Swiss and Palatine-German cultural heritage. They have also clung to this heritage more tenaciously than most nonsectarian

Pennsylvania Germans. They thus retain certain nonmaterial cultural characteristics, such as the use of German Bibles and German hymnals in their worship services; and also certain material cultural traits, such as the Swiss "bank barns," which were characteristic of the Pennsylvania German "church people" (Lutheran and Reformed, largely) a hundred years ago. Evidence of this is seen in every aspect of life: thus, a century ago Pennsylvania Germans played the game of "corner ball," and the Amish still play it; most persons of Pennsylvania German derivation now speak English in the home, but the Amish still use the dialect; nonsectarian Pennsylvania Germans now have automobiles, tractors, and electricity, whereas the Amish reject these. These Amish characteristics are not only now signs of their separation from the modern world, but they are also ties linking them to their culture-historical past. In fact, one of their present sanctions, aside from the scriptural sanction, is the group's appeal to its own history. A characteristic Amish attitude is "If it's old it's good, but if it's new it's bad." This attitude is not, of course, peculiarly Amish, but the extent to which it motivates their life is cardinally characteristic.

One of the most obvious survivals of their material culture-historical past is their Swiss-German "bank barn." These barns are two-story structures built near a bank of ground, or if built on level land, an incline or "bank" of earth is built to lead to the second-story barn floor. Teams can thus easily pull the hayrack or wagon onto the barn floor. The lower story supplies stalls for livestock; the upper story consists of hay and straw mows, granary rooms, and the central floor is used, if necessary, for the storage of farm machinery and other equipment. The second-story barn floor is put to two additional uses by the Amish: here teenagers have their occasional barn-floor dances and "play parties" and here also worship service is held in the summer when the warmer weather makes this possible. Funerals are also sometimes held on the barn floor, especially when the house is too small to accommodate the expected congregation. (An Amish funeral is a worship service, differing from their regular service in that hymns are not sung—sometimes they are read, rather than sung—and the sermons eulogize the deceased, if this is possible, or at least moralistically admonish the relatives as well as others in attendance. English friends often attend these services; the preacher is often a visiting bishop; and the occasion is seized for emphasizing the Amish tenets of nonconformity to and separation from the world.)

When funerals and other worship services are held in the barn, the Amish farmer and his sons spend several days in thoroughly cleaning the barn and it contents: stalls will be whitewashed; stables cleaned; manure hauled away; the barn floor swept; everything put in its place; harness cleaned, greased, and repaired; clean straw spread over the barnyard; the manure pile cut square and covered with straw, if it is not hauled away; horses and cows curried and all barn-housed livestock thoroughly cleaned. For orderliness and cleanliness are marks of a good Amish farmer, and male visitors examine the barn as meticulously as an Amish housewife inspects her host's home.

Another architectural feature of the Swiss barn is the "forebay," also called the overshot or overhang. Usually the south or sunnyside of the barn is constructed so that the second story projects several feet over the lower story. The forebay is on the opposite side of the barn from the bank that leads to the barn floor. The overhung enclosure is often paved with flat stones, more recently with concrete. This outdoor but protected area is a pleasant place for repairing harness, wagons, buggies, and various types of farm machinery. In the spring and fall, it is also a favorite gathering place for the men and boys on Sunday mornings as they await the beginning of the worship service.

When the Amish couples arrive in their buggies for the worship service, the womenfolk go directly into the house (fig.15.2). The men and boys drive the buggy toward the barn, where the sons of the host place the buggy in a convenient place and put the horse in the barn. The menfolk then gather at the forebay, where they stand under the projecting second story until the ministers appear. The bishop then kisses the preachers and the deacon, after which the men proceed to the service, approximately in the order of their age. Boys are permitted to remain at the barn until the second

Fig. 15.2. Amish Buggies (Two Horses Are Never Used Because This Would Be Both Unnecessary and "Proudful")

hymn begins, at which time they must enter "church" and take their places on the backless homemade wooden benches. In the service the sexes sit separately, which was, of course, formerly the custom in churches, and which custom survives among this sect. The seating arrangement for each sex is also affected by age. A mark of the patriarchal organization of Amish society is that the men sit in front, with the women behind them, or even in a separate room more removed from the ministers than the men. Another mark of their patriarchalism is that the ministers are always men. Women may nominate candidates for the "lot," from which the preacher or deacon is selected; but the nominees must be men.

All horses are placed in the barn during the worship service. The eastern Amish protect their livestock whenever possible, and are shocked at what they consider the neglectful practice of midwestern and farwestern farmers pasturing and range feeding stock without providing adequate shelter. Amish barns must thus be large in order to house all larger livestock; Amishmen also like barn floors large enough to accommodate an entire congregation when "preaching" is held on the barn floor. They also have large crops to be stored in the barn, for theirs are not cash-crops to be sold, but feed crops to be stored until consumed on the premises. They have also lagged somewhat in adopting the practice of baling hay and straw, and when these are stored loose in mows, one must have, of course, more space. Even barns built in Big Valley since baling has been introduced have been larger than necessary, now that large storage space is not so essential. The force of tradition is also seen in the arrangement of barn facilities, especially in the lower story. Agricultural economists have called their barns "inefficiently planned," but this is small concern to an Amishman with a family-ful of sons who help him do the chores. Boys must be kept out of mischief, they say, and the best way to do this is to provide them with work to do.

Amish barns in Big Valley are usually painted red; white paint, however, is gradually being introduced. The conservative "Nebraska" Amish of Big Valley do not paint their barns (nor their houses) at all. Unlike nonsectarian Pennsylvania German farmers, the Amish never decorate their barns with painted designs. Their barns thus lack the "hex signs," which have recently enjoyed the apoplectic approval of certain superstition-struck commentators impressed with the "quaintness" of Pennsylvania German culture. If an Amishman were to buy a barn with hex signs on it, he probably would not bother to eradicate them with fresh paint; he would wait until the barn needed repainting, and then refrain from the frivolity of reproducing such signs.

Another conspicuous feature of rural Amish material culture is the large size of their houses. If a farm has a small dwelling, it will be added to, or a second structure will be built. Two houses associated with a large barn are commonly found, although the more usual practice is to build additions to the dwelling already on the property. The second, usually smaller, house is known both as the "tenant house" and as the "grossdawdy" or "grossmutter" house, and its twofold purpose is revealed by these names. It is occupied by a newly married son or daughter with his or her spouse, until they become established on a farm of their own. It is also the unit to which parents retire when their last (usually youngest) son or daughter marries, with the newlyweds assuming operation of the family farm. The Amish thus follow an ultimogeniture or "junior right" (as distinguished from a primogeniture) pattern of inheritance: as older children marry they acquire farms of their own, with the last-to-marry child, his mate, and eventually his own large family, inheriting occupancy of the family homestead. The parents then retire to the grossdawdy house, probably earlier in age than is generally true for non-Amish-American farmers.

Three factors account for the large size of Amish houses: the separate apartment (in lieu of a second dwelling) for the retired couple, the fact that Amish families are considerably larger than non-Amish rural families, and because an Amish family aspires to a house large enough to accommodate preaching services in the home. When the local congregation grows too large to gather in available Amish homes, the church (by which the body of believers is always meant, for they lack "church houses," as they call them) is divided into two districts, so that the now smaller worshiping groups can meet in the homes of members. The division is on a geographical basis, made necessary also by their horse-and-buggy transportation, for no family should have to drive too far to preaching. One Amish church in Big Valley has for some years been divided into three districts for the same reasons; and the same is true elsewhere in larger Amish communities in Lancaster County, Pennsylvania; and in Ohio, Indiana, and Iowa.

Several features of their home interiors are also affected by their at-home preaching practice. Thus, doors between downstairs rooms are wide so they may be swung open, or even removed from their hinges, so that all worshipers may see and hear the ministers. Some Pennsylvania Amish homes have removable panels in the walls of downstairs rooms, which are taken out for worship service so the preachers may be better heard. In order to conserve space, downstairs halls and closets are often lacking in Amish homes; hats, coats and shawls (Amish women wear shawls, rather than coats) are hung on pegs, nails, and hooks conveniently placed for this purpose.

Amish homes are also necessarily large because of the need they feel for two kitchens, one for winter and another for summer use. Both of these are large, for they serve the dual purpose of dining room and living room for

the large families. Attached to the summer kitchen is a woodshed, and often a room for the family bake-oven. There is also a "sitting room" for the accommodation of visitors: it is also called the "living room," although the kitchen shares in serving this purpose. There is sometimes a downstairs bedroom, usually used by an older relative who may live with the family. Regardless of how large the family may be, a spare bedroom—the "good room," they call it—is available for the accommodation of frequent winter visitors. Visiting may fairly be called the main recreational activity of the Amish; it goes on throughout the year, but particularly during the winter months, when farm work is less demanding. The large families of the Amish, the far-flung distribution of the kinship group, and the emphasis placed on the bond of kinship have built up and deeply ingrained the visiting pattern as a highly evaluated aspect of their social life.

Plainness prevails in the house furnishings, as in other aspects of Amish life. Walls are painted in solid colors or have wallpaper of simple design. Due to the sect's disapproval of living likenesses and "graven images," family photographs are lacking, as are also the bric-a-brac so often characteristic of American lower- and middle-class households. Although a conservative rural people, Amish homes lack the old-time family photograph album. To intentionally and willfully pose for a photograph would subject the culprit to meidung in some Amish churches. The home is also conspicuously lacking in nonreligious books and periodical literature.

All conservative Amish homes lack central heating systems, and most lack bathrooms. A few Big Valley homes now have the latter, with running water supplied by gravity from surrounding mountain springs. If an Amish farmer were to buy an English farmhouse equipped with a furnace and wired for electricity, he would remove these facilities. If he were to rent a farm from an English owner, he would remove the light bulbs and refrain from using the furnace. There is, however, one Old Order Amish church in Big Valley whose members have had electric lights for several years and also two years ago accepted automobiles. So far, neighboring Old Order congregations have not done likewise, but these innovations may be portents of the future. When an Amish church adopts these facilities and also builds a meeting house, it then comes to be known in the vicinity (and also to students) as "New Order" or "Church Amish."

The yard surrounding the house is kept clean and well trimmed by the womenfolk—by the mother and her daughters, or by younger sons if daughters are lacking in number (in lieu of daughters, small sons also help their mother in the kitchen). Both the vegetable garden and a large and colorful flower garden, the two often combined, are the pride of the Amish housewife. Tree trunks, stone walls, fences, and small buildings are whitewashed by the men in the summer months. In the immediate vicinity of the dwelling there is a woodshed (if detached from the house), a spring house, a smoke house for the curing of meat, a shelter to contain the bake-oven, the ubiquitous outdoor privy; and farther removed, in the vicinity of the barn, there is a buggy house, an equipment or tool shed, a workshop for the men, one or more chicken houses, range shelters for chickens and pigs, a pigpen, and often a brooder house for raising chicks (which are now usually purchased in quantities from commercial hatcheries). A thirty-year English neighbor of a Pennsylvania Amish community has written that the typical Amish homestead appears like a miniature village. . . . Outbuildings are many, (with) sometimes as many as fifteen or twenty separate structures scattered around the main buildings." The Amish farmer, moreover, usually keeps these buildings well painted and in a good state of repair. Well-tended fields, good crops, well-groomed and well-fed livestock, large barns, commodious houses, strong fences, and neat and substantial outbuildings are the material marks of a successful farmer and a good citizen of Amishland.

Although the casual observer may see Amish culture as a curious compound of conservative customs, more perceptive perspective reveals a people committed to a way of life that may have certain values for non-Amish Americans. For one thing, they may be counted among the best—old-fashioned, one must say—farmers of the nation. A Pennsylvania jurist has reminded us that, in spite of their refusal to fight our wars, and in spite of their eschewal of our higher education, the Amish are "usually out of trouble and should be reckoned among our best citizens." Their own most highly esteemed values are family, faith, and farming— "these three, but the greatest of these" for them is their faith, for it underlies the other two. It is fair to say that all else in life with them is minor and marginal. Their lives are marked, as one of their own group once stated, by a striving for "order, sufficiency, and peace." These they have for us also to strive for. They are, indeed, as they want to be, and they say themselves, "Die Stillen im Lande"—the "quiet ones on the land," who as solid, substantial, successful tillers of the soil have made their unobtrusive contribution among us for now nearly three centuries.

# 16

# The Traditional
# Upland South Cemetery

## Donald G. Jeane

The Upland South folk graveyard is a distinctive type of rural burial ground particularly associated with the dispersed hamlets and scattered farmsteads of upland sections of the southeastern United States (fig. 16.1). In western Louisiana and eastern Texas, this is a well-drained region of second-growth forest, a reminder of the vast virgin pine stands that were encountered by the first settlers and accounted for the popular regional name "piney woods." Settlement in the area began in the late-eighteenth and early-nineteenth centuries, and appears to have been well established by 1850.

The regional landscape is peppered with these rural folk graveyards. Many are now associated with a church or are relatively near one, but many are also found well off major roads in seemingly isolated locations. Some are relic family cemeteries near deserted homesteads. Others appear to be isolated for no apparent reason and are large enough to suggest that they were not intentionally started in an unfrequented place. Many in this category are on roads that have since fallen into disuse, the roadbed so altered by weathering and vegetation that it is recognizable only to the trained eye. Most of the cemeteries in the region predate the construction of churches. Churches were often shared by more than one denomination after being built, but were generally not constructed until circuit riders became frequent in the area or until a particular congregation obtained a permanent minister. The cemeteries are almost always located on high ground, for

Reprinted by permission from *Landscape* 18 (1969): 39–41.

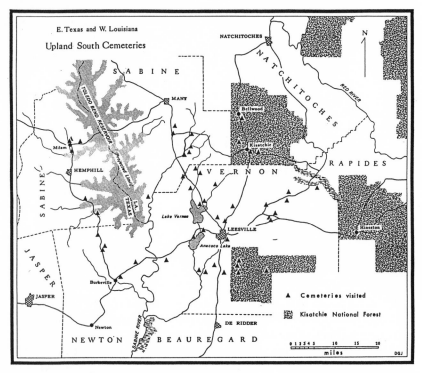

Fig. 16.1. Distribution of Upland South Cemeteries in Western Louisiana and East Texas

drainage. There, one can dig a grave on the day following a heavy rain if need be. In wet weather when the approaches to many of these cemeteries are nearly impassable, the graveyards themselves remain relatively dry.

The most unusual characteristic of the cemeteries in the region is the traditional practice of "scraping" the cemetery, or clearing it of vegetation, and the subsequent mounding of the graves with fresh dirt, gravel, or sand, giving each grave the appearance of a fresh burial. The scraping of the graveyard has traditionally taken on aspects of a group or family ceremony. The participants all bring shovels, hoes, and rakes. The men hoe, mound the graves, and carry away the grass. The women then sweep or rake the cemetery. Formerly, they used brush brooms, usually of dogwood. The women bring food prepared at their homes and there is dinner on the grounds. Many cemeteries still have benches and tables to one side for this purpose. Often someone preaches. Thus, the annual homecomings or graveyard workings serve not only as a means of maintaining the cemetery, but as a social gathering for the area or as a family reunion drawing kin from considerable distance. The original purpose of the practice of mounding is hard to ascertain. One purpose might have been identification. Formerly, according to local accounts, few tombstones were used and graves were often marked only with a piece of wood or a natural unworked stone. Had the graves not been banked, their locations might have been lost if the simple markers had been knocked out of place and the graves covered with grass. Mounding the graves made it possible to find them for repair. A second purpose might have been compensation for natural washing and settling, for when extra cover is applied periodically, there is less chance of an unsightly, open grave occurring during the lapse between graveyard workings. In many cemeteries, a pile of dirt is still located in or near the grave area for the use of persons wishing to repair their kin's burial places in the traditional manner (fig. 16.2).

Some of the graveyards have been roughly divided into old and new sections: the old part is maintained in the traditional manner, but the addition is allowed to grass over and is then mowed. Even if the cemetery has changed to the extent that it is entirely grassed, it is often possible to determine the boundaries of the older section. The grass there tends to be sparse since most of the topsoil necessary for plant growth and nutrition has been scraped off through years of repeated working.

Erosion has become a common problem in all piney-woods burial

Fig. 16.2. Mounded Grave with Shell Decoration

grounds, particularly in the scraped ones on steep slopes. Several methods have been used to combat it—including ridging with sand or earth and placing bricks, stones, and other subjects in contour fashion to catch water and to control runoff.

The family plot marked off within a community burial ground is a recent innovation in the region. Graveyards in this area began as family burial places and spread to include the family as it became enlarged by marriage with other families in the community. Although graves were generally grouped by families, there was no formal demarcation of any kind. As the community grew, land was added and the site came to be used by several families. The more remote the cemetery, the fewer family plots one finds. In the newer graveyards, the plots are marked in a grid pattern and present an orderly appearance; in older cemeteries, the pattern is more nearly random. In some graveyards, the plots are marked only with a stake or a pipe at each corner. Older plots may have a brick-lined perimeter, while more recent ones are surrounded by cinder blocks or even a low concrete wall adorned with a small fence. Some of the older plots have ornate wrought iron fences around them. These usually enclose the plot of a prominent or affluent family and are common in the older burial grounds. Such enclosures may contain as few as one or as many as fifteen graves.

Graves in the Upland South cemeteries are oriented very close to an east-west axis. One informant explained that this orientation was in preparation for the Second Coming of Christ; by burial with feet to the east, the faithful can rise facing the Saviour.

A few of the upland folk cemeteries have burials above ground, a practice more commonly associated with the French of south Louisiana. The dates on the markers show them to be recent in comparison to the rest of the graves, and they are usually at some distance from the core areas of the original graveyards. They were often the mark of affluence. Sometimes a grave is found with a superstructure resembling a crypt, yet with the part above ground filled with stones. These crypts were apparently built at a later date over earlier subterranean burials.

In the folk cemetery, the use of uninscribed wood and stone as grave markers is common. If two carved wooden planks are used, they most often have a rounded top at the head and diamond-shaped top at the foot (fig. 16.3). Unfinished stone markers range from slabs at each end to a form resembling stacked plates. The stone varies in color from black to reddish-brown, and in parts of Arkansas, Texas, and Louisiana is iron rock or a sandstone known locally as "flintrock." The older markers are fast becoming rare because of decay and replacement by more stylish stone monuments. Obelisk markers are not abundant in the traditional cemeteries and are usually attributed to wealthy people. Most, however, seem to be Woodmen of the World monuments. These are widespread and at least one or two can be found in most cemeteries.

Many other styles of grave markers are found in these old burial places, especially the more remote ones. Among them are cast-iron plates fitted with a piece of glass and an engraved sheet of paper giving information about the deceased. Others are made from turpentine cups, from strap-iron in the form of a cross or from ceramic insulators from abandoned turpentine plants. A large amount of petrified wood is also in use as decoration and as grave markers. In many of the older graveyards, homemade tombstones are clearly evidenced by reversed letters, misspelled words, and uneven lines.

In some of the more rural cemeteries, the old tombstones are laid aside, but not destroyed, and are replaced by new granite markers as the residents become able to buy commercial stones. Many older residents of the area claim that the stones are replaced because the new granite markers resist weathering. Many argue the "drippings" from cedar and mimosa cause the old marble to turn black, but old stones can be found that are not near cedar, mimosa, or any other tree, and yet have turned completely black. In a number of cemeteries, the old stones have been painted silver to offset the blackening.

As a general rule, decoration is left to the discretion of the family and, as a result, the variety of decorations is great. Shells are common, some graves have no decoration except the ubiquitous artificial flower (fig. 16.2). Many, however, include such adornments as telephone-line insulators or plastic bleach bottles used to outline the plot and to hold flowers; glass canning jars turned upside down and used as a border or covered with aluminum foil and used as a flower container; and coffee cans, also covered with aluminum foil, used to hold flowers. One grave the author discovered had a drinking glass and a pitcher of water neatly placed upon a flat stone near the monument while another was covered with dishes. Flags are often placed on veterans' graves at Memorial Day. The decorations on children's graves are especially diverse, and include marbles, toy cars, airplanes, light bulbs, metal-tipped vacuum tubes from radios and television sets, and broken pieces of colored glass. Photographs of the dead are coming to be an increasingly common ornamentation. On the older stones, these are black and white or sepia; the newer ones are color prints.

The grave shed, a distinctive decoration thought to have been widespread in former times, is becoming increasingly rare, for new sheds are not being built to replace the ones that decay (fig. 16.4). Frequently, old post holes, buried footings, and remnants of wood around the graves mark the location

Fig. 16.3.  Uninscribed Wooden Grave Markers (Round Top for Head and Diamond Top for Feet)

Fig. 16.4.  Upland South Cemetery Grave Shed

of sheds that have disappeared without being replaced. Generally, the shed is very simple in design, consisting merely of a gabled roof supported by corner posts and a few crossbeams. Some specimens are enclosed with various kinds of siding, ranging from wire to a more elaborated style with scalloped cornice trim, shake roof, and pickets. The exact origin of the shed is an unsolved question. According to local informants, they were built to keep out pigs or other animals that might root up the graves. Some sources state that the Indians practiced a very crude form of shed-building to protect the grave from rain.

Traditionally, the cemeteries were landscaped with cedars, gardenias, and crepe myrtle. As a graveyard expanded, pine and oak of various species in the surrounding woodlands were often left standing and became incorporated in the graveyard planting. Often the original plants survive long after a cemetery is abandoned, and throughout the region, a seemingly wild stand of cedar or crepe myrtle invariably turns out to mark the site of an old graveyard or homesite. Today, planting consists mostly of mimosa, arbor vitae, and ornamental roses and azaleas.

The graveyards are changing. The traditional twice-a-year homecomings are now held only once a year, if at all. The scraped and mounded gravesites with their vertical markers, which gave the old graveyard its austere and distinctive look, are yielding to flat, easily mowed expanses of grass with flat bronze marker plates, a more stylish and contemporary "memorial garden" form in which the cemetery is landscaped and maintained by a hired staff. Indeed, in a few years the old folk graveyard may be only a memory.

# 17

# Modern Navajo Cemeteries

## Stephen C. Jett

The Navajo are an Athapaskan-speaking group whose ancestors migrated from present-day western Canada to the American Southwest about five hundred years ago, where they were heavily influenced by Puebloan cultures.[1] Today, the Navajo are the country's largest reservation-Indian population, occupying an area the size of West Virginia in the states of New Mexico, Arizona, and Utah. Their "traditional" economy came to combine subsistence farming, raising of livestock (especially, goats and sheep), and hunting (the latter becoming obsolescent around the turn of the twentieth century). Today, wage work, public assistance, and arts and crafts are major sources of income.

Navajo burial practices have altered dramatically during and since World War II. The features of contemporary Navajo graveyards derive from Euroamerican models, yet also are to some degree distinctive in terms of the particular forms and combinations of features utilized. Further, they reflect, in part, age-old Athapaskan beliefs and thus are not to be viewed as being as radically different in terms of fundamentals as superficialities might suggest.

### Traditional Navajo Burial Practices

Although the Navajo conception of a soul's afterlife (in Ch'iiditah,[2] "Ghostland") is vague, like other Athapaskan-speaking Indians, traditional Navajos fear ch'iidi: the evil residue or "ghosts" of the dead.[3]

Reprinted by permission from the author and *Material Culture* 28 (1996): 1–23.

Formerly, Navajo burials were individual and often secret, and there were no ceremonies for the soul of the dead, no postmortem extrafamilial observances, and (normally) no group burial grounds.[4] Infant corpses were disposed of on small platforms in trees. The corpse of any older person would be placed in a cliff crevice and covered with rocks to prevent disturbance by scavengers; occasionally placed in a special masonry structure in a cliff shelter; or, more commonly, inhumed, head toward the north, the grave being unmarked or covered by a cairn or a pile of brush to protect from scavengers. Sometimes, the grave would be signaled by an arrangement of poles, and/or by the intentionally broken (ghost-contaminated) shovel and any other tools used, plus certain of the deceased's possessions, such as a sacrificed horse and saddle.[5] In addition to the literal killing of the horse (and, sometimes, sheep), the material possessions would often be "killed"—mutilated—perhaps to allow them to join the deceased but, more explicitly, to discourage theft (in any case, they could not be used by heirs, owing to being ghost-tainted).[6] These physical indications were largely incidental to the burial and warned others away from a ghost-polluted place but were not commemorative in nature.

There was no practice of visiting graves—indeed, they were avoided so as not to interfere with the dead or risk ghost contamination—or of leaving offerings at subsequent times. If a suitable crevice was not available and the ground was too frozen to dig in, the body might be buried beneath the hogan floor; this dwelling would then be sealed and abandoned or burned, as would any hogan where a death occurred (other than of an infant or a senile, wasted old person), owing to ghost fear. But despite such fear, "corpse powder" (for witchcraft) and jewelry buried with the deceased in any of these situations would sometimes be stolen by grave-robbers, mainly (male) "witches," who, through perverted ritual, are immune from ill effects.[7]

## Early Trader and Missionary Burials

As Anglo traders and Christian missionaries came to the reservation beginning in the late-nineteenth century, an increasing number of Navajos turned to them (and sometimes, to government employees) to bury the dead.[8] Yet this change in mortuary practice was less out of admiring imitation of Anglo ways or from burgeoning Christian conviction (by no means all of the burials in mission graveyards were of Christians) than for more traditionally pragmatic reasons. Boards and locally made coffins came to be available through the Bureau of Indian Affairs and the tribal government, and although traditional burials continued to take place, and doubtless still do, coffins early came to be appreciated for their protection of the body from scavengers (being bothered by same could cause ghost problems, and sometimes shipping crates were employed).[9] Of especial importance, if the traders or missionaries did the burying, no Navajo burial party would have to undergo ghost-protection purification rites.[10] Further, interment in a graveyard proximate to the mission afforded better security against grave-robbers.[11] Initially, trader and missionary burials were performed gratis, but today fees are charged by the missionaries (traditional traders are almost a thing of the past).

By 1950, there were twenty-six mainline Protestant and several Catholic missions, and by 1977, there were sixty-two of the former. According to Lamphere, "In the 1960s, most Navajos (in the Sheep Springs, New Mexico, area) died in the hospital; the body was taken to a funeral home where it was embalmed and placed in a casket. Most families arranged for missionaries to bury the deceased."[12]

## Modern Navajo Funerary Practice

Mission burial grounds appear to have had their inception in the 1890s.[13] Cemetery burials began to be widely accepted beginning with World War II, at which time the first commercially made caskets were shipped to the reservation by the armed forces, for the interment of war dead. The trend toward cemetery burials has accelerated since about 1960, and by 1968 there were some forty formal mission and chapter (community) cemeteries in the Navajo Country.[14] Extremely well-attended public gatherings before and during the burial service, employment of morticians, use of expensive commercially manufactured caskets carried by pallbearers, viewing of the deceased, and eulogies in the church, have become common, the long service being followed by a feast. Obituaries are published in the Navajo Times, and graves are often visited and tended indefinitely, with real and plastic flowers being offered. There is a mortuary at Tuba City, Arizona (and probably others elsewhere in the Navajo Country), and there are even a few Navajo funeral directors.[15] Cremations—foreign to traditional Navajo culture—occur but are rare.[16]

These changes in funerary practice are, at least superficially, very radical. During the period of development of these trends, Navajos have been becoming increasingly acculturated, and considerable numbers have adopted the outward forms of Christianity, with considerably smaller numbers accepting conventional Christian beliefs as well, and the infrastructure for

"Christian" burials is now firmly in place, unlike in the past.[17] The fast-growing native evangelical churches explicitly reject traditional Navajo religious practice, and this may extend to old-style burial observances.[18] However, there is reason to believe that it is still largely—or, at least, importantly—the traditional reasons, not acculturative ones, that are involved in these dramatically changing mortuary practices. The increasingly elaborate funerals and aboveground grave furniture seem to be partly for reasons of display (including to appear "modern"), but are primarily to honor the dead. All this was certainly influenced by Anglo and Hispano values and practice and by the spread of the introduced non-ghost-oriented Native American Church (peyote cult); but for the Navajo family, conspicuously honoring the dead symbolizes how much he or she was loved and has the specific benefit of appeasing the *ch'iidi* by giving the deceased a good "sendoff." Deep, sometimes cinder-block-lined graves, and hermetically sealed caskets, may even be seen as sealing in the ghost as well as excluding tampering by witches. The notion of ghost-protection is reinforced by the continuing custom of erasing footprints around the grave, as in traditional practice, so that the ghost cannot follow the pallbearers. Too, personal possessions (including the odd television set) are still interred, and are sometimes mutilated.[19] Griffen reported the abandoning or trading-in of the pickup truck that was used to transport the coffin and was, consequently, contaminated.[20] Therefore, these manifestations of customs new to the Navajo may actually in part reflect the strength of ancient and persistent Athapaskan beliefs rather than adoption of novel ones.[21] Christianity—perceived by many Navajos as just another "way" (*-ji*) or ceremonial complex to be added to, and practiced side by side with, strictly tribal ones—may be seen as providing practices affording supernatural protection against ghost sickness.[22]

## Physical Characteristics of Modern Navajo Cemetery Graves

The Indian Health Service has long underwritten burials of people dying in its hospitals, and Bureau of Indian Affairs schools have supplied coffins.[23] In 1943, the War Department, with the cooperation of the Navajo Tribe, established a ten-acre veterans' cemetery at Ft. Defiance, Arizona, and community cemeteries were authorized by the tribe in 1958; the first was established at Kinlichee, Arizona, in 1960.[24] As mentioned, during this century a number of Christian missions have created their own graveyards, often but not always near the mission; and besides these and the newer, nondenominational community cemeteries, there are a few family burial grounds among Christian and Native American Church-practicing Navajos.[25] A 1968 survey indicated that of some two thousand Navajoland cemetery burials, "only 7 percent had headstones, while 61 percent had no markers whatsoever. The remaining 32 percent had such markers as wooden crosses, metal-tag devices or traditional items such as saddles and cradle boards."[26] In the late 1980s, the bulk of the graves in the Navajo section of the Ramah, New Mexico, Mormon cemetery were without permanent markers.[27]

Despite the developments described above, and despite academic interest in changing Navajo funerary practices and acculturation in general, no one other than Keith Cunningham has, to my knowledge, heretofore discussed the physical character of modern Navajo cemetery graves beyond Ward and Brugge's statement and the occasional mention of tombstones, and almost no photographs have been published.[28] Accordingly, from 1993 to 1995, I examined nine Navajo cemeteries: in Arizona, the Ft. Defiance Navajo Veterans' Cemetery, the Tuba City community cemetery, the Chinle community cemetery, and mission cemeteries at Rock Point (Lutheran), Del Muerto (Presbyterian), and Emmanuel Mission (nondenominational Protestant), and in New Mexico, the San Juan Mission Cemetery (Episcopal) just south of Farmington, and at Rehoboth (Christian Dutch Reformed), and Cañoncito (Tohaajilee Baptist Mission).

Military-veteran status carries prestige among the Navajo, and the Ft. Defiance Navajo Veterans' Cemetery has probably been a major influence on adoption of Christian-style burials. Here (and in mission cemeteries), World War II and later war dead were not only buried but were provided with a standard armed-services-supplied tombstone, a Veterans Administration-supplied American flag, and a military honor guard, and were eulogized for their sacrifice to their country. Certainly, all this pomp exerted strong appeal and encouraged civilian funerals.[29]

Physically, most Navajo cemeteries (the Cañoncito one excepted) are surrounded by post-and-wire fencing to exclude livestock. There is no overall landscaping; wild native plants grow up largely unimpeded, and there are few, if any, plantings other than the occasional iris plant (fig. 17.1).

Although, as mentioned, Cunningham stated that at the Mormon mission cemetery at Ramah, "The bulk of Navajo graves have no permanent markers of any kind," in the modern Navajo cemeteries I examined there were markers at most (but by no means all) graves, and Griffin illustrated a painted wooden cross, commercial and homemade headstones, religious figurines, stone-slab and cinder-block borders, petrified wood, and plastic flowers, many on mounded graves.[30] Markers at the heads of graves include military and other standardized commercial headstones of concrete or

Fig. 17.1. Standardized White-Painted Wooden-Cross Markers, Welded-Pipe Entry with Cross, and Volunteer Vegetation (Rock Point, Arizona)

stone and metal tags ("plaques") on standards; the names and dates of the deceased are impressed on these tags or written on paper inserted into the frames. A variety of other, commercially carved tombstones also appear, some with decorations, such as images of Navajo weavers, deer, cattle, sheep, and horses—the last of which could simply reflect Navajo love of horses, cowboying, and rodeo, but which also may be a modern manifestation of the horse-sacrifice tradition (which continued occasionally to be done in connection with "Christian" burials).[31] One inscription on a stone depicting a horse read, "SOMEDAY WE SHALL RIDE AGAIN." Of course, Christian themes, such as praying hands, crosses, and religious personages, are also depicted on commercial stones.

Homemade cast-concrete markers (at Rehoboth, sometimes with cast-bronze plaques) occur, and one torch-cut steel sheet attached to a stone slab was seen at Rehoboth, where welded steel fencing was also well developed, perhaps reflecting a school welding program; a steel-horse silhouette was included (fig. 17.2). Also common are mass-produced or homemade white-painted or unpainted wooden crosses or boards as well as slabs of local sandstone with the deceaseds' names painted on or incised; sometimes, mottoes appear, such as "WE ALL LOVE AND MISS YOU BRO," although only one Navajo-language inscription was noticed (at the McCarrell Memorial). Footstones are sometimes seen. No saddles, cradleboards, or the like were observed, although other observers reported possessions, including tack, being placed in the grave.

"Whenever possible, or permitted by the cemetery plan, the traditional (north-south) patterns of burial orientation are maintained," according to

Fig. 17.2. Flat Grave with Hand-Cut Steel Plaque, Metal Tag, Plastic Flowers, and Bar-Steel Fence at Rehoboth, New Mexico (Note Silhouette of Horse)

Ward and Brugge, although Christian-style east-west oriented graves (head toward the west) were the rule in cemeteries I examined, except at Tuba City.[32] Flush Navajo graves certainly occur, but graves are, more often than not, prominently mounded (the mounds being reduced by erosion over the years) (fig. 17.3). More often than not, the earth is bare, but—flush or mounded—graves are not infrequently covered with: sandstone slabs; local gravel; imported crushed rock or volcanic cinders, rarely in designs (e.g., a cross); and, occasionally, with cobbles and/or petrified wood (figs. 17.4 and 17.5). On one raised grave, Astroturf had been laid down. Graves may be outlined with stones, (fig. 17.3) especially cobbles, and/or cemented vertical

Fig. 17.3. Mounded, Cobble-Girt Graves with Standardized White-Painted Wooden-Cross Markers at Farmington, New Mexico (Note Whirligig in Foreground)

Fig. 17.4. Left-Hand Grave is Raised but Flat with Wooden Cross, Plastic Flowers in Mug, Juniper Bushes, and Cinderblock Wall, While Right-Hand Grave Is Surrounded by a Steel-Bar Fence (Rehoboth, New Mexico)

or horizontally coursed field stone, cut-stone slabs, or cinder blocks; (fig. 17.4) poured-concrete curbing (balks), occasionally with bits of petrified wood set in; or picket or post-and-rail or vertical-board wooden fencing, (fig. 17.5) snow-fencing, post-and woven-wire fencing, bar-iron fencing, a steel-post-and-chain barrier, or low wire or cast-plastic garden-border fencing. In a few cases at Rehoboth, there were raised concrete-slab-covered graves with cinder-block retaining walls topped by coping, and a few simple concrete-slab coverings were seen at Tuba City.

Fig. 17.5. Flat Grave with Wooden-Cross Head and Foot Markers, Ground Cross in White Crushed Stone on Volcanic Cinders, and Low Unpainted Picket-Fence *Cerquita* (Rehoboth, New Mexico)

Navajo graves are sometimes decorated with planted iris or cut flowers but more often with plastic flowers, occasionally in purchased arrangements to read something like "Mom" or to depict the United States flag.[33] At Rehoboth, and only there, small juniper shrubs were also occasionally planted, and one grave had two dead rosebushes. Commercially made Christian-religious and secular figurines and flower vases of ceramic or cement or steel cans occur, and veterans' graves frequently sport large or small United States flags, which, over time, tend to shred in the strong winds. The helmet of an interred Vietnam veteran was laid on one rather elaborate grave. A number of coffee mugs were seen, sometimes functioning as vases, but in one case a mug appeared with eating bowls. Stuffed animals, dolls, and other toys occur now and then, especially, but not exclusively, on children's graves, and the odd whirligig exists.

## Comparison with Non-Navajo Cemetery Graves

Comparison with several Anglo cemeteries in the region revealed Navajo cemeteries' somewhat greater similarity to the Mormon burial ground at Bluff, Utah, right across the San Juan River from the reservation, than to other Anglo burial grounds, including ones at Blanding, Utah, and Flagstaff, Arizona, and the community cemetery at Stanley, New Mexico, on the Plains a considerable distance away. Like many Navajo graves but unlike most other Anglo ones, Bluff's graves tended to be slightly mounded and outlined with cobbles. Like graves in Blanding and Flagstaff (where tree-studded lawn covered the cemetery grounds), graves at Stanley were flush; a few had rock or cinder-block borders enclosing a flat crushed-stone or volcanic-cinder covering, manifestations said by the caretaker to be recent, not traditional there; both commercial headstones and homemade board markers were present. No grave fences were noted, but I have often seen them in nineteenth-century Anglo cemeteries in the West. Whirligigs were seen both at Bluff (Anglo) and at Farmington (Navajo).

In addition to essentially all-Anglo or all-Navajo cemeteries, I also examined the McCarrell Memorial near Chambers, Arizona. This is a local, stone-walled, largely Anglo, private burial ground, but there is also a section devoted to Navajo graves (identified by surnames and given names). The typical Anglo graves had commercial or folk headstones and concrete-curb or stone borders with gravel inside and, sometimes, chunks of petrified wood set in; only a few were mounded. Some sported planted iris, and two had whirligigs. The Navajo graves were mostly mounded, some with low wooden or metal fencing; markers were wooden crosses, one homemade sandstone marker, and commercial stones, and, like Anglo graves, there were plastic flowers.

Only one, small, Hispano *camposanto* (at San Luis, New Mexico, in the Rio Puerco valley) was examined in detail for comparison, but there is also some relevant literature. Hispano graveyards are largely a product of the American period, burials previously having been largely under church floors. In common with most Navajo graveyards, such cemeteries are fenced against animals; are essentially without landscaping and vegetated largely with wild plants; and have homemade wooden crosses and head markers, homemade and commercially made headstones of rock and concrete, as well as protective picket, wrought iron, and wire grave fencing (*cerquitas*), plus religious statues, plastic flowers, and certain possessions of the deceased (e.g., dolls, eating utensils); but graves are normally unmounded and grave orientation is irregular.[34] An exception to Hispano graves being unmounded is recorded by Jordan, who found mounds to be the rule in far west Texas, and concrete curbing further to the east. Stone-slab-covered mounds were also observed in Texas.[35] Graves were aligned west-east at San Luis, and also in evidence were steel crosses, concrete curbing, completely concrete-covered graves (but no gravel), and metal tags.

Comparison with Puebloan graveyards was interesting. A Laguna Indian (Keres) cemetery at Encinal, New Mexico, shared a number of traits with Navajo ones, including: mounded graves, although these had no borders other than one low picket fence; wooden crosses and commercial headstones; iris; Christian figurines; plastic flowers; and a few small American flags. Less similar was the Hopi graveyard at Corn Rock on Second Mesa, Arizona (seen from the exterior), which had mounds of imported stones over the graves, some unpainted wooden crosses, and one sandstone slab, but no commercial markers; one grave had a low picket fence, and there were some, but not many, plastic flowers. Grave orientation appeared to vary from northeast-southwest to northwest-southeast. At the entrance, at least, there were numerous Hopi potsherds on the ground.

At this stage, it is not possible fully to trace the specific cultural and geographical connections of each individual feature of Navajo graveyards, but clearly most are directly or indirectly of Anglo-American origin. For instance, mounding of graves was common in pioneer cemeteries of the Upland South as far west as Texas (and, no doubt, elsewhere). "Mounds served several purposes. One, of course, was grave location. Since markers were wooden, or of local stone, decay or displacement could result over time in the gravesite being lost. A more practical value in mounding was compensation for settling of the grave," according to Jeane.[36] Of course, mounding also relieved people of the task of disposing of the earth displaced by the coffin. More substantial markers and wooden rails to outline plots came in later.

As in New Mexico, in a Southern-California Mexican-influenced New Mexico-derived Spanish-American cemetery, early markers were nearly all wooden (mainly, crosses); stone markers began in the late-nineteenth century, and curbing began at the end of the century, succeeding wooden-fence *cerquitas*.[37] The picture in Texas is similar, where steel crosses have also been noted, as has the practice of embedding objects in the concrete curbing, something occasionally seen among the Navajo. Widespread use of concrete markers began in the 1920s.[38] According to Sanborn, "Stone gravemarkers did not become popular in New Mexico Territory until the 1880s, when a wave of immigration arrived in New Mexico with the railroad. Among the immigrants were French and Italian (architectural) stonecutters . . . who also carved marble headstones for the wealthy. Local people copied this art in local materials—sandstone and limestone. . . . Concrete has remained the most popular material since the turn of the century."[39] Brown documented round-topped wooden slabs, folk and commercially cut headstones, cast-concrete markers, steel-pipe crosses, picket-fence surrounds, incorporation of petrified wood, lamb symbolism for children, and use of toys and stuffed animals in Anglo-Western cemeteries, and painted wooden crosses, wooden tablets, homemade and commercial stones, cast-concrete markers, bar-metal fences, religious figurines, and plastic flowers in Hispano graveyards.[40] The "typical" Navajo cemetery would seem to be directly influenced by both Anglo and Hispano traditions: from the former, for example, headstones, mounding, and planting of iris; and from the latter, wooden crosses, concrete markers, *cerquitas*, and other outlining. Still, despite their variability and the derivative nature of virtually all features of Navajo cemeteries, in their combinations and emphases, at least, such cemeteries remain distinct from those of other ethnicities.

## Final Thoughts

The present article provides an overall introduction to, and view of, modern Navajo cemeteries. I have not made an attempt to provide a quantitative or comprehensive survey of the full suite of modern Navajo graves and graveyards. Nor, beyond general suggestions, have I endeavored to fully trace the origins of individual features and their variations in frequency according to time, place, religious affiliation of the cemeteries, and so forth. There remains plenty of scope for a future, more thorough study, which I will leave to other scholars. However, I believe that the present article is useful in drawing attention to a somewhat distinct and almost undescribed form of American mortuary landscape, in setting same in cultural context, and in defining the basic characteristics of post–World War II Navajo burial grounds.

## Notes

1. Stephen C. Jett and Virginia E. Spencer, *Navajo Architecture: Forms, History, Distributions* (Tucson: University of Arizona Press, 1981), 1–7.

2. Boldface for Navajo vowels herein represents nasalization.

3. Leland C. Wyman et al., *Navajo Eschatology* (University of New Mexico Bulletin 377, Anthropological Series 4, 1942); Berard Haile, *Soul Concepts of the Navajo* (Vatican City: Tipografia Poliglotta Vaticana, 1943), 88–89; Gladys A. Reichard, *Navajo Religion: A Study of Symbolism* (New York: Pantheon Books, 1950), 126–27; Kerndall A. Blanchard, *The Economics of Sainthood: Religious Change among the Rimrock Navajos* (Rutherford, N. J.: Fairleigh Dickinson University Press, 1977), 191; Charlotte J. Frisbie, ed., "Introduction to Special Symposium on Navajo Mortuary Practices and Beliefs," *American Indian Quarterly* 4 (1978): 304; David M. Brugge, "A Comparative Study of Navajo Mortuary Practices," *American Indian Quarterly* 4 (1978): 312–13; Mary Shepardson, "Changes in Navajo Mortuary Practices and Beliefs," *American Indian Quarterly* 4 (1978): 385 and 387; Richard J. Parry, *Western Apache Heritage: People of the Mountain Corridor* (Austin: University of Texas Press, 1991), 90.

4. Albert E. Ward and David M. Brugge, "Changing Contemporary Navajo Burial Practices and Values," *Plateau* 48 (1975): 31–33; Joyce Griffin, *Navajo Funerals, Anglo Style* (Flagstaff, Ariz.: Museum of Northern Arizona Research Paper 18, 1980); Gerald E. Levy, "Changing Burial Practices of the Western Navajo: A Consideration of the Relationship between Attitudes and Behavior," *American Indian Quarterly* 4 (1978): 397; Shepardson, 385; Haile, 88.

5. Haile, 88–89; Ward and Brugge, 31–33; Brugge, 314–15; Shepardson, 385; Jett and Spencer, 205–7.

6. Albert E. Ward, "Navajo Graves: Some Preliminary Considerations for Recording and Classifying Reservation Burials," *American Indian Quarterly* 4 (1978): 337; Shepardson, 386; Lloyd M. Pierson, "Death in the Desert or the Day We Buried the Navajo," in *Of Pots and Rocks: Papers in Honor of A. Helene Warren*, eds. Melika S. Duran and David T. Kirkpatrick (The Archaeological Society of New Mexico, 1995), 137–40.

7. Haile, 88 and 90; Ward and Brugge, 34–35; Brugge, 313–14, 316, 318;

Shepardson, 385; Pierson, 138; Cecil Calvin Richardson, "The Navajo Way," *Arizona Highways* 71 (1995): 2–4.

8. Shepardson, 388; Ward, "Navajo Graves: Some Preliminary Considerations for Recording and Classifying Reservation Burials," 340.

9. Shepardson, 388; Ward, "Navajo Graves: Some Preliminary Considerations for Recording and Classifying Reservation Burials," 371.

10. Ward and Brugge, 35–37, 39–40; Levy, 398; Pierson, 137–38.

11. Dorothea Leighton and Clyde Kluckhohn, *Children of the People* (Cambridge, Mass.: Harvard University Press, 1948), 92.

12. Louise Lamphere, *To Run after Them: Cultural and Social Bases of Cooperation in a Navajo Community* (Tucson: University of Arizona Press, 1977), 162.

13. Albert E. Ward, *Navajo Graves: An Ethnoarchaeological Reflection of Ethnographic Reality* (Center for Anthropological Studies, 1980), 30.

14. Ward and Brugge, 36–37.

15. Lamphere, 162–65; Ward, "Navajo Graves: Some Preliminary Considerations for Recording and Classifying Reservation Burials," 341; Keith Cunningham, "The People of Rimrock Bury Alfred K. Lorenzo: Tri-Cultural Funerary Practice," in *Ethnicity and the American Cemetery*, ed. Richard E. Meyer (Bowling Green, Ohio: The Popular Press, 1993).

16. Ward and Brugge, 39.

17. Levy, 400; Charlotte J. Frisbie, "Temporal Change in Navajo Religion: 1868–1900," *Journal of the Southwest* 4 (1992): 457–514. See also Shepardson, 391–92.

18. Frisbie, "Temporal Change in Navajo Religion: 1868–1900," 491.

19. Ward and Brugge, 37–39; Shepardson, 388–89, 393; Levy, 397; Lamphere, 163; Ward, "Navajo Graves: Some Preliminary Considerations for Recording and Classifying Reservation Burials," 337.

20. Griffin, *Navajo Funerals, Anglo Style*, 13.

21. Shepardson, 390–92; Levy, 400–403.

22. Ward and Brugge, 40.

23. Levy, 398–99; Ward, "Navajo Graves: Some Preliminary Considerations for Recording and Classifying Reservation Burials," 340.

24. Ward and Brugge, 36–37.

25. Shepardson, 390; Ward and Brugge, 39.

26. Ward and Brugge, 37.

27. Keith Cunningham, "Navajo, Mormon, Zuni Graves: Navajo, Mormon, Zuni Ways," in *Cemeteries and Gravemarkers: Voices of American Culture*, ed. Richard E. Meyer (Ann Arbor, Mich.: UMI Research Press, 1989), 202.

28. Cunningham, 1989; Cunningham, 1993; Ward and Brugge, 37.

29. Shepardson, 390–94; Ward and Brugge, 36.

30. Cunningham, "Navajo, Mormon, Zuni Graves: Navajo, Mormon, Zuni Ways," 202; Griffin, *Navajo Funerals, Anglo Style*, 19–26.

31. Shepardson, 389.

32. Ward and Brugge, 39.

33. Shepardson, 390.

34. Roland Dickey, *New Mexico Village Arts* (Albuquerque: University of New Mexico Press, 1970), 209–12; Robert Brewer and Steve McDowell, *The Persistence of Memory: New Mexico's Churches* (Santa Fe: Museum of New Mexico Press, 1990), 49, 91; Nancy Hunter Warren, "New Mexico Village Camposantos," *Markers* 4 (1987): 115–29; Laura Sue Sanborn, "Camposantos: Sacred Places of the Southwest, " *Markers* 6 (1989): 158–79; Susan Hazen-Hammond, "Camposantos: Dios Da y Dios Quita," *New Mexico Magazine* 64 (1986): 31; Terry G. Jordan, *Texas Graveyards: A Cultural Legacy* (Austin: University of Texas Press, 1982), 65–88.

35. Jordan, 70, 72–73.

36. Jordan, 16–19; D. Gregory Jeane, "The Upland South Folk Cemetery Complex: Some Suggestions of Origin," in *Cemeteries and Gravemarkers: Voices of American Culture*, ed. Richard E. Meyer (Ann Arbor, Mich.: UMI Research Press, 1989), 113.

37. Warren, 116. See also Russell J. Barber, "The Agua Mansa Cemetery: An Indicator of Ethnic Identification in a Mexican-American Community," in *Ethnicity and the American Cemetery*, ed. Richard E. Meyer (Bowling Green, Ohio: The Popular Press, 1993), 16–63.

38. Jordan, 70–71, 75–83.

39. Sanborn, 166.

40. John Gary Brown, *Soul in the Stone: Cemetery Art from America's Heartland* (Lawrence: University Press of Kansas, 1994), 18–19, 40, 43–44, 46, 123, 125, 138, 175, 229, 232–35.

# Part VI: Folk Medicine

Folk medicine may be divided into two branches: natural and magico-religious. The first represents human use of the natural environment with the seeking of cures from herbs, plants, minerals, and animal substances. The second type uses charms, holy words, and holy actions to cure diseases. Magico-religious healing is based on supernatural powers for healing and the mediation of that power through material objects as well as human healers.

Natural folk medicine, often called "home remedies," is passed down from generation to generation. It has been utilized for chronic health problems (e.g., colds, indigestion, burns, sores, headaches, fevers, and general aches and pains) more frequently than acute ones. Women are generally regarded as the folk healers, especially "granny women" used as midwives in childbirth, although men are also sought for help. A major part of this branch is herbal—based on the plants of woodland and field. Herbal specialists are often known as "yarb doctors" or "root doctors." The natural healer also draws upon mineral and animal substances, including such items as mud, animal organs, and even human urine and excrement.

Both chapters in part 4 deal with natural folk medicine. The beliefs associated with folk medicine are considered nonmaterial, while the substances and objects used are part of material culture.

*Folklife regions* based on folk medicine include the two discussed in chapters 18 and 19—Mexican and Upland South. The Rio Grande Valley of the Mexican folklife region is where *curanderos* (curers) rely on a variety of medicinal plants to cure illnesses. The southern Appalachians of the Upland South folklife region is one of the major source regions for botanical drugs in the United States.

The *origin and diffusion* theme is portrayed in chapter 18. Some of the medicine used by *curanderos* is derived from plants brought to the New World from Europe, the Near East, and the Mediterranean lands, especially by the Spaniards in the sixteenth and seventeenth centuries. In general, folk medicine combines elements from various origins including African and European cultures, Greek classical medicine, and voodoo beliefs from Haiti. These influences diffused from various sources to America in the seventeenth and eighteenth centuries.

The theme of *folklife ecology* is no better illustrated than in the natural branch of folk medicine because of the use of plants and animal substances

233

obtained from the natural environment. In chapter 18, a variety of wild and garden plants (flowers, bark, roots, and leaves) are used in curing illnesses. Ginseng, one of the plants discussed in chapter 19, is especially suited for the coves of southern Appalachia. The prime locations for ginseng are found on the north-facing "wet" sides of these depressions.

Folk medicine and folk religion maintain a strong interrelationship typifying the *folklife integration* theme. Folk healing practices, especially in the Upland and Lowland South folklife regions, have synthesized within the framework of fundamentalist Christianity and provide the participants with a broad belief system allowing them to explain illnesses and cures.

The *folk landscape* theme is expressed in the tangible objects and facilities associated with folk medicine, including boticas/botanicas, herbal stores, and voodoo outlets.

Folk medical traditions and practices appear to have been rejuvenated in the United States. This increased interest in folk medicine and folk healers is partly because of a lack of access to modern medical care and the expense incurred. Herbalists, bone setters, and granny women (midwives) are still in great demand, and commercial drug stores throughout the United States have sections stocked with ingredients that can be used for "home remedies." Although exact statistics on the distribution and frequency of folk medicine are unavailable, the practice has been, and remains, widespread, particularly among the poor in both rural and urban areas.

# 18

# Plants in the Folk Medicine of the Texas-Mexico Borderlands

## Clarissa T. Kimber

Wild and garden plants are essential elements in the folk medicine practiced by Mexicans and Mexican Americans along the border between Texas and Mexico. After recognition of illness, the first remedies used are teas, poultices, or baths prepared from plants.[1] Flowers, leaves, stems, bark, roots, chunks of wood, and even the whole plant are used in curing a variety of illnesses. Although views vary among members of the Mexican-American community on the relative importance of natural and supernatural causes of disease, and the efficacy of medicinals as compared with faith, women with families turn to the tried, familiar botanicals as the first defense against illness. *Curanderos* use in their practice a variety of remedies employing a great many medicinal plants.[2] Informants in Laredo report that medical doctors sometimes prescribe these same herbs for their poor patients unable to afford the cost of over-the-counter drugs. The majority of these plant medicines are obtained from vendors specializing in these products. However, some of the plant sources of the most common folk remedies come from the fields, roadsides, or are grown in dooryard gardens readily available for the family in any emergency. In the summer of 1971 a study was designed and begun to recover the still extant ethnopharmacology of wild and cultivated plants in the folk medicine of northern Mexico and southern Texas.

Reprinted by permission from the *Proceedings of the Association of American Geographers* 5 (1973): 130–33.

This chapter reports the herbal medicines found in use and the plants from which they are derived. The folklore of disease—its cause, prevention, and cure—as pieced together from interviews with lay folk, curers, medical doctors, and public health officials is used to explain the sources and persistence of the plants in use in the modern folk culture.

## The Herbal Medicines

Over 400 medicinal names were found along the border. Two hundred and seventy samples of 113 different medicines were obtained by purchase in *boticas*, markets, grocery stores, and corner drugstores, and as gifts from housewives. Visual inspection revealed that a small number (eight) of the herbal medicines are being sold under more than one name. The same plant may furnish two botanicals, that is, the leaves called by one name and reputed excellent for one purpose while the root is called by another name and used for a different purpose. For the most part, one vernacular name is used consistently throughout subunits in the region. This is true of both the wild plants collected locally and for imports from Mexico. Of the medicinals and herbarium specimens collected, some 290 plants have been identified to species. Eighty-four families contribute medicinals but about two-fifths of them come from seven families (table 18.1).

The botanicals are used in preparing poultices, infusions, and baths. Families known for a large number of species possessing aromatic essential oils and alkaloids such as the mints and verbenas are understandably important as sources of decoctions and infusions. The fresh or dried leaves of *Salvia* species are used to alleviate stomach distress, aid in digestion, as a tonic, or chewed with salt for digestive upsets. Seeds are ground to make

**Table 18.1: Most Important Families for Medicinal Plants in the Texas-Mexico Borderland**

| Compositae | 33 species | in | 25 genera | |
|---|---|---|---|---|
| Leguminosae | 27 species | in | 20 genera | (*Cassie* 3 spp) |
| Labiatae | 20 species | in | 12 genera | (*Salvia* 6 spp) |
| Euphorbiaceae | 14 species | in | 6 genera | (*Croton* 5 spp) |
| | | | | (*Euphorbia* 3 spp) |
| Umbeliferae | 10 species | in | 9 genera | |
| Verbenaceae | 9 species | in | 3 genera | (*Lippia* 5 spp, *Verbena* 3 spp) |
| Solanaceae | 7 species | in | 4 genera | |
| 7 families | 120 species | | 79 genera | 6 imp. genera |

*Source:* Field Data Collected by Author

refreshing teas and to relieve constipation. Saponins and alkaloids so characteristic of the potato relatives account for the strong contribution of this family. Euphorbs are well-known purgatives and sedatives. The seeds of *Croton* species, ground to a powder are made into a decoction drunk as a purgative while the powdered leaves of one species is used directly on the skin as a mosquito repellant and in baths to relieve fevers. *Euphorbia* species are used to counter attacks of diarrhea. Crushed fresh leaves are applied to rashes and minor skin erruptions. Legumes contain saponins and glucosides. They are commonly used as purgatives, cathartics, laxatives, and diuretics. *Cassia* species are used in poultices for sores and ulcers of the skin, to combat dropsy, and act as a vermifuge. The carrot family contains many herbs with volatile oils and aromatic seeds. They are commonly used in cooking but medicines prepared from them are reputed to act as stimulants, emmenagogues, expectorants, antisyphilitics, and vermifuges. The roots of the wild carrot are mascerated and used as a poultice for ulcers on humans and livestock. The sunflower family is the one best represented with species in the region. The uses of these composites are extremely varied.

According to vendors, a few species account for the majority of medicinals sold. The sixteen most commonly sold botanicals are listed in table 18.2. Those preceded with an asterisk in the table are exotic plants either from Europe or South America. Yet so completely are they part of the folk

**Table 18.2: Most Important Medicinals Obtained from Commercial Sources (In Order Listed by Vendor)**

| | |
|---|---|
| * 1. | manzanilla (camomile)-*Matricaria chamomilla* L. |
| * 2. | ruda (rue)-*Ruta graveolens* L. |
| * 3. | romero (rosemary)-*Rosmarinus officinalis* L. |
| * 4. | poléo (pennyroyal)-*Mentha pulegium* L. |
| * 5. | sávila (aloe vera)-*Aloe barbadensis* Mill. |
| 6. | muicle (firecracker bush)-*Jacobinia spicigera* Bailey |
| * 7. | yerba buena (peppermint)-*Mentha piperita* L. |
| * 8. | albahaca (basil)-*Ocimum* spp. |
| * 9. | rosa de Castilla (rose)-*Rosa* spp. |
| 10. | estafiate-*Artemisia mexicana* Willd. |
| *11. | borraja (borage)-*Borago officinalis* L. |
| 12. | gordoloba (cudweed)-*Gnaphalium* spp. |
| 13. | governadora (creosote bush)-*Larrea divaricata* Cav. |
| *14. | yerbanís-*Pimpinella anisum* L. |
| 15. | ceniso (purple sage)-*Leucophyllum texana* Benth. |
| *16. | pirúl (Brazilian pepper tree)-*Schinus molle* L. |

*Source:* Field Data Collected by Author

medicine perceived as part of their Mexican heritage that informants will speak of *manzanilla* as "an old Indian remedy." Furthermore, it can be noted that all but one of the exotic species identified have Linnean names, which indicates a knowledge by Europeans of these plants by the eighteenth century.

## The Source Regions of the Medical Flora

When the source area of each species in use was identified from the literature and tabulated (table 18.3), the proportion of native plants to the whole is much higher than that among the most commonly purchased plants. Examination of table 18.3 shows that three-fourths of the plants are native to the New World and one-fourth are local, indigenous to the borderlands.[3] One-eighth are, or could be, derived from Europe and the Near East. Two are cosmopolitan species meaning that they could have been derived from Europe or the New World. The other, very small geographical contributions are from Africa south of the Sahara, the Pacific, and the Americas north of the borderlands. Together these three last groups account for less than 3 percent of the total species list. These distributions lead one to suppose that the plants were derived from the source areas of the populations ancestral to the modern Mexican and Mexican American: the Spaniards of the sixteenth and seventeenth centuries and the Indians of the lands that became Mexico.

Table 18.3: Origins of Medicinal Plants Used in the Texas-Mexico Borderlands

| | |
|---|---|
| OLD WORLD | |
| 14 | Mediterranean lands and western Asia |
| 18 | Europe north of the Mediterranean |
| 2 | Africa south of the Sahara |
| 20 | Orient, Southeast Asia, and Indonesia |
| 2 | Pacific strictly speaking |
| 25 | Eurasian and plants given a general Old World origin |
| | |
| NEW WORLD | |
| 4 | Americas north of the Borderlands |
| 86 | Texas-Mexico Borderlands |
| 117 | Americas south of the Borderlands |
| | |
| COSMOPOLITAN | |
| 2 | species |

*Sources:* Correll and Johnston (1970), Bailey (1949), and Martinez (1969)

## Theory of Disease and Healing

Discussions about causes of disease and correct curing procedures generally led to an eventual distinction between natural causes and supernatural causes, but during the investigations conducted both by the author and by assistants from the folk community, the informant always seemed to blur the distinctions between emotional illness, emotionally derived sickness, and somatic disease. Natural-causes type diseases would be treated by natural means, but often in a patterned manner implying magic or religious ritual, that is, three cups of tea for three days; taking of a medicine for forty days. The necessity for harmony between natural and supernatural is thought essential to health and welfare. Disease and misfortune is usually thought to involve some disharmony between the two realms of human experience. This is similar to what Rubel and Madsen reported in their earlier study in the central part of the valley.[4]

The hot-cold balance is occasionally referred to and remedies may be designed to restore "the balance" by the administration of the proper hot or cold antidote. However, the concept of "hot" and "cold" was very imperfectly expressed by virtually all informants and rarely voluntarily raised except as being characteristics of foods, or human states of being. No one could give a well-formulated doctrinal statement. Strong anger is reported as causing sickness, vomiting, and diarrhea. Both this and the "hot-cold" concept or theory are relicts of Hippocratic medicine introduced into Mexico by the Spaniards in the sixteenth century.[5]

Plants are not only used in the preparation of herbal medicines, but soft branches of plants such as muicle and pirul are used to stroke the body when a *curandero* is cleansing the patient. Romero is often used as an incense of purification in religio-magical rituals as well as in the sickroom. Fresh flowers are an important part of the preparation of the house or room prior to elaborate curing rituals in the home. Bouquets of real and plastic flowers are left at shrines such as that of Don Pedrito Jamarillo or at the shrine of San Juan de la Valle.

Comparisons of the herbal remedies collected along the border with those reported in the literature for Mexico and sixteenth-century Spain show considerable parallels in remedies for specific diseases.[6] Modern herbal medicine compilations printed in Spain are found in Mexican bookstores as well as in the more elaborate herbal shops. Whether there is a market for these books in Spain today is not known. Nonetheless, references by certain informants to the way it is done in Spain suggests that some persons perceive that source region as important.

Comparisons of the modern or recently collected remedies with those collected in the 1930s show a shift away from herbal remedies for infections, broken bones and sprains, whereas those for the common cold, skin irritations, and earache and stomach disorders remain the same.[7] On the other hand, herbal treatments for high blood pressure, diabetes, and cancer have increased. There is limited evidence that the complement is not fixed. New plants may enter the pharmacopoeia, such as eucalyptus, which was introduced to Mexico in the nineteenth century.

Virtually all plants in the pharmacopoeia of the Mexican Americans can be accounted for by (1) the empirical testing of the indigenous flora for useful medicines, (2) the importation of Iberian herbal medicines by the fifteenth- and sixteenth-century conquerors and settlers, and (3) the introduction of medical plants from those parts of the world where Spain conducted trade regularly.

Foster writes that the folk level is no better illustrated than in the realm of folk medicine.[8] According to Foster, the unity of Spanish-American folk medicine is due to the acceptance of scientific medical knowledge in greatly simplified forms of the time of the conquest. He pointed out that his work shows that half or more of the herbs commonly used in folk medicine in Latin America today were prescribed by Spanish physicians of the sixteenth century. And when we recall that the Spanish crown was most anxious to collect the rich medical herbal lore of the Aztecs, whom contemporary Spaniards conceded was superior to that of Spain, it would seem that it is safe to conclude that the persistence of the plants in the ethnopharmacopoeia of the Texas-Mexico borderlands is due to the persistence of folk elements in a culture undergoing considerable change in which the constructs associated with disease and curing are traditional forms having strong roles in the folk culture.

## Notes

1. William Madsen, *Society and Health* (Austin: University of Texas Press, 1961), 20.

2. George I. Sanchez, *Forgotten People: A Study of New Mexicans* (Albuquerque, N.M.: Calvin Horn Publisher, 1940), 34; Margaret Clark, *Health in the Mexican-American Culture: A Community Study* (Berkeley: University of California Press, 1959), 242; and Fordon Schendel, *Medicine in Mexico: From Aztec Herbs to Betatrons* (Austin: University of Texas Press, 1968), 131.

3. Richard L. Nostrand, "The Hispanic-American Borderland: Delimita-

tion of an American Culture Region," *Annals of the Association of American Geographers* 60 (1970): 638–61.

4. Arthur J. Rubel, "Concepts of Disease in Mexican-American Culture," *American Anthropologist* 62 (1960): 795; William Madsen, *The Mexican-Americans of South Texas* (New York: Holt, Rinehart and Winston, 1964), 18.

5. George Foster, "Relationships between Spanish and Spanish-American Folk Medicine," *Journal of American Folklore* 66 (1953): 210.

6. Foster, "Relationships between Spanish and Spanish-American Folk Medicine"; Madsen, *Society and Health*; William Madsen, "Hot and Cold in the Universe of San Francisco Tecospa, Valley of Mexico," *Journal of American Folklore* 8 (1955): 123–39; Rubel, "Concepts of Disease in Mexican-American Culture"; and Isabel Kelly, *Folk Practices in North Mexico* (Austin: University of Texas Press, 1965).

7. Estelle Friend and William Friend, "Plant Lore of the Rio Grande Country," unpublished manuscript written c. 1937.

8. George Foster, "What Is Folk Culture?" *American Anthropologist* 55 (1953): 168–70.

# 19

# Root Digging in the Appalachians: The Geography of Botanical Drugs

## Edward T. Price

The blessings of antibiotics have been accompanied by harsh economic side reactions for the crude-drug dealers and collectors of roots, barks, and herbs in the Southern Appalachians. Even the antibiotics, however, serve to remind us that most medicine has been founded directly on plant lore. Gathering drugs from the wild has steadily lost ground to cultivation and synthetic imitation; but it survives on both domestic and commercial scales in parts of the United States.

### Development and Decline of American Medical Botanicals

Determining the medicinal plants and their uses was a part of the pioneer's task of learning to live in North America. John Josselyn, writing in London in 1672 after a visit to New England, described a score of curative American herbs, most of which are still in use; but Thomas Glover, chirurgeon, after a visit to Virginia about the same time, felt that the medical possibilities of the flora there had not been given much attention by the colonists.[1]

Many of the colonists' remedies were adopted directly from Native Americans, so that the settlers had an opportunity to obtain instruction in the use of plants available on the spot.[2] Several of those reported by Josselyn

Reprinted by permission from *The Geographical Review* 50 (1960):1–20.

were Indian cures; Glover also recognized that American Indians had learned much about "the nature and uses of their plants, but they use no correctives to take away the flatuous, nauseous, and bad qualities of them."[3] From domestic medicine scores of American Indian remedies came to the attention of professional physicians, who gradually adopted the ones they considered effective. That Peter Smith found it advantageous in 1812 to entitle his book *The Indian Doctor's Dispensatory* attests to a persistent faith in the advantages of prior familiarity.[4] Professional physicians probably played the greater part in developing the use of American relatives of European plants that the Indians had not used.

The medicinal plants include, in addition to the natives, a good representation of the naturalized adventives that have sprung up in old fields and along fence rows and roadsides, some of them as escapes from cultivation. Josselyn and Glover both reported a number of imported weeds, and Peter Kalm noted many during his mid-eighteenth-century travels.[5] Indeed, it is likely that European weeds preceded European settlement in many areas.

During the nineteenth century, the development of medicine became mostly a matter for professionals. Chemists were isolating the alkaloids and other substances that gave the plants their most potent properties. While the doctors winnowed a few of the best cures from the many they were discarding, the school of Eclectic medicine fought a rear-guard action to keep a large number of remedies on the market.[6] This, they believed, would implement their philosophy of treating patients rather than diseases.

American wild plants and their preparations have almost disappeared from the United States Pharmacopoeia.[7] Many are still listed in the National Formulary, but sixteen were dropped between the 1942 and 1946 editions, and seven more before 1950.[8] Flurries of interest nevertheless develop over possibilities of new applications. In 1947 root diggers were busy collecting the normally abundant wild-yam root (*Dioscorea villosa*) from the Appalachian forests to meet a demand based on the vain hope that its cortisone yield might be comparable with that of some of the Latin-American species.[9] Two or three years later, interest arose in the long-familiar American false-hellebore (*Veratrum viride*) as a cure for hypertension, and frantic efforts were made to collect it until experimentation proved it inadequate.

Many common remedies never reached the pharmacopoeia. The perversities of plant distributions create a need for several plants to fulfill each purpose if a user is to be able to collect his or her own cures. Long lists of plants and their uses can be quickly compiled by inquiring of farm folk concerning remedies available to them. The geography of these domestic remedies in this country has not been worked out; it must involve an interesting complex of cultural patterns superimposed on the natural plant distributions.

The largest number of plants are classified vaguely as tonics or bitters, but many for almost every purpose are listed in the medical books. The catalogue of a modern herb house that includes probably more than two hundred American products among its wares lists these uses for some common botanicals: blue-flag root (*Iris versicolor*), alterative, resolvent, laxative, diuretic; mullein leaves (*Verbascum thapsus*), demulcent, diuretic, anodyne, antispasmodic, vulnerary; agrimony herb (*Agrimonia gryposepala*), mild astringent, tonic, stomachic; liver herb (or liverleaf) (*Hepatica americana, H. acutiloba*), tonic, astringent, hepatic, pectoral. Other drugs are specifics for certain diseases or conditions; for example, pinkroot (*Spigelia marilandica*) is used as a vermifuge.[10]

Many of the botanical materials are used as flavoring or as minor ingredients in "ethical" pharmaceuticals. They are more likely to form the chief ingredients in proprietary or patent medicines. A glance at the labels on the tonic shelf in any drugstore will reveal them as important constituents of many preparations such as Swamp Root, Cardui, or Lydia Pinkham's compound. A change in the formula of one of these compounds may have startling results on the demand for, and price of, a particular herb.

A band of the faithful stick loyally to "natural" herb cures. None is more ardent than the old collector on an east Tennessee mountain who told me, "The good Lord has put these yerbs here for man to make hisself well with. They is a yerb, could we but find it, to cure every illness." This optimistic belief had long been reinforced by the widespread doctrine of signatures, which held that each remedy could be identified by some mark indicative of its function; for example, the trilobate leaf of a certain small green plant suggested the shape of the liver, and liverleaf accordingly became a leading liver tonic.[11]

## Characteristics of American Medicinal Plants

More than a thousand American plants have been used medicinally either in aboriginal times or later. A large number can be found in nearly any part of the country. Both the ethnobotanical literature and modern compilations of plants from limited areas are almost encyclopedic in the large numbers of medicinal plants reported.[12] Yet most of the common medicinal plants belong primarily to the deciduous forests. The higher rainfall and certain other factors have probably made these areas more productive sources. Perhaps more important, the plants that were to become standard in our national materia medica would most likely have been available in the areas where settlement first occurred and where American culture was largely developed.

For this study, I have compiled data on 148 medicinal plants that have had commercial value within the present century.[13] A quarter of the group are natives of Eurasia that have become naturalized in this country. The majority of these Old World species are weedy herbs, and conversely the majority of all the weedy medicinal plants in the United States are Old World species. Most of the weeds were long-established pests of European agriculture and were quick to settle in the congenial American environment provided where the forests had been cleared for settlement. Several of our most familiar weeds have medicinal use; among those not already mentioned are mustard (*Brassica* spp., seeds), dock (*Rumex crispus*, roots), yarrow (*Achillea millefolium*, tops), and hoarhound (*Marrubium vulgare*, leaves and tops). Their uses are ancient, and we tend to depend mostly on imports from Europe for our commercial supply of them.

On the other hand, the familiar and violently poisonous Jimson weed (*Datura stramonium*), thought to be native to the Caspian lands, was apparently not well known in Europe when it showed up in this country.[14] Although it became known to the Indians as the "white people's plant," the ignorance of Europeans concerning it is attested by the story of those Jamestown settlers who unwittingly gained immortality in its name (Jimson being a corruption of Jamestown) by trying to use the thorny plant as a potherb.[15] Later Americans used it domestically as a pain- and asthma-relieving favorite, and atropine, the principal constituent of its preparations, was subsequently identified and isolated.

However, a number of the medicinal weeds are native, among them butterfly weed (*Asclepias tuberosa*), whose roots have a variety of medicinal uses but were once cooked and eaten by the Indians; boneset (*Eupatorium perfoliatum*, leaves); horseweed (*Erigeron canadensis*, herb; now naturalized in Europe and Asia); maypop (*Passiflora incarnata*, herb); pokeberry (*Phytolacca americana*, root; this plant also has many uses as a food and dye); and queen of the meadow (*Eupatorium purpureum*, root). Wormseed (*Chenopodium ambrosioides* var. *anthelminticum*) was originally a native of the American tropics; its fruit yields a volatile oil.

More than half of the native American plants on the list are reported to have been used medicinally by one or more Indian tribes. At least sixteen, and probably many more, of the native American plants are parallel species of the same genera used in Old World medicine, and more than half of these were known to the Indians. For example, Canada wild ginger, *Asarum canadense*, has a number of uses but was not so effective an emetic as A.

*europaeum*; and Oregon hollygrape, *Berberis aquifolium*, provides a bark used for its tonic properties, whereas *B. vulgaris* and other species were used in ancient Europe and India for treating eye diseases. Half a dozen species seem to have been native in both hemispheres, but I have found no record of identical pre-Columbian uses for them.

More than two-thirds of all the medicinal species are herbaceous. The modern search for alkaloids has suggested that they are more common in herbs than in woody plants.[16] Among woody medicinal plants, there are twice as many trees as shrubs. The plant parts used, in order of importance, are root, herb and leaves, stem bark, root bark, seeds and berries, and flowers. Roots outnumber herbs two to one among Indian uses, but the reverse is true of European introductions. Many of the European adventives are annuals, which have less opportunity to develop sizable roots and to store chemicals in them. If the Indians had a partiality for root digging, it may have been passed on to the settlers. There is some tendency yet for men to assume the harder and more lucrative work of collecting the native roots and barks, while the women give their attention to gathering the weedy European herbs around the house and along the roads. This division of labor may stem from pioneer days, when the more widely adventuring men were in the better position to pick up Indian lore, whereas the women were carriers and preservers of the domestic ways of the Old World.

Most of the plants have been in use a long time. Many are traceable to ancient Europe, and many may be assumed to have been old among the Indians. Writers of the period 1750–1830 have provided abundant material on most of the plants now in use and on many more.[17] I have found only three plants for which evidence is at hand to support a recent adoption (since about 1800).[18] These are the saw palmetto (*Serenoa serrulata*), whose berries are reported as coming into use about 1879 after sick animals feeding on them had been observed to grow well;[19] Carolina jessamine, discussed below; and hop tree (*Ptelea trifoliata*), which provided a now obsolete substitute for quinine and was introduced into medical literature by Rafinesque.

What are the fundamental controls, one may wonder, that cause some plants to be used for medicinal purposes and others to be relegated to the realm of neutral stuff? On the human side, we should have to understand the process of culture evolution itself to know why people use certain plants and ignore others of equally great or small real worth. Historical accident must have played a large part. On nature's side, we must assume that many plants have valuable properties and that others have properties that people have thought indicate value. But what determines which plants have these properties? The distribution of the medicinal plants through the plant kingdom is so random that we can only be reminded of the multiple diversities of evolution. Of the plants listed in *Gray's Manual of Botany*, about one species in twenty-eight appears on my list.[20] The nonflowering plants (Pteridophyta) are weakly represented, one fern (*Dryopteris marginalis*) in more than a hundred species. Conifers are strong, five out of twenty-five (witness the common uses for turpentine, juniper berries, and pine bark). Monocotyledons are weak, about one in every eighty, mostly bulbs. The largest gap in the whole division of spermatophytes occurs in the grasses, which offer a single introduced species, quack grass, in medicinal demand.

Most of the medicinal plants are dicotyledons. Among them the legumes, medicinally important in the tropics, offer here only two medicinal species—American senna (*Cassia marilandica*) and yellow wild indigo (*Baptisia tinctoria*)—out of 180 listed in the family. The most notable concentration occurs in the order Ranunculales, a tenth of the 127 species being on my list, nearly all natives.[21] A nearly identical concentration occurs among seven successively listed families rich in forest trees.[22] The Compositae (sunflower family) and Labiatae (mint family) contain more medicinal species than any other family, nineteen and eleven respectively, but the majority in each are introduced rather than native.[23]

## Names Given to Medicinal Plants

Many of our feelings about the plants we use are reflected in the name we give them. Each plant on the list has been called by a large number of names that refer to different aspects of our association with it. In the following examples it is easy to distinguish several ideas among the names and also certain groups of names that represent variations of a single sound. The American mountain ash, *Sorbus americana*, is known as service tree, American rowan (probably meaning "red") tree, roundtree, mountain sumac, dogberry, quickbeam, winetree, witchwood, life-of-man, mozemize (Algonquian for "moose bush"), and missey-moosey.[24] And the pokeberry is known as pocan (a Virginia Indian word for "dye," equivalent to "puccoon"), scoke, coakum (probably a Massachusetts corruption of the Tarascan "mechoacan"), pigeonberry, garget (a Middle English word for "throat"; the reference is either to a disease of the throat in swine or cattle or to a disease of cow's udders that the plant was used to cure), inkberry, American nightshade, cancer jalap, and redweed.

It has not been possible to collect data on local names applied to the various plants, but I shall give examples of some of the common types of names, especially those that have readily understandable meanings. Many of the common names reach back into the Anglo-Saxon past and, though occasionally used, lack general meaning for most Americans. The most usual plant names, scientific or common, are descriptive, and often the description is visual.

The generic names of about a tenth of the plants suggest medical usage: for example, *Solidago* (goldenrod), "to make whole or solid"; *Tussilago* (coltsfoot), referring to its curative effect on coughs; *Symphytum* (comfrey), "grown together." The common names more often suggest medicinal uses, among them ague bark, quinine tree, cancer jalap, kidneyroot, asthma weed, emetic herb, eyebright, feverwort, birthroot, toothache tree, nerve-root, coughweed, cramp-bark tree, soldier's-woundwort, and maiden's-relief. And there are many more.

Frequently the popular names are identical or nearly identical in meaning with the generic names, with no indication whether the English follows the Latin or vice versa: passion flower and *Passiflora*, dogbane and *Apocynum*, wolf's foot and *Lycopus*, moonseed and *Menispermum*, Venus's-shoe or lady's-slipper and *Cypripedium*, snowflower and *Chionanthus*.

Certain compound terms arouse one's curiosity: "nature's mistake" for the dogwood; "bad man's oatmeal" for the poison hemlock (*Conium maculatum*), supposedly the same plant that provided Socrates' death drink; "old-maid's-nightcap" for the wild geranium; "quiverleaf" or "auld-wives'-tongue" for the aspen.

Indian names are surprisingly few considering the Indians' use of plants; they include *wahoo*, from the Dakota for "arrowwood"; *pipsissewa*, Algonquian for "it breaks it into small pieces"; *puccoon*, a term for dye-yielding plants in Virginia; *cohosh*, Algonquian for "it is rough."

Some of the proper names used are biblical in origin: apple of Sodom, Noah's ark, Sampson snakeroot, Aaron's-rod, Adam's-flannel, balm of Gilead poplar, Jacob's-ladder, and sage of Bethlehem. Others commemorate physicians (Bowman's root and Culver's physic), Indian tribes (Choctaw-root, Seneca snakeroot), saints (St.-Bennet's-herb, St.-Benedict's-thistle), or figures from Greek mythology (Hercules'-club, Venus's-shoe). Animals also figure prominently: pigeonberry, partridgeberry, chickenberry, deerberry, crane's-bill, dove's-foot, wake-robin, bumblebee root, lambkill, hog apple, ox balm, robin runaway, mouse-ear, squirrel cup. And some names have a regional connotation: Virginia poke, Canada tea, Scotch mercury.

Certain suffixes are used over and over: *-tree* and *-bush* are added to other names; *-root* and *-wood* emphasize certain parts of the plant (bitterroot, birthroot, spicewood, canoewood); *-weed* appears often (gypsyweed, butterweed, milkweed); *-wort*, Middle English for "plant," is common (quillwort, motherwort, ragwort, huskwort); and *-bane* appears occasionally attached to whatever the plant will repel (bugbane, fleabane, ratbane).

Nonmedicinal uses suggest that many of the plants have been multipurpose and have probably been in use for a long time: pegwood, spindle tree, canoewood, spoonwood, leatherwood, ropebark, tanbark tree, cabinet cherry, tallowberrry, candleberry, inkberry.

In spite of this plethora, people have always had trouble finding new names for plants and often fall back on other plants—Indian shamrock, Texas sarsaparilla, false valerian, velvet dock. A few new names, however, have been derived by folk etymology: benjamin bush, from the generic name *Benzoin*; shoe-make, from sumac; beaumont root, apparently from Bowman's root, reversing the process perhaps. Pennyroyal is thought to derive from the Latin *pulegium*, though the phonic connection is hardly evident.

## Collecting Areas and Distributing Points

In the United States, the gathering of drug plants is chiefly, but not exclusively, a Southern industry. Most of the Southern drug plants are also native over the entire deciduous woodland; indeed, Cincinnati was the drug collection center until after the Civil War, and the Shaker colonies, mostly in the North, were among the chief packagers and distributors of drug materials.[25] Retreat of the deciduous forests, which shelter many of the plants, to the mountainous areas combined with the labor availability of the poor mountain farmer to make the southern Appalachians, and to a small extent the Ozarks, the chief centers of collection.

The dealers who buy crude drugs and distribute them wholesale to manufacturers, smaller distributors, and exporters are shown on figure 19.1. These are the main warehouses where drugs are received and stored and represent the chief "funnels" between the complementary processes of collection and distribution. I believe the map to be complete for the type of dealer described. There are several other collection points in east Tennessee, but so far as I know they are tributary to the dealers indicated. I have visited nearly all the drug houses shown. Although this industry has no directory, the people in it are well acquainted with their competitors and provided information about other firms. The map also represents the distribution of the scattered collection activity better than any other measure available.

The crude-drug industry is highly concentrated in the mountain area comprising the neighboring parts of Kentucky, West Virginia, Virginia, Tennessee, and North Carolina. The Blue Ridge is reported in most of the

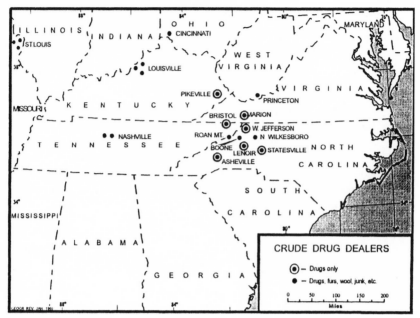

Fig. 19.1.  Distribution of Crude Drug Dealers

literature as the main area; some sources attribute as much as three-fourths of all collection to the Blue Ridge, but that figure seems too high, even if the entire Blue Ridge province is included.[26] Only four of the major dealers are located in the Blue Ridge province, though others draw some of their wares from it. The usual explanation of this concentration of the industry is that the Blue Ridge harbors the greatest variety of medicinal plants; such a statement would probably be valid if applied to the southern Appalachians as a whole, but it is almost impossible to verify for a small area. As was previously noted, most of the plants are widely distributed. The mountain environment provides a refuge for forest survival, a diversity of habitat, and relatively high rainfall. Braun says the forest of greatest diversity in dominant tree species is in the Cumberland Mountains.[27] The Blue Ridge, with somewhat more rainfall, higher elevations, and more fertile soils, may offer a more suitable habitat for the sensitive herbs of the forest floor.

The drier Ozarks form a poor second in drug production, since suitable herb-growing habitats are restricted to the more favorable sites for soil, slope, and exposure. Virtually all the herbs had dried up by early August in the drought of 1954, for example.

Crude-drug production in western North Carolina received a boost during the Civil War when a Confederate laboratory was established at Lincolnton.[28] A few years later, the first of the modern drug houses was founded by the Wallace Brothers at Statesville. By about 1900, three or four companies were operating in Ashe County, in the northwest corner of the state; competition proved tough, and some of them moved to other localities, leaving only the Blue Ridge Drug Company at West Jefferson today. One of the largest dealers is R. T. Greer and Company, with warehouses now in Statesville and in Marion, Virginia, and Pikeville, Kentucky; the Greer Drug Company at Lenoir is an offshoot controlled by another branch of the same family. S. B. Penick and Company, an international trader, claiming to be the world's largest botanical drug house, has a big warehouse at Asheville and also contracts for the purchases of some of the other dealers.

A large part of the raw material received is delivered to the warehouse by the collectors. One may bring in a handful of ginseng on the Saturday shopping trip, or a sack of cherry or slippery-elm bark, or a truckload of maypop herb. More remote collectors send in their herbs by parcel post or express or sell them to rural stores, feed and seed establishments, or junk dealers in their own localities; these in turn have agreements to supply the drug houses.

In the cities west of the Appalachians, the crude-drug trade in mostly in the hands of dealers in furs, hides, wool, and beeswax. Their collection areas are wide, usually covering several states. Most of their drugs are shipped to them, but some dealers operate trucks on regular routes to pick up roots and barks from rural stores or from the more regular collectors.

All the dealers put out price lists from time to time and send them to collectors who have furnished materials in the past. The prices fluctuate greatly with supply and demand. A dealer may raise the price on an item for which he or she has a large order to ensure an adequate supply, or the dealer may cut the price or stop buying if the dealer is overstocked.

A typical drug house is a three-story warehouse with a few thousand square feet of storage space on each floor. The most important pieces of equipment are the scales for weighing the drugs and the baling press for packaging them. The drugs are typically packed in sacks and barrels or piled on the floor to await sorting or disposition. The drug house is filled and surrounded with a fragrant blend of the odors of its many contents. Three or four employees are usually enough to take care of the work.

Some of the drugs are handled in quantities of hundreds of thousands of pounds a year; for others a few pounds will supply the market. Figures are not available on the total volume of trade, which is probably about three million dollars a year. Most of the dealers were finding business slow in the summer of 1954, and most of the collectors found prices either disappointing or unattractive. Some saw the lapse as a permanent consequence of the ruthless effectiveness of the new medicines. Others, long used to the ups and downs of the market, expected good times again when the surplus stocks were exhausted. In 1959, prices of many of the drugs were higher; others were lower. The volume of business is reported as continuing to decrease.

## The Collectors

Few collectors make their living primarily from gathering roots, barks, and herbs, though I have talked with many who did so at some previous time. Some have spent certain seasons traveling around with a truck, trying to find and exploit the richest hunting grounds. The mountain dweller is a victim of both hidden and evident unemployment. The marginal farmer who cannot keep productively busy on his or her small farm and the migrant who is home again after the layoff at a Piedmont rubber plant or a Texas oil field take advantage of their spare time to spend days in the woods and to gain a little needed cash. Many thousands of people contribute to collection of the total crop.

Both men and women take part in the work of collection. Children may earn spending money for themselves and will often work resources not sufficiently attractive for adults (sometimes with undesirable consequences for conservation). A typical return from a day of collecting is not more than two or three dollars, this to be balanced against an outlay for shoe leather and torn clothing in what cannot be called an easy job. The collector's tools vary with the quarry. A grubbing hoe is needed for large roots, some sort of trowel for small ones. Bark can be peeled with a sharp knife, perhaps after the tree has been cut with an ax; herbs can usually be collected by hand. The gunnysack is the common receptacle for the take. All drugs must be dried before marketing (fig. 19.2). If collectors work on a small scale, a shed roof or a bare rock may provide sufficient drying area. Some roots must be split or sliced to facilitate drying, and some of the barks will bring a better price if the outer layers are scraped off (rossed).

Seasons of collection vary with the farm workload, the persistence of the collector, and the nature of the material. Collectors who are heavily dependent on income from this business must work from early spring to late fall, regardless of when the plants are in best condition to be collected. Roots are best dug in the fall, when the active ingredients are concentrated in them and the loss of weight through drying is at the minimum. Barks are

Fig. 19.2.  Drying Ginseng in Southern West Virginia

best gathered in the spring, when they can be easily peeled. Herbs are gathered at different times, often when in flower.

## The Plants and Their Products

A few examples will tell more about the roots and herbs than statistical generalizations. Ginseng (Panax quinquefolium), though virtually ignored as a cure in the United States, is collected for sale to the Chinese (90 percent of current exports go to Hong Kong, 5 percent to Malaya) and is the most valuable of all wild drug plants in the United States, either in dollar volume or in price per pound. Ginseng exports total more than 100,000 pounds a year, and current prices paid collectors are $12 to $16 per pound. The generic name Panax reflects the plant's status as a panacea among the Chinese, who value the root for its gnarled and twisted appearance (fig. 19.2) and for its frequent resemblance to the human body or its members.

The discovery that American ginseng could be sold as a supplement to the native Chinese supply is credited to a Jesuit in Canada, early in the eighteenth century.[29] It formed an important catch crop for the frontier farmer, who could sell it as a by-product of forest clearing. Ginseng is a sensitive herbaceous perennial that demands a rich mull soil and well-watered woodland shade. Through most of its range summer drought restricts it to north slopes and sheltered coves. It will not survive much disturbance of the forest. It persists in the collecting grounds because of certain qualities. The seeds do not sprout until the second spring after their ripening in the fall, and in some years the roots may not send up the shoots that guide the diggers to them. Moreover, the seasoned collector will leave the smallest plants, whose roots are too small to have much value, and will scatter the seeds over the ground if he or she digs the roots in the fall.

A steady increase in price has accompanied the gradual depletion of the plant.[30] Most of the ginseng is dug sporadically, but a few collectors are able to bring in the better part of a pound in a day and may make a living from it during the season. The high price on the root helps to make a sport rather than a task of the search for the graceful plant with the bright-green leaves, divided palmately into five leaflets. Many a mountaineer will hunt ginseng who does not feel it worthwhile to dig other roots. The digging of ginseng is pleasantly combined with squirrel hunting in the fall, when the greater part is collected. Ginseng is, in fact, though not in law, a fugitive resource; it becomes the property of the finder regardless of on whose property it may be growing.[31]

West Virginia seems to be the leading ginseng state, with Kentucky second. The nonfarming country of southern West Virginia and parts of eastern Kentucky has an abundance of rich forests. The plant is not yet on the edge of extermination, for the dealers notice a marked increase of ginseng collection with unemployment in the coal fields. Many other states contribute substantially to ginseng production, south and east to the inner margin of the Coastal Plain, west into Oklahoma, and north into Canada.

Probably more people have dreamed of cultivating ginseng than have ever dug it in the woods. Thousands have tried, but few have succeeded, much less made the twenty thousand dollars an acre a simple calculation shows to be possible. The plant is not ready to dig for about six years; it must be grown under shade and is affected by drought and many diseases. Probably more cultivated ginseng is marketed than wild, but the price received for the larger and smoother cultivated root is much lower. Fromm Brothers near Hamburg, Wisconsin, have been the most successful cultivators recently;[32] Rafinesque earlier reported the Shakers as cultivators of ginseng.

Goldenseal or yellow root (*Hydrastis canadensis*) is respected both for its curative properties and for the price it brings, long second only to that of ginseng. Unlike ginseng, which the collectors look upon as a Chinese whimsy, goldenseal is considered a sure cure for sores in the mouth and an aid for many stomach troubles, and it has also been used in the treatment of certain venereal diseases. Some Indians used it for a dyestuff (yellow puccoon), the Cherokees for a cancer cure, but American doctors were slow to recognize its value.[33] Its habitat is similar to that of ginseng, but gathering has probably reduced the supply even more. The price of goldenseal has often run from $5.00 to $6.00 a pound, but it was less than $1.50 in 1954 and is nearly $3.00 now. Goldenseal also has been cultivated, sometimes with considerable profit. Goldenseal and ginseng have both been cultivated in Oregon and Washington in recent years.

Mayapple or mandrake (*Podophyllum peltatum*) is a common forest plant whose root is used as a purgative and in the preparation of the resinous material podophyllin. Its discovery is credited to the Cherokees. Long after it had become an important medicine in North America, a relative in India with nearly identical properties was put to use.[34] The market for mandrake root, which formerly reached half a million pounds a year, is now down to less than half that.

Bloodroot or red puccoon (*Sanguinaria canadensis*) has been listed in the formulary for a long time. The root, which exudes a red juice, is used as a stimulant and an emetic and in many home compounds for colds. The plant is abundantly available in the woods. The price has been above fifty cents a pound recently, but the prices of fifteen to twenty-five cents a pound current a few years ago could hardly reward the effort of digging roots that may run as many as two hundred to a pound. Another common plant is known as black cohosh or cohosh bugbane (*Cimicifuga racemosa*). This plant sends up a stem three to six feet in height and is easily spotted, but in some years it brings only two to ten cents a pound. Other species of *Cimicifuga* were used as insect repellents in Europe, but black cohosh is probably best known as a constituent of Lydia Pinkham's compound, reminiscent of the old Indian designation of it as "squaw root."

Carolina jessamine (*Gelsemium sempervirens*) is a woody vine of the bottom forests of the Southeast. The properties of its roots were discovered accidentally when a servant gave some to a sick Mississippi planter. The potent alkaloids nearly killed the man, but his fever vanished. The root became a constituent of a famous "electrical febrifuge" of the day.

The American falsehellebore (*Veratrum viride*) was early recognized as a substitute for its European relative (*V. album*). Indians used it for wounds and aches and as an ordeal test. Peter Kalm reports two unusual applications: a decoction of the root was used to poison seed corn to keep birds from eating it (it was said to make blackbirds dizzy); and placed on a comb (it was considered useful in killing lice).[35] During the Revolution it was substituted for the European species used by patients afflicted with gout. A potent and dangerous drug, hellebore is now kept on the restricted list.

Mad-dog skullcap (*Scutellaria lateriflora*) is a bitter mint that had some use for insomnia. In 1772 it was introduced as a cure for rabies (as other mints seem to have been in many lands). For a generation or more it continued to be used as a leading antihydrophobic before it was at last proved ineffective.

Several barks are handled in large volume. Wild black cherry (*Prunus serotina*), obtained in clearing pastures, is frequently used in cough sirups. Sassafras is a pest quick to come in on cleared land; most of the sassafras-root bark is a by-product of clearing. Sassafras tea is an old-fashioned spring tonic for purifying the blood and is still produced by several companies. The flavor of sassafras may also be detected in root beers. White pine (*Pinus strobus*) bark, also used in cough sirup, is usually a by-product of lumbering.

A number of important drugs grow in habitats not found in the Appalachians. Passionflower vine, or maypop, grows as a weed in Piedmont cotton fields just as blackroot (*Veronicastrum virginicum*) does in bottom fields along the Mississippi. A small quantity of cotton-root bark (*Gossypium hirsutum*) is still marketed; among the slaves it was a conveniently available abortifacient. A few prairie species such as *Echinacea angustifolia* are collected. Pinkroot (*Spigelia marilandica*), a vermifuge taken mixed with senna, and earlier known to the Cherokees, is rare north of Alabama and Georgia. A nearly identical plant in east Tennessee (*Ruellia ciliosa*), has often been confused with the genuine plant, which once brought the attractive price of $1.25 a pound.[36] Pipsissewa (*Chimaphila umbellata, C. maculata*) is a low herb most common in the pine forests of lowland Maryland and Delaware. It forms a constituent of some root beers and is also used medicinally.

Cascara buckthorn (*Rhamnus purshiana*) is a small tree of the Pacific Northwest, first identified on the Lewis and Clark expedition and known to settlers by the biblical term Chittim wood.[37] The laxative effect of its bark, apparently known to the Indians, was introduced to medicine by Dr. Bundy, an eclectic of Colusa, California; Parke, Davis used the bark in preparations in 1877.[38] Its Eurasian relative, *Rhamnus cathartica*, was in use in Europe before the Norman Conquest. The bark, usually obtained by cutting down the tree, is aged for a year after drying in the shade. Production amounts to a million or two pounds a year at the rate of perhaps ten pounds per tree, and the native stand has gradually diminished. Cascara buckthorn probably accounts for a larger dollar volume of sales than any other American wild drug plant except ginseng; exports run a few hundred thousand pounds a year, two-thirds going to Britain.

Although the root and herb industry is slowly declining, a number of its products are still in demand. Americans will be slow to give up completely the long reliance on many of their plants. As collection slows, many species will have a chance to regain their original abundance and to play their natural part in the forest community, no longer threatened with exhaustion or extinction. Those still in demand will have to fight it out with the price and the labor supply. The prices quoted will be only enough to induce collectors to bring in the proper quantity. But the labor supply for collecting work may well disappear before the demand for the plants is eliminated.

# Notes

1. Josselyn excerpts appear in H. W. Felter (ed.), "The Genesis of the American Materia Medica," *Lloyd Library Bulletin No. 26, Reproduction Series No. 8*, 1927. Among the cures mentioned are "Blew Flower-de-luce" (probably *Iris versicolor*), "To provoke Vomit and for Bruises"; "White Hellebore" (*Veratrum viride*), for "Wounds and Aches Cured by the Indians. For the Toothache. For Herpes milliares"; "Ravens-Claw" (*Geranium maculatum*), "admirable for Agues"; and a concoction mixed from sundry ingre-

dients, including sassafras (*Sassafras variifolium*) root and three Old World weeds—catmint (*Nepeta cataria*), sow thistle (*Sonchus* sp.), and enula campana (*Inula helenium*); Thomas Glover, "An Account of Virginia, Its Scituation, Temperature, Productions, Inhabitants and Their Manner of Planting and Ordering Tobacco," *Philosophical Transactions of the Royal Society of London* ( 20 June, 1676), reprinted by Basil H. Blackwell (Oxford, England, 1904), 16, 18, and 26.

2. Some sixty drugs used by American Indians are said to be in the modern materia medica and in formulae prepared by drug houses according to M. E. Pickard and R. C. Buley, *The Midwest Pioneer: His Ills, Cures, and Doctors* (Crawfordsville, Ind.,1945), 40.

3. Glover, 26.

4. Peter Smith, *The Indian Doctor's Dispensatory* (Cincinnati, 1913). Reprinted as *Lloyd Library Bulletin No. 2, Reproduction Series No. 2*, 1901.

5. Walter Conrad Muenscher, *Weeds* (New York: Macmillan, 1952), 26. Muenscher notes that among weeds of recent medicinal use mentioned by Josselyn are quack grass (*Agropyron repens*), dandelion (*Taraxacum officinale*), and mullein (*Verbascum thapsus*). Most of the medicinal plants mentioned by Glover were European weeds. See also Peter Kalm, *America of 1750: Peter Kalm's Travels in North America; The English Version of 1770* (New York: Wilson-Erickson, 1937). Among medicinal weeds mentioned by Kalm are narrow dock (*Rumex crispus*), burdock (*Arctium lappa*), and mullein. Mullein provided leaves for tea for dysentery and a root decoction for injection into cattle wounds infested with worms; American Swedes tied the leaves around their feet and arms when suffering from ague.

6. The *Eclectic Medical Journal* (1836–1937) and the *Eclectic Medical Gleaner* (1889–1912), both published in Cincinnati, devoted their issues to a variety of medical topics, including copious notes on herbal remedies.

7. *The Pharmacopoeia of the United States of America*, 15th revision, Easton, Penna.: Mack Printing, 1955.

8. *The National Formulary*, 7th ed. (Washington, D.C.: American Pharmaceutical Association, 1942); 8th ed. (1946); 9th ed. (1950).

9. D. S. Correll et al., "The Search for Plant Precursors of Cortisone," *Economic Botany* 9 (1955): 327–40.

10. Catalog No. 852, The Old Fashioned Herb Company, Pasadena, California.

11. The doctrine of signatures was systemized by Theophrastus von Hohenheim (1493–1541) in Alexander Nelson, *Medical Botany* (Edinburgh, Scotland: E & S Livingstone, 1951), 375.

12. For example, 440 species were considered by Ernst T. Stuhr in "Medicinal Plants of Florida," *Journal of the American Pharmaceutical Associa-*

*tion* 17 (1928): 761–66, and 1160 in *Manual of Pacific Coast Drug Plants* (Lancaster, Penna., 1933). About 250 are listed as having some commercial demand in Leo Roy Tehon, "The Drug Plants of Illinois," *Illinois Natural History Survey Circular 44*, 1951; and 307 were listed by B. B. Smyth, "Preliminary List of Medicinal and Economic Kansas Plants with Their Reputed Therapeutic Value," *Kansas Academy of Sciences* 18 (1901–2): 191–209.

13. In selecting the list of plants in current use, I have relied chiefly on "American Medicinal Plants of Commercial Importance," *United States Department of Agriculture Miscellaneous Publication No. 77*, 1930, and on several earlier publications by Alice Henkel, "Weeds Used in Medicine," *United States Department of Agriculture Farmers' Bulletin 188*, 1904; "Wild Medicinal Plants of the United States," *United States Bureau of Plant Industry Bulletin 89*, 1906; "American Root Drugs," *United States Bureau of Plant Industry Bulletin 107*, 1907; "American Medicinal Barks," *United States Bureau of Plant Industry Bulletin 139*, 1909; "American Medicinal Leaves and Herbs," *United States Bureau of Plant Industry Bulletin 219*, 1911; and "American Medicinal Flowers, Fruits, and Seeds," *United States Department of Agriculture Bulletin 26*, 1913.

14. John U. Lloyd, *Origin and History of All the Pharmacopeial Vegetable Drugs, Chemicals and Preparations* (Cincinnati, 1921), vol. 1, 323–24; see also *The Eclectic and General Dispensatory* (Philadelphia, 1827), 163: "This annual plant is a native of America, but is now naturalized to this country [England] . . . growing on dunghills and by roadsides." Kalm, vol. 1, 81, observed it in America as a frequenter of habitats occupied by different weeds in Sweden.

15. Lloyd, 323–24.

16. J. J. Willaman and B. G. Schubert, "Alkaloid Hunting," *Economic Botany* 9 (1955): 147.

17. For example, Jonathan Carver, *Travels through the Interior Parts of North America, in the Years 1766, 1767, and 1768* (London: n.p., 1781) and Constantine Samuel Rafinesque, *Medical Flora; or, Manual of the Medical Botany of the United States of North America*, 2 vols. (Philadelphia: Atkinson & Alexander, 1828–1830).

18. I have not attempted to cite references for all the information about medicinal plants and their uses. Sources consulted frequently and not elsewhere specified include the following: Oliver Perry Medsger, *Edible Wild Plants* (New York: Macmillan, 1939); Charles Frederick Millspaugh, *American Medicinal Plants* (New York: Dover, 1974); and Walter Conrad Muenscher, *Poisonous Plants of the United States* (New York: Macmillan, 1949).

19. John U. Lloyd, "History of the Vegetable Drugs of the Pharmacopoeia of the United States," *Lloyd Library Bulletin No. 18, Pharmacy Series No. 4* (1911): 71.

20. *Gray's Manual of Botany*, 7th ed. (New York: American Book Company, 1908).

21. Families and some of their prominent species include Ranunculaceae, goldenseal (*Hydrastis canadensis*); black cohosh (*Cimicifuga racemosa*); Berberidaceae, blue cohosh (*Caulophyllum thalictroides*); Lauraceae, sassafras, spicebush (*Lindera benzoin*); Menispermaceae; Magnoliaceae.

22. The six families with medicinal plants are Salicaceae (willow), Myricaceae (wax myrtle), Juglandaceae (walnut), Betulaceae (birch), Fagaceae (oak, beech), and Urticaceae (nettle).

23. Other families worthy of note, with the number of their medicinal species, are Ericaceae, six; Rosaceae, five; Scrophulariaceae, five; Liliaceae, four; Solonaceae, three; Umbelliferae, three; Araliaceae, three; and Araceae, three.

24. I have drawn most heavily on the copious lists of names in the "American Medicinal Plants of Commercial Importance," *United States Department of Agriculture Miscellaneous Publication No. 77* (1930), but have supplemented these when new names have emerged. The lists were evidently taken in great part from publications of the 1750–1830 period. There is no reason to believe that all the names listed in *Publication No. 77* are in current use, and there is some question as to whether certain of them have ever been used in this country. I can say for my collection only that it consists of English-language names applied to the plants at some time. Meanings and derivations of common names have come most frequently from *Webster's New International Dictionary*, meanings of generic names from *Gray's Manual of Botany*.

25. C. O. Ewing and E. E. Stanford, "Botanicals of the Blue Ridge," *Journal of the American Pharmaceutical Association* 8 (1919): 16–26. See also John U. and C. G. Lloyd, "*Hydrastis canadensis*," *Lloyd Library Bulletin No. 10, Reproduction Series No. 6* (1908): 89–90. Cincinnati is mentioned as the distribution center, and a Shaker is quoted on the early commercial history of goldenseal. Rafinesque, 20, makes frequent reference to Shakers as distributors of particular products. Many American drugstores in recent years have exhibited a series of pictures telling the history of pharmaceuticals, which have featured the role of the Shakers. The work of John U. Lloyd (1849–1936) on botanical drugs, his many writings about them, and the establishment of the Lloyd Library devoted to botany and medicine are all products of Cincinnati's importance in the drug trade. The earlier writings of Daniel Drake (1785–1852) had also contributed both to knowledge of domestic medicines and to their availability in Cincinnati.

26. For example, Ewing and Stanford.

27. Emma Lucy Braun, *Deciduous Forests of Eastern North America*

(Philadelphia: Blakiston, 1950). Her explanation relates the large variety of tree species to the long period of undisturbed development on remnants of the Schooley peneplain.

28. Newspapser clippings on file in the Asheville Public Library.

29. Maurice Grenville Kains, *Ginseng-Its Cultivation, Harvesting, Marketing, and Market Value, with a Short Account of Its History and Botany* (New York, 1914), 3; and A. R. Harding, *Ginseng and Other Medicinal Plants*, rev. ed., (Columbus, Ohio: Published by author, 1908), 43–44. A description and drawing of ginseng had been published in 1713 by Father Jartoux, a missionary in China, in "The Description of a Tartarian Plant Called Ginseng, with an Account of Its Virtues," *Philosophical Transactions of the Royal Society of London* 28 (1713), 237–47. Father Jartoux suggested that, if the plant was to be found elsewhere, Canada would be a likely place because its forests and mountains resembled those in northern China. According to Kains, a Father Lafitau saw the article, sought the plant in Canada, and discovered it near Montreal in 1716. In Harding's account, Father Jartoux himself came to Canada to find the ginseng. In either case, trade in American ginseng developed only a few years after the publication of Father Jartoux's article.

30. Kains, 47, and Harding, 125–26. Quoted prices rose from $.52 cents in 1858 to $2.13 in 1888, $3.66 in 1898, and $7.50 in 1913. The top export reported by Kains and Harding was more than 400,000 pounds, in 1878, but Louis O. Williams, "Ginseng," *Economic Botany* 11 (1957): 344–48, reports the official 1862 figure of 622, 761 pounds—surprising for a country split by war, but possibly including an accumulation from the year before.

31. A special law was passed in West Virginia to forbid digging or prospecting for ginseng on someone else's land in counties wishing to be included in the provision in Kains, 140. Several states have laws forbidding digging of ginseng in spring and early summer when the root is less valuable and before the seeds have ripened in Kains, 138–39.

32. Katherine Sutherland Pinkerton, *Bright with Silver* (New York: Sloane, 1947 rev. ed., 1953). In 1951, Fromm Brothers were reported to have eighty-one acres planted.

33. Lloyd, "*Hydrastis canadensis*," 86, 152, 154, and 155.

34. Ramgopal Chatterjee, "Indian Podophyllum," *Economic Botany* 6 (1952): 342–54: Nelson, 396.

35. Kalm, 249 and 257.

36. W. W. Stockberger, "The Drug Known as Pinkroot," *United States Bureau of Plant Industry Bulletin 100*, Part V (1907): 41–44. Another species (*Spigelia anthelmia*) is known as a vermifuge in the West Indies and Africa. See E. G. B. Gooding, "Facts and Beliefs about Barbadian Plants," *Journal of Barbados Museum and Historical Society* 9 (1942): 192–94.

37. Proceedings of Conference on the Cultivation of Drug and Associated Economic Plants in California, Los Angeles, California, 28–29 December, 1943, 81.

38. Lloyd, "History of the Vegetable Drugs of the Pharmacopoeia of the United States," 68.

# Selected Bibliography

## Part I: Folk Architecture

Ensminger, Robert F. *The Pennsylvania Barn: Its Origin, Evolution, and Distribution*. Baltimore, Md.: Johns Hopkins University Press, 1992.
The most scholarly, exhaustive, and recent study on a folk architecture type that has been covered by virtually every folklore discipline, including architectural historians, cultural geographers, folklorists, and anthropologists.

Glassie, Henry. *Pattern in the Material Folk Culture of the Eastern United States*. Philadelphia: University of Pennsylvania Press, 1968; *Folk Housing in Middle Virginia: A Structural Analysis of Historic Artifacts*. Knoxville: University of Tennessee Press, 1975.
From one of the most prolific folklife scholars (see chapter 1), these two works are among his most innovative and brilliant in terms of meticulous analyses and convincing observations of the evolution of the Western mind. Both are absolutely essential reading and contain extensive bibliographies.

Hubka, Thomas C. *Big House, Little House, Back House, Barn: The Connected Farm Buildings of New England*. Hanover, N. H.: University Press of New England, 1984.
A book-length study that fills the gaps proposed by Zelinsky in chapter 3.

Jordan, Terry G. *American Log Buildings: An Old World Heritage*. Chapel Hill: University of North Carolina Press, 1985. Terry G. Jordan, and Matti Kaups. *The American Backwoods Frontier: An Ethnic and Ecological Interpretation*. Baltimore, Md.: Johns Hopkins University Press, 1989. Terry G. Jordan, Jon T. Kilpinen, and Charles F. Gritzner. *The Mountain West:*

*Interpreting the Folk Landscape.* Baltimore, Md.: Johns Hopkins University Press, 1997.
Cultural geographer Jordan has distinguished himself as the contemporary authority writing on folk architecture, especially on European antecedents of log construction. In the Jordan-Kaups book, chapter 6, "Log Construction," and chapter 7, "Backwoods Folk Architecture," are most valuable. The Jordan-Kilpinen-Gritzner collaboration covers log dwellings, log outbuildings, and log carpentry traditions in chapters 2 to 4 as well as wooden fences in chapter 5. All three works with Jordan as lead author contain an impressive list of references.

Kniffen, Fred B. "Louisiana House Types," *Annals of the Association of American Geographers* 26 (1936): 179–93; "Folk Housing: Key to Diffusion," *Annals of the Association of American Geographers* 55 (1965): 549–77; Fred B. Kniffen, and Henry H. Glassie. "Building in Wood in the Eastern United States: A Time-Place Perspective," *Geographical Review* 56 (1966): 40–66.
Kniffen is *the* pioneer in American folk architecture. Kniffen's two classic articles elevated the topic by classifying and naming folk house types that others continue to use. The 1965 article summarizes almost thirty years of study on folk buildings and identifies the three hearths (New England, Middle Atlantic, and Lower Chesapeake) as the source areas for American folk houses. Kniffen and Glassie present a detailed analysis of horizontal log construction and theorize that log construction diffused to the Upland and Lowland South via the Germans and Scotch-Irish.

McAlester, Virginia, and McAlester, Lee. *A Field Guide to American Houses.* New York: Knopf, 1984.
This widely acclaimed guide is the most useful publication for identifying architectural styles in the United States. For folk architecture, the most valuable section is chapter 2, "Folk Houses," which covers Native American, Pre-Railroad, and National folk house types. The diagrams, maps, photographs, and bibliography provide additional enhancement to the text.

Marshall, Howard Wight. *American Folk Architecture: A Selected Bibliography.* Washington, D.C.: American Folklife Center, 1981.
Although dated, this is still the most complete bibliography on folk architecture found in one publication. Marshall divides the bibliography into five sections: Theory and General Works, Antecedents to American Building, Regional Works, Museums and Historic Preservation, and Field Documentation.

Noble, Allen G. *Wood, Brick, and Stone: The North American Settlement*

*Landscape.* Amherst: University of Massachusetts Press, 1984. 2 vols.; *To Build in a New Land: Ethnic Landscapes in North America.* Baltimore, Md.: Johns Hopkins University Press, 1992. Allen G. Noble, and Richard K. Cleek, *The Old Barn Book: A Field Guide to North American Barns and other Farm Structures.* New Brunswick, N. J.: Rutgers University Press, 1995.

The 1984 prize-winning two-volume series is a must for all folk architecture enthusiasts. Volume 1 covers houses, while volume 2 includes barns and other farm structures. The 1992 volume edited by Noble contains twenty-two original essays by twenty noted contributors. The Noble and Cleek work is the most recent account of barns and is valuable as a guide to identifying barn types.

Roberts, Warren E. "Folk Architecture," in *Folklore and Folklife: An Introduction,* ed. Richard M. Dorson. Chicago: University of Chicago Press, 1972.

An exceptional definition of folk architecture as compared to academic architecture. Log-building construction techniques are explained and illustrated with diagrams and photographs.

Upton, Dell, ed. *America's Architectural Roots: Ethnic Groups That Built America.* Washington, D.C.: Preservation Press, 1986; Dell Upton, and John Michael Vlach, (eds.). *Common Places: Readings in American Vernacular Architecture.* Athens: University of Georgia Press, 1986.

Upton has edited a worthwhile introduction to ethnic landscapes of America representing a wide variety of groups from African Americans to Ukrainians. The Upton and Vlach edition is composed of twenty-three previously published articles by notable folk architecture scholars including Kniffen, Glassie, Roberts, and Upton.

## Part II: Folk Food and Drink

*American Heritage Cookbook and Illustrated History of American Eating and Drinking.* New York: Simon & Schuster, 1984.

Drawn from historical sources and magnificently illustrated with numerous photographs and reproductions of artwork, this often-cited volume includes a series of essays on various regional and ethnic cuisines of the United States along with menus and recipes.

Bourke, John Gregory. "The Folk-Foods of the Rio Grande Valley and of Northern Mexico," *Journal of American Folklore* 8 (1895): 41–71.

This was the pioneering effort by a folklorist to study foodways. It remained the only scholarly work on traditional foods for fifty years.

Brown, Linda Keller, and Mussell, Kay, eds.. *Ethnic and Regional Foodways in the United States: Performance of Group Identity*. Knoxville: University of Tennessee Press, 1984.
An outstanding collection of essays authored primarily by anthropologists and folklorists, it is widely cited in the foodways literature. Readers should also consult authors' special volume of the *Journal of American Culture*.

Camp, Charles. *American Foodways: What, When, Why, and How We Eat in America*. Little Rock, Ark.: August House, 1989.
Authored by a folklorist, this volume in the American Folklore Series, edited by W. K. McNeil, is a culmination of Camp's earlier work in *Journal of American Culture* and *American Quarterly*. This is a must for students interested in American foodways. Contains an excellent bibliography.

Cummings, Richard Osborn. *The American and His Food: A History of Food Habits in the United States*. Chicago: University of Chicago Press, 1940 (reprint, New York: Arno Press, 1970).
Although dated, a scholarly account of the history of the American diet. American traditional foods are discussed from an authoritative perspective and given thorough detail.

Cussler, Margaret, and de Give, Mary L. *Twixt the Cup and the Lip: Psychological and Socio-Cultural Factors Affecting Food Habits*. New York: Twayne Publishers, 1952.
Based on extensive fieldwork by the authors in the early 1940s, this book remains a classic study of food patterns in the rural South. A series of outstanding photographs enhances the text.

Gutierrez, C. Paige. *Cajun Foodways*. Jackson: University Press of Mississippi, 1992.
One of the best recent studies of regional/ethnic foodways. Author based her writing on extensive fieldwork with a folkloristic and cultural anthropology perspective. Food jokes, food festivals, and symbolic aspects of Cajun dishes are described. See also Gutierrez' essay in the Brown-Mussell book.

Hilliard, Sam Bowers. *Hog Meat and Hoe Cake: Food Supply in the Old South, 1840–1860*. Carbondale: Southern Illinois University Press, 1972.
Hilliard, a historical-cultural geographer, bases his research on historical diaries, manuscript collections, and travelers' accounts from the period

preceding the American Civil War. One of the most thorough and original studies on nineteenth-century Southern diets. Well-illustrated with
thirty-five maps, it is an outgrowth of his earlier article in the *Annals of
the Association of American Geographers* article on pork and the repro-
duced essay in chapter 7 of this anthology.

Jones, Michael Owen, Giuliano, Bruce, and Krell, Roberta, eds. *Foodways
and Eating Habits: Directions for Research.* Los Angeles: California Folklore Society, 1983.
A collection of articles written by folklorists that provides an excellent
overview of issues in foodways research. Based on a special issue of *Western Folklore.*

Levenstein, Harvey A. *Revolution at the Table: Transformation of the American Diet.* New York: Oxford University Press, 1988; *Paradox of Plenty: A
Social History of Eating in Modern America.* New York: Oxford University
Press, 1993.
Authored by a historian, these two volumes provide the best and most
recent history of American food from the late nineteenth century to the
present. Chapter 2 in the 1988 book gives an incisive account of tenant
farmers' diets and discusses "dirt-eaters" in the South. Highly recommended because of the author's writing style and research techniques.

Shortridge, Barbara G., and Shortridge, James R. "Cultural Geography of
American Foodways: An Annotated Bibliography," *Journal of Cultural
Geography* 15 (1995): 79–108.
This bibliography contains 135 entries from the more than 1,250 this
wife-husband team of cultural geographers have collected in a master list
for their geography of foodways seminar at the University of Kansas. They
are authoring an anthology on this topic for Rowman & Littlefield
Publishers.

Sokolov, Raymond A. *Fading Feast: A Compendium of Disappearing Regional Foods.* New York: Farrar, Straus, and Giroux, 1981; *Why We Eat
What We Eat: How the Encounter between the New World and the Old
World Changed the Way Everyone on the Planet Eats.* New York: Summit
Books, 1991.
These two books have achieved national notoriety because of Sokolov's
contributions to *Natural History* magazine and are widely quoted in both
academic and popular literature. The 1991 book presents a comparative
analysis between Old and New World contributions to the American diet.

Yoder, Don. "Folk Cookery," in *Folklore and Folklife: An Introduction*, ed.
Richard M. Dorson. Chicago: University of Chicago Press, 1972; "Histor-

ical Sources for American Traditional Cookery," in *Discovering American Folklife*, ed. Don Yoder. Ann Arbor, Mich.: UMI Research Press, 1990. Studies on folk cookery by a leading folklorist on American foodways. Yoder examines preparation, morphology, and preservation of food as well as social functions in folklife. His research on Pennsylvania folk culture focuses on such individual foods as sauerkraut, mush, and schnitz.

## Part III: Folk Music

Ancelet, Barry. *Cajun Music: Its Origins and Development*. Lafayette: Center for Louisiana Studies, 1989. Barry Ancelet, and Mathe Allain. *Travailler, c'est trop dur: The Tools of Cajun Music*. Lafayette: Lafayette Natural History Museum Association, 1985.
Ancelet and his colleagues have forged the best studies in Cajun music from south Louisiana. Fiddle, accordion, and *tit fer* (triangle) constituted the original triumvirate of Cajun folk music, however, the *frottoir* (rubboard) has subsequently replaced the triangle as rhythm instrument. The fiddle diffused from Canada by way of Acadian diaspora, while the accordion was introduced by German settlers after the Civil War.

Carney, George O., ed. *The Sounds of People and Places: A Geography of American Folk and Popular Music*, (3rd ed.). Lanham, Md.: Rowman & Littlefield, 1994.
A collection of twenty previously published articles contributed by cultural geographers who have researched American music. Folk music selections concentrate on such genres as blues, bluegrass, gospel, zydeco, jazz, Ozark ballads, and Woody Guthrie's Dust Bowl ballads. Includes more than fifty maps on American folk music.

Jackson, George Pullen. *White Spirituals in the Southern Uplands*. Chapel Hill: University of North Carolina Press, 1933 (reprint, New York: Dover, 1965). "Some Factors in the Diffusion of American Religious Folksongs," *Journal of American Folklore* 65 (1952): 356–69.
Jackson's book on the shape-note tradition is the foundation for any further study. His seminal work in 1933 is the most quoted authority on the subject of spirituals. The 1952 article is widely acclaimed among cultural geographers from Kniffen to Jordan because of its series of diffusion maps.

Lomax, Alan. *The Folk Songs of North America in the English Language*. Garden City, N.Y.: Doubleday, 1960; *The Land Where the Blues Began*. New York: Random House, 1993.

Lomax is one of the premier authorities on folk music both in America and throughout the would because of his Cantometrics project on world folk music. The 1960 book presents a regionalization of five styles of American folk music accompanied by two helpful maps. The 1993 book is Lomax's recent analysis of the Mississippi Delta country blues. An excellent videotape of the same name is from the *American Patchwork Series* on public television. Highly recommended for classroom use.

Malone, Bill C. *Country Music, U. S. A.* (rev. ed.) Austin: University of Texas Press, 1985. *Singing Cowboys and Musical Mountaineers: Southern Culture and the Roots of Country Music.* Athens: University of Georgia Press, 1993.

Malone is *the* authority on country music from its inception to the present. The 1985 book is the beginning point for all those who want to study country music. Both books give the folk music roots before the commercialization of country music. Both publications are well documented and contain extensive bibliographies and discographies.

Oliver, Paul. *The Story of the Blues.* New York: Chilton, 1969; *Aspects of the Blues Tradition.* New York: Oak Publications, 1970.

An incisive interpreter of the blues, this British scholar's works are among the most authoritative and carefully documented accounts of this American folk music genre. Readers interested in the blues should start with the 1969 book. His introduction to the 1970 book provides an analytical overview of the blues tradition.

Paredes, Américo. *A Texas Mexican Cancionero: Folksongs of the Lower Border.* Urbana: University of Illinois Press, 1977.

Authored by an eminent folklorist, this volume examines the *canción*, a folk song of a romantic or introspective nature, sung by Mexicans in the borderland region.

Randolph, Vance. *Ozark Folksongs.* 4 vols. (rev. ed.) Columbia: University of Missouri Press, 1980.

A monumental work unparalleled in its scope by any other collection from a particular region. Based on intensive fieldwork in the 1920s, Randolph gives full texts as well as names and location of informants.

Robb, John Donald. *Hispanic Folk Songs of New Mexico.* Albuquerque: University of New Mexico Press, 1954; *Hispanic Folk Music of New Mexico and the Southwest.* Norman: University of Oklahoma Press, 1985.

These two volumes present the most valuable regional collection on this genre of American folk music. Included are sacred, secular, and instrumental music with informative notes on each type as well as complete texts and English translations.

Rosenberg, Neil. *Bluegrass: A History*. Urbana: University of Illinois Press, 1987.
   The title is deceptive because this volume is the most comprehensive study of bluegrass ever written. A folklorist, Rosenberg has authored the definitive history of this folk music genre. The starting point for those readers interested in bluegrass is this meticulously researched book of 447 pages.

Schuller, Gunther. *Early Jazz: Its Roots and Musical Development*. New York: Oxford University Press, 1968; *The Swing Era: The Development of Jazz, 1933–1945*. New York: Oxford University Press, 1989.
   These two works constitute the most perceptive analyses of jazz from its inception through the Big Band era. As insightful guides to jazz, these books offer musical analysis of the genre and place the music into the American cultural context.

## Part IV: Folk Sports and Games

Beezley, William H. "Locker Rumors: Folklore and Football," *Journal of the Folklore Institute* 17 (1980): 196–221.
   An examination of the occupational code of professional football players. It provides a treatment of the folktypes of coach and team joker shared by players.

Brunvand, Jan Harold. *The Study of American Folklore: An Introduction*. New York: W. W. Norton, 1968.
   See chapter 15, "Folk Games," for an analysis of games involving manipulation of objects (balls) and variations of organized sports such as baseball ("Work-Up" and "Flies and Grounders") and basketball ("Round the World" and "H-O-R-S-E").

Coffin, Tristram P. *The Illustrated Book of Baseball Folklore*. New York: Seabury Press, 1975.
   One of the few book-length studies by a professional folklorist devoted to sports. Coffin examines slogans, aphorisms, anecdotes, superstitions, and legends surrounding the entire body of folk traditions in professional baseball.

Culin, Stewart. "Street Games of Boys in Brooklyn, New York," *Journal of American Folklore* 4 (1891): 221–37; *Games of North American Indians*. Washington, D.C.: Bureau of American Ethnology, 1907.
   As an American anthropologist, Culin was one of the pioneers in sports and games folklore. His 1891 article focuses on several variations of base-

ball played by boys in Brooklyn. Culin's classic work on Native American games was recently reprinted by the University of Nebraska Press (1992) in two volumes.

Eisen, George, and Wiggins, David W., eds. *Ethnicity and Sport in North American History and Culture.* Westport, Conn.: Greenwood Press, 1994. A recent collection of readings that deals with a neglected facet of sport.

Gmelch. George. "Magic in Professional Baseball" in *Games, Sports, and Power,* ed. Gregory P. Stone. New Brunswick, N.J.: Transaction Books, 1972.
A much-cited essay comparing the use of ritual, magic, and taboo by professional baseball players in batting, pitching, and fielding.

Hufford, Mary T. *Chaseworld: Foxhunting and Storytelling in New Jersey's Pine Barrens.* Philadelphia: University of Pennsylvania Press, 1992. From a folklorist perspective, this is the best local study in recent years on a sport covered in this anthology. Includes the ritual surrounding the activity of foxhunters in the folk region (Pine Barrens) and reports some fascinating stories associated with the sport.

Peterson, Elizabeth. "American Sports and Folklore," in *Handbook of American Folklore,* ed. Richard M. Dorson. Bloomington: Indiana University Press, 1983.
Focuses on a variety of sports from a folkloric viewpoint ranging from professional football to rock climbing. Peterson calls for folklorists to study the content, style, and form of sports heros, legends, jokes, and customs related to the social, cultural, and historical contexts in which they occur.

Raitz, Karl, ed. *The Theater of Sport.* Baltimore, Md.: Johns Hopkins University Press, 1995.
An outstanding compilation of thirteen original essays by noted sports geographers. Organization of the anthology centers on sports and leisure landscapes and their social and cultural contexts, the use of space by sports, and the association of sport with place. The essays include the sports of baseball, soccer, cricket, tennis, basketball, football, golf, stock car racing, rodeo, foxhunting, thoroughbred horse racing, and climbing.

Rooney, John F., Jr. *A Geography of American Sport: From Cabin Creek to Anaheim.* Reading, Mass.: Addison-Wesley, 1974; *The Recruiting Game.* Lincoln: University of Nebraska Press, 1987, Rooney, John F., Jr., and Pillsbury, Richard. *Atlas of American Sport.* New York: Macmillan, 1992. Rooney is *the* pioneer in the geography of American sports including both individual and team sports. He has compiled an exhaustive data base for his works. All three publications are richly illustrated with maps and photographs and should be consulted by every student of folk sports and games.

Sutton-Smith, Brian. "Sixty Years of Historical Change in the Game Preferences of American Children," *Journal of American Folklore* 74 (1961): 17–46. *The Folkgames of Children*. Austin: University of Texas Press, 1972; Brian Sutton-Smith, and Elliott M. Avedon, (eds.). *The Study of Games*. New York: Wiley, 1971.
Sutton-Smith is an eminent authority on games. As a sports sociologist, his work emphasizes the structural development of complexities of social interaction in games and sports.

## Part V: Folk Religion and Cemeteries

Clements, William M. "The Folk Church: Institution, Event, Performance," in *Handbook of American Folklore*, ed. Richard M. Dorson. Bloomington: Indiana University Press, 1983.
The author is the leading authority on the folk church based on fieldwork as a participant observer. He identifies ten characteristics of the folk church and views folk religious services as event and performance, including singing, preaching, ritual, and testimony. Clements concludes that the folk church is the basic unit in American folk religion.

Crowley, William K. "Old Order Amish Settlement: Diffusion and Growth," *Annals of the Association of American Geographers* 68 (1978): 249–64.
One of the few geographical accounts on the Amish, this study provides some background on Amish religious customs, but the primary emphasis is on settlement patterns and cultural diffusion of this folk religion through an excellent series of maps.

Danielson, Larry. "Religious Folklore," in *Folk Groups and Folklore Genres: An Introduction*, ed. Elliott Oring. Logan: Utah State University Press, 1986.
A helpful overview that discusses the question of what factors distinguish religious folklore from institutionalized religious practices and beliefs. It contains a useful bibliography.

Hostetler, John A. *Amish Society*, 4th ed. Baltimore, Md.: Johns Hopkins University Press, 1993.
An in-depth history and folkloric analysis by the co-author of chapter 15. Approaches the Amish as an insider who clearly details their folk culture.

Howard, Guy. *Walkin' Preacher of the Ozarks.* New York: Harper Brothers, 1944, reprint 1976.
An informal account of an itinerant country preacher's travels as he walked some four thousand miles a year visiting with and preaching to Ozark hillfolk.

Hurston, Zora Neale. *Mules and Men.* Bloomington: Indiana University Press, 1978.
Voodoo beliefs and rituals in African-American culture are provided in a vivid account of the author's apprenticeship to hoodoo "doctors" in Louisiana (pp. 193–252).

Jeane, D. Gregory. "The Upland South Cemetery: An American Type," *Journal of Popular Culture* 6 (1978): 895–903; "Rural Southern Gravestones: Sacred Artifacts in the Upland South Folk Cemetery" in *Markers IV*, ed. David Watters. Lanham, Md.: University Press of America, 1987.
Author of chapter 16, Jeane is the foremost authority on cemeteries in one of the major folklife regions in the United States—the Upland South. Characterized by hilltop location, small size, preferred vegetation species, unique decorations, and ceremonies of piety, Jeane concludes that the Upland South cemetery is a distinctive American graveyard type.

Jordan, Terry G. *Texas Graveyards: A Cultural Legacy.* Austin: University of Texas Press, 1982.
Despite its state-based title, one of the most scholarly assessments of "necrogeography," or regionality of burial practices. Jordan's thorough fieldwork includes analyses of traditional Southern cemeteries as well as Mexican and German graveyards. Laced with numerous photographs and maps.

Kane, Stephen. "Ritual Possession in a Southern Appalachian Religious Sect," *Journal of American Folklore* 87 (1974): 293–302. "Snake Handlers," in *Encyclopedia of Southern Culture*, eds. Charles Reagan Wilson and William Ferris. Chapel Hill: University of North Carolina Press, 1989.
Kane is the authoritative scholar on the religious sects of southern Appalachia, which use snake handling as a part of their folk religion rituals.

Lawless, Elaine. *God's Peculiar People: Women's Voices and Folk Traditions in a Pentacostal Church.* Lexington: University Press of Kentucky, 1988.
Author focuses on Pentacostal Holiness oral traditions and customs. Describes and analyzes traditional expressive verbal art in the Pentacostal service, especially personal testimonies and glossolalia (speaking in tongues).

Meyer, Richard E., ed. *Cemeteries and Gravemarkers: Voices of American Culture.* Logan: Utah State University Press, 1992.
Folklorist Meyer has organized twelve original essays into four sections: Icon and Epitaph, Origins and Influences, Ethnicity and Regionalism, and Business and Pleasure. An important contribution to folk gravestone and cemetery studies and demonstrates what modern scholars are researching in this field.

Yoder, Don. "Official Religion Versus Folk Religion," *Pennsylvania Folklife* 15 (1965–1966): 36–52. "Symposium on Folk Religion," *Western Folklore* 33 (1974): 1–87.
Yoder, one of the pioneers to study folk religion, proposes three levels of religion: official or organized religion based on theology and liturgy, popular religion centered on the lay person's version of religion, and folk religion focused on traditional beliefs and customs that exist parallel or below official religion. Edited by Yoder, the symposium articles include his definition of folk religion that originally appeared in *Western Folklore.*

## Part VI: Folk Medicine

Brendle, Thomas R., and Unger, Claude W. *Folk Medicine of the Pennsylvania Germans: The Non-Occult Cures.* Norristown: Proceedings of the Pennsylvania German Society, 1935.
A classic work that presents some of the most detailed analyses of the disease theory of one of the oldest ethnic groups in the United States. Includes a valuable annotated bibliography.

Clark, Margaret. *Health in the Mexican-American Culture: A Community Study.* Berkeley: University of California Press, 1959.
A study based on intensive fieldwork in the Mexican-American community of San Jose, California. It is one of the best local studies to place folk medicine within its full cultural context. Provides a useful glossary and bibliography.

Hand, Wayland D. *Popular Beliefs and Superstitions from North Carolina.* Vols. 6 and 7. Durham, N.C.: Duke University Press, 1961, 1964; *American Folk Medicine: A Symposium.* Berkeley: University of California Press, 1976; *Magical Medicine: The Folkloric Component of Medicine in the Folk Belief, Custom, and Ritual of the Peoples of Europe and America.* Berkeley: University of California Press, 1980.
Volumes 6 and 7 from the Frank C. Brown Collection of North Carolina Folklore deal with traditional beliefs, including those emphasizing folk

medicine. The 1976 symposium consists of twenty-five papers, edited by Hand, on a variety of ethnic and regional folk medicine traditions from different academic disciplines and considered the most comprehensive view of folk medicine up to the 1970s. The 1980 compilation by Hand is a collection of twenty-three previously published essays on a broad range of supernatural healing practices.

Hufford, David. "Folk Healers," in *Handbook of American* Folklore, ed. Richard M. Dorson. Bloomington: Indiana University Press, 1983.
Discusses folklore approach to natural and supernatural healing and folk psychiatry. Readers should also consult Hufford's other works in the comprehensive bibliography on folk medicine.

Kiev, Ari. *Curanderismo: Mexican-American Folk Psychiatry.* New York: Free Press, 1968.
Examines an older form of folk medicine that has continually reaffirmed its validity in modern times among members of an ethnic group who live in both rural and urban areas. (See Kiev's other books in the comprehensive bibliography on folk medicine.)

Kirkland, James et al., eds. *Herbal and Magical Medicine: Traditional Healing Today.* Durham, N.C.: Duke University Press, 1992.
One of the best recent collections on folk medicine in modern society. Specialists in folklore, anthropology, clinical medicine, and ethnobotany contribute ten essays on medical beliefs and practices.

Madsden, William. *The Mexican Americans of South Texas.* New York: Holt, Rinehart and Winston, 1964.
One of the most concise analyses of the theory and practice of traditional medicine among Mexican-Americans in the Southwest. See especially chapter 8, "Sickness and Health;" chapter 9, "Witchcraft;" chapter 10, "Curers and Physicians;" and chapter 11, "Folk Psychotherapy."

O'Connor, Bonnie. *Healing Traditions: Alternative Medicine and the Health Professions.* Philadelphia: University of Pennsylvania Press, 1995.
A recent study that demonstrates how important an understanding of traditional healing practices can be in treating ailments that have no reliable "formal" cures to expect from standard medical practices.

Paredes, Américo. "Folk Medicine and the Intercultural Jest," in *Spanish Speaking Peoples of the United States,* ed. June Helm. Seattle: University of Washington Press, 1968.
Folklorist Paredes introduces a complex layering of Mexican-American folk tradition, including *curanderismo* (the system of folk curing) and *casos* (belief tales that revolve around the practice of *curanderismo*).

Puckett, Newbill Niles. *Folk Beliefs of the Southern Negro.* Chapel Hill: University of North Carolina Press, 1926.
This classic work includes the study of "conjuring" (conjure-doctors) and "hoodoo" for African-American healing practices. Puckett contends that African-American medical beliefs are derived from African and European origins.

Randolph, Vance. *Ozark Magic and Folklore.* New York: Dover, 1964.
Along with North Carolina, this is the best regional-based investigation of superstitions. Chapter 6 details the home remedies of the "yarb doctors" and "granny women" of the Ozarks. Cures range from the cathartic powers of the May apple root to ragweed tea for diarrhea. Chapter 7, "The Power Doctors," outlines the work and context of the magic healer in a regional setting.

Wilhelm, Eugene J., Jr. "The Mullein: Plant Piscicide of the Mountain Folk Culture," *Geographical Review* 64 (1974): 235–52. "Those Old Home Remedies," *Mountain Life and Work* 44 (1968): 20–23.
One of the few cultural geographers who has studied folk medicine, Wilhelm conducted intensive fieldwork in the Blue Ridge Mountains during the 1950s and 1960s. Both articles are based on his compilation of 210 medicinal plants used domestically in the twentieth century.

Wolf, John Quincy. *Life in the Leatherwoods.* Memphis: Memphis State University Press, 1974.
The chapter "Medical Science in the Leatherwoods" (pp. 87–99) is full of valuable information on folk medicine, herbs and remedies, ailments, and early backwoods doctors. Lists more than fifty "yarbs" and the remedies concocted from them.

Yoder, Don. "Folk Medicine," in *Folklore and Folklife: An Introduction,* ed. Richard M. Dorson. Chicago: University of Chicago Press, 1972.
Divides folk medicine into two branches—natural folk medicine and magico-religious folk medicine. The first involves the seeking of cures from herbs, plants, minerals, and animal substances of nature. The second uses charms, holy words, and holy actions to cure disease.

# Index

# About the Contributors

*Malcolm L. Comeaux* is professor of geography at Arizona State University. His Ph.D. is from Louisiana State University and his research specialties include historical and cultural geography.

*Loyal Durand, Jr.,* served on the geography faculty at the University of Tennessee-Knoxville from 1944 to the time of his death in 1970.

*Richard V. Francaviglia* is director of the Center for Greater Southwestern Studies at the University of Texas-Arlington. He holds a Ph.D. in historical-cultural geography from the University of Minnesota.

*Dennis A. Frate* is research professor in the Research Institute of Pharmaceutical Sciences at the University of Mississippi. His Ph.D. is in medical anthropology from the University of Illinois.

*Henry H. Glassie* is College professor of folklore in the Folklore and Folklife Institute at the University of Indiana. His Ph.D. is from the University of Pennsylvania.

*Charles F. Gritzner* is Distinguished Professor of Geography at South Dakota State University, where he specializes in cultural geography and geographic education. His Ph.D. is from Louisiana State University-Baton Rouge.

*Fred Hawley* is professor and head of the department of criminal justice at Western Carolina University-Cullowhee. He holds a Ph.D. in criminal justice from Florida State University.

285

*Sam Hilliard* is emeritus alumni professor of geography at Louisiana State University-Baton Rouge. His Ph.D. is from the University of Wisconsin-Madison in historical and cultural geography.

*John A. Hostetler* is emeritus professor of anthropology and sociology at Temple University and former director of the Center for Anabaptist and Pietist Studies at Elizabethtown College.

*Donald G. Jeane* is professor of geography and chair at Samford University in Birmingham, Alabama. His Ph.D. is from Louisiana State University-Baton Rouge.

*Stephen C. Jett* is professor of geography at the University of California-Davis. He holds a Ph.D. from Johns Hopkins University.

*Jon T. Kilpinen* is assistant professor of geography at Valparaiso University, where he specializes in historical-cultural geography. He received his Ph.D. from the University of Texas-Austin.

*Clarissa T. Kimber* is professor of geography at Texas A & M University. Her Ph.D. is from the University of Wisconsin-Madison in biogeography.

*Maurice A. Mook* was emeritus professor of anthropology at Pennsylvania State University until the time of this death in 1973.

*Edward T. Price* is emeritus professor of geography at the University of Oregon. His Ph.D is from the University of California-Berkeley.

*Karl B. Raitz* is professor of geography at the University of Kentucky. He holds a Ph.D. from the University of Minnesota.

*Donald E. Vermeer* is professor of geography at California State Polytechnic University-San Luis Obispo. His Ph.D. is from the University of California-Berkeley.

*Roger L. Welsch* is emeritus professor of folklore at the University of Nebraska-Lincoln. He has served as essayist for *CBS Sunday Morning* and columnist for *Successful Farming* magazine.

*Wilbur Zelinsky* is emeritus professor of geography at Pennsylvania State University, where he specializes in historical-cultural geography. His Ph.D. is from the University of California-Berkeley.

# About the Editor

*George O. Carney* is Regents Professor of Geography at Oklahoma State University where he has taught introductory cultural geography since 1969. His other teaching interests include music geography, the history and philosophy of geography, and historic preservation. He holds degrees from Central Missouri State University (B.A. in geography and M.A. in history) and Oklahoma State University (Ph.D. in American social history). He has authored more than seventy publications, including seven books and numerous journal articles, monographs, and book reviews. He has been awarded grants from both public and private agencies including the National Endowment for the Humanities, National Endowment for the Arts, National Park Service, Atlantic-Richfield Foundation, and the Smithsonian Institution. His honors include awards for both teaching and research: *Journal of Geography* Best Content Article, National Council for Geographic Education Distinguished Teaching Award, Oklahoma State University Regents Distinguished Teaching Award, American Association for State and Local History Certificate of Commendation, Association of American Geographers Applied Geography Award, AMOCO Foundation for Undergraduate Instruction, and the George H. Shirk Memorial Award for Historic Preservation in Oklahoma. In 1996, he won the prestigious Ray and Pat Browne National Book Award given by the American Popular Culture Association for *Fast Food, Stock Cars, and Rock 'n' Roll: Place and Space in American Pop Culture* (Rowman & Littlefield, 1995). His folk culture maps have appeared in such diverse outlets as the *Washington Post*, the *Encyclopedia of Southern Culture*, and the Public Broadcasting System (PBS) network.